Death in Medieval England

an archaeology

First published 2001

PUBLISHED IN THE UNITED KINGDOM BY:

Tempus Publishing Ltd
The Mill, Brimscombe Port
Stroud, Gloucestershire GL5 2QG
http://www.tempus-publishing.com

PUBLISHED IN THE UNITED STATES OF AMERICA BY:

Arcadia Publishing Inc.
A division of Tempus Publishing Inc.
2 Cumberland Street
Charleston, SC 29401
1-888-313-2665
http://www.arcadiapublishing.com

Tempus books are available in France, Germany and Belgium
from the following addresses:

Tempus Publishing Group	Tempus Publishing Group	Tempus Publishing Group
21 Avenue de la République	Gustav-Adolf-Straße 3	Place de L'Alma 4/5
37300 Joué-lès-Tours	99084 Erfurt	1200 Brussels
FRANCE	GERMANY	BELGIUM

© D.M. Hadley, 2001

The right of D.M. Hadley to be identified as the Author
of this work has been asserted by her in accordance with the
Copyrights, Designs and Patents Act 1988.

All rights reserved. No part of this book may be reprinted or reproduced or utilised in any form or by any electronic, mechanical or other means, now known or hereafter invented, including photocopying and recording, or in any information storage or retrieval system, without the permission in writing from the Publishers.

British Library Cataloguing in Publication Data.
A catalogue record for this book is available from the British Library.

ISBN 0 7524 1470 4

Typesetting and origination by Tempus Publishing.
PRINTED AND BOUND IN GREAT BRITAIN

Contents

List of illustrations — 4

Acknowledgements — 7

1 Introduction — 9

2 The geography of death — 17

3 Preparation for burial and beyond: deathbeds, wills and funerals — 56

4 Graves — 92

5 Remembering the dead: memorials, commemoration and care of the soul — 125

6 The living and the dead — 174

Bibliography — 185

Index — 190

List of illustrations

Text figures

1 Grave cover from Kirkdale (Yorks)
2 Grave marker from York Minster
3 Sarcophagus from St Alkmund, Derby
4 Carved panel from Wirksworth (Derbs)
5 Fragments of carved panel from South Kyme (Lincs)
6 Location of Anglo-Saxon cemeteries at Ripon (Yorks)
7 Church and mausoleum at Repton (Derbs)
8 Cemetery at Crayke (Yorks)
9 Burials at Addingham (Yorks)
10 Anglo-Saxon church and cemetery at Pontefract (Yorks)
11 Burial truncated by walls of the church at Pontefract (Yorks)
12 Map of 'Viking' burials in England
13 Burials from Whitton (Lincs)
14 Burial from Fillingham (Lincs)
15 Burials from St Mary, Doncaster (Yorks)
16 Preferred place of burial as indicated in wills from Yorkshire and Nottinghamshire, 1389-1475
17 Villages in Lincolnshire with more than one church
18 The location of the hospital of St Leonard, Grantham (Lincs)
19 Skeleton showing signs of leprosy from the hospital of St Leonard, Grantham (Lincs)
20 Cross-shaft with inscription from Thornhill (Yorks)
21 Stone sculpture with inscriptions from Thornhill (Yorks)
22 Burial disturbed by later burial from Pontefract (Yorks)
23 The Percy tomb from Beverley Minster (Yorks)
24 Depiction of Hell from the west front of Lincoln Cathedral
25 Depiction of Hell on a tympanum from York
26 Guildhall in York
27 Silver cross set in the nasal piece of a helmet from Benty Grange (Derbs)
28 Excavations of the pre-Norman cemetery at York Minster
29 Burial in parts of a boat from York Minster
30 Locks from coffins excavated at Ripon (Yorks)
31 Burial with cobbles set around the head from the church of St Andrew, York
32 Coffin from Barton-on-Humber (Lincs)

List of illustrations

33 Double burial from the church of St Andrew, York
34 Warrior on Anglo-Saxon sculpture at Norbury (Derbs)
35 Burial of priest from St Leonard's Chesterfield (Derbs)
36 Lead paten from Chesterfield (Derbs)
37 Burial from the Augustinian friary at Hull (Yorks)
38 Burial from the Augustinian friary at Hull (Yorks)
39 Burials in stone coffins at the Gilbertine priory of St Andrew, York
40 Grave lined with tiles from the Gilbertine priory of St Andrew, York
41 Burial marked with a stone marker at the Gilbertine priory of St Andrew, York
42 Double burial from St Helen-on-the-Walls, York
43 Reconstruction of a coffin from the cemetery at Jewbury, York
44 Anglo-Saxon sculpture from Bakewell (Derbs)
45 Anglo-Saxon sculpture from Hackness (Yorks)
46 Anglo-Saxon sculpture from Repton (Derbs)
47 Anglo-Saxon sculpture from Bradbourne (Derbs)
48 Inscribed lead plaque from Kirkdale (Yorks)
49 Sculpture *in situ* above a grave at St Mark's, Lincoln
50 Excavation of later Anglo-Saxon cemetery at York Minster
51 Sculpture and burials from York Minster
52 Sculpture and burials from York Minster
53 Cross-shaft from Nunburnholme (Yorks)
54 Cross-shaft from Leeds (Yorks)
55 Cross-shaft from Kirklevington (Yorks)
56 Sculpture from Levisham (Yorks)
57 Cross-shaft from Middleton (Yorks)
58 Fragment of a hogback monument from Dewsbury (Yorks)
59 Grave cover from Dewsbury (Yorks)
60 Grave covers in the porch at Bakewell (Derbs)
61 Grave covers in the porch at Bakewell (Derbs)
62 Grave slabs reused as window lintels from Baslow (Derbs)
63 Grave cover from Darrington (Yorks)
64 Alabaster slab commemorating Elizabeth Fitzherbert at Norbury (Derbs)
65 Monument to Nicholas Fitzherbert at Norbury (Derbs)
66 Brass from Sprotborough (Yorks)
67 Brass from Tideswell (Derbs)
68 Brass from Cowthorpe (Yorks)
69 Monument to Ralph and Elizabeth Fitzherbert at Norbury (Derbs)
70 Effigy of Sir Henry Fitzherbert at Norbury (Derbs)
71 Window glass from Thornhill (Yorks)
72 Tomb from Tideswell (Derbs)
73 Effigy from Sprotborough (Yorks)
74 Effigies from Tideswell (Derbs)
75 Collar on effigy at Harewood (Yorks)
76 The wives of Nicholas Fitzherbert at Norbury (Derbs)

List of illustrations

77 Tomb of John Barton at Holme (Notts)
78 Alabaster monument to Sir Godfrey Foljambe and his wife at Bakewell (Derbs)
79 Window depicting St Christopher from All Saints, North Street in York

Colour plates

1 Carved panel from Hovingham (Yorks)
2 Burial near chapel from Flixborough (Lincs)
3 Inscribed lead plaque from Flixborough (Lincs)
4 Grave goods from barrows in Derbyshire and Yorkshire
5 A burial aligned south-north cut by a later burial aligned west-east at Kellington (Yorks)
6 Burial mounds at Heath Wood, Ingleby (Derbs)
7 Burials at Fillingham (Lincs)
8 Burials at Wigber Low (Derbs)
9 Skull excavated at Towton (Yorks)
10 The visit of Christ to Hell from a fifteenth-century wall painting from Pickering (Yorks)
11 Wall painting at Blyth (Notts)
12 A devil listening to gossiping women on a wall painting from Melbourne (Derbs)
13 Peasants labouring on the land in window glass from Dewsbury (Yorks)
14 Painted panel from Newark (Notts)
15 Tomb in the churchyard at Loversall (Yorks)
16 The blessing of Joan Fitz Payn from the Gray-Fitz Payn Book of Hours
17 Coffin and depiction of Hell from the Luttrell Psalter
18 Sir Geoffrey Luttrell preparing to go off to battle from the Luttrell Psalter
19 Window glass from St Mary Magdalene, Newark (Notts)
20 Window from All Saints, North Street, York
21 Members of the Fitzherbert family praying in a window-glass at Norbury (Derbs)
22 St Anne teaching the Virgin to read on a window from Norbury (Derbs)
23 The Seven Corporal Acts of Mercy from a wall painting at Pickering (Yorks)
24 Wooden tomb of Sir Roger Rockley at Worsborough (Yorks)
25 Excavations of a skeleton in progress at Grantham (Lincs)

Acknowledgements

This book relies upon the assistance and advice of a number of students, colleagues and friends. I am grateful to those students who joined me in my travels around the region during the summer of 1999, and helped me to collect material for the book: Michelle Bosco, Cathy Cook, Neil Dransfield, Kate Gibson, Bob Hamilton, Alison Jackson-Bass, Laura Johnson, Craig Martin, Pam McInally, Fiona Keith-Lucas, Rachel Nowakowski, Lesley Richmond, Martha Riddiford, Suzy Thomas, Jane Travis, and Norma Wade. My thanks go to Andrew Chamberlain, Glyn Davies and Jo Buckberry for their efforts at Fillingham. Jo Buckberry has also pointed me in the direction of a number of sites following her own work in the region, and has helped me to clarify my thoughts on the Anglo-Saxon period. I am grateful to Robert Swanson for initial bibliographic orientation on the later Middle Ages, and for answering various queries along the way. Many people have generously helped by providing photographs from their personal collections, and I would like to thank Martin Biddle, Julian D. Richards, Kevin Leahy, Phil Sidebottom, Alison Walster, Stuart Wrathmell, and, in particular, my colleague Andrew Chamberlain whose slide collection has been raided on numerous occasions (and not always with his knowledge!) during the writing of this book. I would like to thank the Royal Commission for Historic Monuments, the British Library, Sheffield Museum, the Humberside Archaeological Trust, West Yorkshire Archaeological Service, ARCUS and the Fitzwilliam Museum for supplying me with photographs — they retain the copyright and this is acknowledged in the captions. I am extremely grateful to Rosemary Cramp who allowed me to reproduce photographs from the British Academy Corpus of Anglo-Saxon Stone Sculpture. I would like to thank Jim Williams for his interest in the project and for taking many of the photographs. The illustrations were drawn by Jo Mincher and Alex Norman. This book is dedicated to Patrick Major, for his good-humoured interest in this project, and for his skilled but utterly unproductive excavation of trench 2 at Fillingham!

1 Introduction

*As you are now, so once were we.
As we are now, so shall ye be*

According to these words spoken in the medieval legend of the *Three Living and Three Dead*, death was the great leveller in medieval society. Everyone would, of course, eventually die. However, not everyone would receive the same treatment at his or her funeral, and not everyone would be commemorated or remembered for generations to come. In fact, death was only a social leveller in theory. In practice, the social divisions based on wealth, rank, profession, and gender would play a major part in the way in which the dead were buried and how they were regarded after their death. This book explores the variety inherent in medieval burial practices, preparation for death, funerals, funerary monuments and commemoration between *c*.600 and 1500. Although the book is primarily concerned with archaeological evidence, it examines a broad range of sources, including not only excavated cemeteries, but also funerary monuments, depictions of death, the dying and the dead in the visual arts, and documentary evidence.

There have been a number of recent studies of death in the Middle Ages, and while excellent introductions to the subject, they are largely limited to particular types of evidence, and to shorter time periods than the present volume. Christopher Daniell has recently discussed the archaeological evidence for burial practices in England between 1066 and 1550, with some reference to documentary sources, but no discussion of funerary monuments. Paul Binski has, in contrast, written about medieval death largely by reference to documentary sources and the funerary monuments of the period. Other books, such as that edited by Peter Jupp and Clare Gittings, have tended to concentrate on documentary sources. These studies also explore the subject on a national or even, in the case of Binski, an international scale, and while such an approach makes for a fascinating study of, for example, some of the finest medieval funerary monuments around, it does tend to overlook the more mundane medieval provisions for the dead.

This book explores medieval death from a new perspective. It uses both a wide selection of evidence and at the same time narrows the focus to a regional study. Studies that emphasize the archaeological evidence traditionally tend to restrict themselves to excavated cemeteries, with occasional reference to funerary monuments. However, there is much more material evidence available to us if we broaden our focus. For example, in the Middle Ages it was expected that death should be prepared for, and the reasons for this preparation and the means by which the soul could be ensured a swift passage to Heaven were made apparent in a variety of contexts. Wall paintings, sculpture and window glass in churches, and manuscript illuminations all have much to reveal about attitudes to death in the Middle Ages, and about the messages that people were given concerning their

Introduction

potential experiences in the afterlife. These various forms of material evidence concerning death may be supplemented by written texts such as wills, church sermons and manuals giving advice on how to 'die well'. The approach adopted in this book permits us to take a look at the wide variety of burial practices, funerary monuments and attitudes to death that are to be found between *c*.600 and 1500, and the regional approach also allows us to see that the variety of evidence is not simply the product of amalgamating the evidence from many regions and countries, but genuinely reflects the variety available to particular groups of people in particular medieval societies. By focusing on a single region we are also able to see what is unique to that region, what is a product of that region and what was imported, and what is a more widespread national phenomenon.

The region chosen roughly corresponds to the English counties of Derbyshire, Lincolnshire, Nottinghamshire and Yorkshire. The wealth of evidence from this region is impressive for the whole of our period of study. There are also regional peculiarities characteristic of these counties, which make this a rewarding region to study, although we have to remember to distinguish what is unique from what is also found widely in other regions. There have been numerous recent excavations of medieval cemeteries in the study region which have provided a wealth of new information, not least because post-excavation work on the skeletal material has enabled us to know the age, sex, health and even the causes of death of individuals buried in these cemeteries. Examples include excavations of the following types of burial:

i) burials in barrows from the seventh century, such as that at Wigber Low (Derbs)
ii) the cemeteries of Anglo-Saxon churches, such as those at Repton (Derbs), Ripon, Addingham and Whitby (Yorks)
iii) Anglo-Saxon cemeteries not associated with a surviving church, such as Thwing (Yorks), Flixborough and Fillingham (Lincs)
iv) Viking burials, such as the cremations under barrows at Heath Wood, Ingleby (Derbs)
v) the cemeteries of later medieval parish churches, both urban (such as St Mark's, Lincoln, and St Helen-on-the-Walls, York), and rural (such as Barton-on-Humber (Lincs), Kellington and Wharram Percy (Yorks))
vi) the cemetery of Jewish communities in York
vii) the cemeteries of later medieval monasteries, such as the Augustinian friary at Hull (Yorks), and the Gilbertine priory at Fishergate in York
viii) the cemeteries of hospitals at Grantham (Lincs) and Chesterfield (Derbs)

There is also a diverse range of funerary monuments across the region dating from as early as the eighth century. These include the elaborate Anglo-Saxon stone sculptures that are a peculiarity of this region. The tenth-century examples provide one of the clearest indications of the cultural influence of the Scandinavian settlers of the later ninth and tenth century, as they incorporate Scandinavian styles and animal ornamentation and images drawn from Norse mythology. Numerous grave slabs, stone and wooden effigies, and tombs survive from the later Middle Ages, and many were made locally. There are also many later medieval brasses, some of which were made locally, which is unusual since brass manufacture in later medieval England was largely limited to London. The existence of a number of brass-workshops in the region has been identified, and these were few and far between outside London. There are also brasses imported from the continent, which came in through the ports of the east coast of the region. The region also possessed the main English workshops producing alabaster monuments in the later Middle Ages, at Chellaston (Derbs) and Nottingham.

There is also a wide range of surviving medieval ecclesiastical art depicting death and the dying. This includes wall paintings, window glass and sculptures in churches, and manuscript illuminations. Finally, there is good documentary evidence relevant to the issues discussed in the book that was produced in or about the region. This includes the writings of the monk Bede in the early eighth century, Anglo-Saxon and medieval wills, saints' *Lives*, and ordinances concerning the provision of post-mortem prayers by the guilds and chantry chapels of the region. The region chosen offers a microcosm of medieval attitudes to, and provision for, death. Moreover, it has its own peculiarities, which make it a fascinating place to explore medieval death.

I have chosen to begin my story in the seventh century. During this century the region acquired a network of major churches, often called 'minsters' both in medieval documents and in contemporary scholarship. These churches had communities of clergy and provided pastoral care to some, although perhaps not all, members of lay society, and soon came to provide places of burial for the laity. However, not everyone was buried in or near churches in the seventh century, and other types of burial, in barrows or in cemeteries remote from churches, were known. It was perhaps not until the tenth century that everyone was normally buried in churchyards. It is often supposed that the Church must have had a major impact on the burial practices of the Anglo-Saxons, and that they must have been forced by the Church to give up cremation and burial with grave goods, which had both been common in the fifth and sixth centuries. However, there is actually no written evidence to suggest that the Church did actively force people to bury their dead in a particular way. As we shall see, whatever churchmen thought about the practice, burial with grave goods continued into the eighth century and was not completely unknown during the following centuries. Moreover, cremation had largely disappeared as a burial rite by the seventh century, and so the churchmen of the region were not faced to any great extent with the one sort of funerary practice that the documentary evidence suggests the Church *did* frown upon.

This book traces the development of burial practices and changing attitudes to death through many tumultuous events. The Viking raids of the ninth century eventually turned into settlement, and the most obvious impact this had on funerary provision concerns the introduction of different burial rites, the disruption, if not destruction, of churches and the artistic influence of the settlers on the stone funerary sculpture produced in the region. The unification of England into a single kingdom under the royal house of Wessex saw the relics of the most holy dead, saints, removed from churches in the region and given to churches further south. In 1066 the Battle of Hastings ushered in a new regime under the Normans, and while the Normans were Christians their activities had a major impact on burial practices as their castles obliterated burial grounds, especially in towns, and their foundation of new parish churches and monasteries provided a variety of new places for the dead to be buried. The outbreak of the Black Death in 1348 saw as many as a third of the population die and new burial grounds had to be consecrated as the survivors struggled to cope with the implications of the drastic loss of population and with the increased need for burial provision. The ways in which people dealt normally with the dead and the ways in which they responded to new and changing circumstances are the main focus of this book.

Throughout the book I have dispensed with normal academic referencing, although I have occasionally cited a particular study where it influenced the argument elaborated in the book. A detailed bibliography is provided at the end of the book, arranged thematically to enable the reader to find the further literature that they are looking for. I have not assumed any prior knowledge on the part of the reader, and the book is aimed not only at the general reader and the student, but also at the researcher, who, while familiar with the general themes, is not familiar with the evidence from this region. The chapters are thematic, and each theme is then discussed more or less chronologically.

The first chapter examines where the dead were buried. The picture that emerges is a diverse one, and it reveals the extent to which burial grounds came into and went out of use between the seventh and the fifteenth century. The burial grounds of the fifth and sixth centuries, with their wealth of grave goods, have traditionally received more attention from Anglo-Saxon archaeologists than the later cemeteries, but we are now able to see that by drawing all of the available evidence together for the first time just how much evidence there is for the locations of cemeteries of seventh- to eleventh-century date. The available documentary evidence means that we know a lot about later medieval burial practices without excavating, yet recent excavations of later medieval cemeteries add much to the picture to be gleaned from the written sources about where, and how, the dead of the later Middle Ages were buried. The second chapter examines the ways in which individuals prepared for death. This includes the sorts of rituals and religious activities which medieval society thought beneficial to the soul, and the ways in which the sought-after 'good death' could be achieved, and the implications of failure in this endeavour. By necessity this means drawing on documentary evidence, but our picture is also considerably enhanced by visual evidence, such as wall paintings, sculpture and funerary monuments. This chapter also examines the evidence we have for funerals.

The third chapter considers the archaeological evidence for graves. This reveals much about the ways in which the dead were placed in the grave, the items that accompanied them and the ways in which the grave was prepared to receive bodies. Although grave goods had largely disappeared from graves by the eighth century, it is not true to say that what went in the grave ceased to be of any interest to society. Artefacts were still sometimes placed in graves, bodies had to be dressed for burial, and grave furniture (including coffins and grave linings and covers) could be elaborate and diverse. Chapter 4 examines the various ways in which the dead were remembered and commemorated and the post-mortem measures that were put in place to ensure the safe passage of the soul of the deceased. The final chapter discusses the opportunities that death afforded the living. The funerary industry created employment for many people, and the death of friends, neighbours and family members created social disruption that often led to new opportunities for employment and landholding for the survivors. In particular, the Black

Death had such a cataclysmic effect on society that the changes in fortunes of the lowly were a subject of much concern for contemporary commentators.

The remainder of this introductory chapter provides a brief outline of some of the issues that we need to consider when addressing the various types of evidence at our disposal.

Archaeological evidence

The region has a wealth of excavated cemeteries. However, some of these were excavated long ago, before the development of modern excavation techniques and recording systems. This is particularly true of the barrow burials and associated cemeteries of the seventh century. Nineteenth-century excavators were prone to excavate through the tops of mounds, to miss what was not centrally placed and to record only the elaborate finds. Often no record, or only a partial account, of excavations survives. The area around the barrows was often not excavated and this means that our perception of them as containing isolated burials is not necessarily accurate. Some other sites, such as the various cemeteries around the minster at Ripon (Yorks), were excavated many decades ago but have only been published recently, after some ingenious detective work on earlier reports. Many cemeteries in the region have only been partially excavated. Some because they were discovered by chance, such as those at Fillingham and Flixborough (Lincs), and others because they were the subject of limited excavation in advance of construction work, such as at Pontefract (Yorks) and Swinegate in York. We have to remember that the digging of graves is an essentially destructive process, and it can be hard to distinguish the different phases of use of a cemetery since later graves often disturb earlier graves. Moreover, deeper graves cannot necessarily be presumed to be the earliest in the sequence, since the depth of graves is a factor determined by the depth to which people in the past thought it necessary or appropriate to dig a grave. This means that the normal laws of stratigraphy (the deeper something is, the older it must be) do not necessarily apply, and our ability to see that a later grave has cut through an earlier one is often hampered by the general levels of disturbance of the site.

Overall in the region there has been a bias towards the excavation and study of early, that is to say fifth- to sixth-century, Anglo-Saxon cemeteries with their rich array of grave goods. In part this reflects the interests of antiquarian excavators, but it also has much to do with the difficulty of identifying and dating cemeteries of a later date. The general absence of grave goods, and more importantly of grave goods that are datable, means that cemeteries of eighth-century and later date are often difficult to date precisely, or even, in some cases, to distinguish from prehistoric or Roman burials. Generally it has been the presence of an associated church or of particular types of grave furniture, and the basic stratigraphy of the site (that is to say, can certain burials be shown to be earlier or later in date than some other datable feature, such as a building?) that has allowed tentative dates to be assigned to cemeteries. However, in recent years our ability to study these later Anglo-Saxon and later medieval cemeteries has been transformed by the availability of radiocarbon dating. Simply put, the carbon isotope known as ^{14}C is absorbed into living organisms from the atmosphere, but when they die the ^{14}C present in the organism begins to decay, at a more or less predictable rate. By measuring the amount of ^{14}C left in a skeleton scientists can estimate the time in the past when the person died. Although this technique cannot give us a precise date, it does allow us to distinguish, say, earlier Anglo-Saxon burials from later Anglo-Saxon burials and later medieval burials. This is an extremely useful technique for archaeologists to be able to draw upon, and throughout this book various cemeteries have been identified as being either Anglo-Saxon or medieval largely on the basis of radiocarbon dating. In all cases I have given the radiocarbon dates as they are given in published accounts of the sites.

Scientific analysis also allows us to distinguish the skeletons of males from females with a high degree of accuracy where the skeleton is relatively complete. Sex can be determined by examining both the pelvis, which is lower and broader in females, and the skull, which has more prominent ridges where the muscles that move the head and lower jaw are attached in males. To a lesser extent the general robustness of the skeleton can also suggest sex. These sex determinants are only relevant for sexing the skeletons of adults. The identification of the sex of pre-pubescent individuals can rarely be attempted from the skeletal evidence. DNA analysis can potentially identify the sex of infants, but is an expensive, and rarely used, option. We can also establish the approximate age at death of an individual. The bones and teeth develop through infancy at predictable rates, and permit relatively accurate estimates of age at death. Scientific analysis also allows us to identify injuries, illnesses and diseases that the individual has suffered from. In this book such analysis has proved useful in identifying, for example, the cemeteries of hospitals from the incidence of leprosy, and the burials of the casualties of battle.

Funerary monuments

The region studied in this book possesses a wide range of types of funerary monument. The elaborate stone sculptures of Anglo-Saxon date are one of its most characteristic features, and much of this sculpture clearly served a funerary purpose, as grave markers and covers. The discovery of some of these sculptures *in situ* above graves, at York Minster and St Mark's in Lincoln, provides conclusive proof of the function of the sculpture, which had previously only been assumed. Close dating is not possible, but stylistic developments and the discovery of some sculptures in archaeological contexts permit some broad date ranges to be established.

Later medieval tombs, grave slabs, brasses and effigies are generally able to be more closely dated. Inscriptions, changing art styles and the fashions depicted on such monuments generally permit us to narrow down the date of the production of a monument, if not to a precise date then at least to a particular century. We have to remember, however, that monuments were sometimes commissioned in advance of, or long after, a person's death, and thus the date of death revealed in an inscription may be misleading about the date of manufacture of the monument. Few, if any, of these later medieval monuments can be shown to be *in situ*, whether above a grave or in the place in the church where they were originally displayed. Many grave slabs have been reused over the centuries for later burials or as building fabric, and tombs, effigies and brasses have clearly been moved.

Artistic evidence

Throughout the book, in addition to funerary monuments, we shall also explore relevant evidence from other artistic contexts. Wall paintings in churches are a useful source of information on medieval views of Hell, Purgatory and the afterlife. The role of saints, who could be expected to intercede on behalf of the souls of the dead, is also commonly depicted in wall paintings. Sculptures of various types and window glass also give us insights into medieval beliefs about saints and the afterlife. Windows were often provided by wealthy patrons and they often incorporate the heraldic devices of the donor, if they do not actually depict the name or an image of the donor. Manuscript illuminations sometimes provide similar information, and they are also important indicators of the ways in which their wealthy patrons wished to be remembered as they commonly depict the patron somewhere in the illuminations. Such types of evidence rarely form part of discussions of medieval death, yet they provide an invaluable guide to medieval attitudes.

Documentary sources

Although this book is primarily about archaeological evidence — both what is buried in the ground and the surviving material culture of medieval society — documents are also used to enhance our picture of medieval death. It is, however, important to remember that documents tend to be more plentiful for the wealthy in society, and also for ecclesiastics and saints. Documents also tend to tell us what was expected to happen, not necessarily what actually did happen. For example, wills explain, often in great detail, what the testator wanted his executors to do, but whether these requests were always carried out is less clear. Sometimes the wishes of a will-maker can be shown to have been ignored. The bequests made to chantry chapels for a priest to pray in perpetuity for the soul of the deceased were often not sufficient for the task, and supplementary bequests had to be made by descendants or friends, or else the role of the chantry priest had to be scaled down in order to ensure some on-going, if less comprehensive, provision. Many of the documents available to us are quite formulaic, and it can be difficult to use them to discuss what really happened as opposed to some literary ideal concerning what should have happened. This is particularly true of saints' *Lives*, since in order for the sanctity of an individual to be established certain events, such as visions and miracles and the continuing incorrupt nature of the body, needed to have occurred. Discussion of death, even in medical texts, is heavily laden with a powerful moral component. Why and how someone died, and the likely fate in the afterlife, were all widely believed to relate to the way in which a person had behaved during their lifetime on earth. The expected rewards of Heaven could also be used as a reason for accepting one's earthly lot, however terrible. Those who played their part in God's divinely sanctioned order of the world would eventually reap their rewards. In sum, documents do not provide a comprehensive picture; moreover, they provide a more useful picture of attitudes and aspirations than of what really happened.

Conclusions

Throughout this book we will examine a variety of types of evidence, and explore each of the main themes from a number of perspectives. Archaeological evidence will be combined with documentary sources, funerary monuments and art historical evidence. We should not suppose that the study of death is a grim experience. On the contrary, medieval attitudes to death consisted of hope and promise for the future. Moreover, the study of death is not solely about the dead. It is also, as St Augustine observed in the early fifth century, quite as much about the living as about the dead.

2 The geography of death

This chapter explores where people were buried between c.600 and 1500 in the counties of Derbyshire, Lincolnshire, Nottinghamshire and Yorkshire. It quickly becomes apparent that not everyone was afforded burial in a churchyard during those centuries. Even in the later Middle Ages when churchyard burial was the norm, some individuals, particularly excommunicates and criminals, were excluded from burial in churchyards. Churchyards both grew and shrank in size, were abandoned, built over and disturbed, and there was clearly no guarantee that the dead would long rest undisturbed in their graves. Furthermore, the Church itself was as likely to be responsible for disturbing the dead as anyone else. This chapter reveals that there was a certain amount of choice about where individuals might be buried, although that choice was limited by such factors as wealth, social status and the parish in which a person resided.

The development of churchyard burial

It has long been argued that by the eighth century the Anglo-Saxons had ceased to cremate their dead or to bury them with grave goods, that they had abandoned their pagan burial grounds and that unaccompanied inhumation in churchyards was from then on the norm. It has also been suggested that the progress from large 'pagan' cemeteries to churchyard burial commonly included an intermediate phase, characterized by small cemeteries closer to the settlement site than the earlier large pagan burial grounds. The burials in such 'intermediary' cemeteries were largely unaccompanied by grave goods, but a few burials might include them. This type of cemetery has come to be known as 'final phase', that is, the final phase of furnished burial. However, while this account of the transformation of burial rites and burial locations may have explained the archaeological evidence available up to the 1970s, more recently excavated evidence suggests a more complex transition to churchyard burial. It is now apparent that even once burial in or near churches began this did not invariably set a pattern that was to persist into the later Middle Ages. Recent excavation also shows that burial practices and forms of commemoration varied greatly from cemetery to cemetery and even within the same cemetery. Moreover, the notion that the growing influence of the Church led to a more egalitarian form of burial is called into question by the survival of elaborate commemorative and funerary monuments, and by the evidence that *where* a person was buried was commonly a reflection of their status. The element of display associated with burial did not cease in the eighth century with the abandonment of grave goods, but was rather transformed and involved an increasing amount of above ground-display (discussed in chapter 5).

1 *Grave cover from Kirkdale (Yorks). This slab is of eighth- or ninth-century date, and may have lain at ground level, but it is also possible that it surmounted a box shrine.* Alex Norman

The inhabitants of religious communities, bishops and kings were certainly sometimes buried in churchyards, or within churches, from at least the late seventh or early eighth century. For example, two children of King Edwin of Northumbria, Æthelhun and Æthelthryth, who died as infants were buried 'in the church of York' (presumably at St Peter's, later to be the episcopal church) in the 620s or 630s. Later, King Ælfwini (d.678), was buried at York, probably at St Peter's. The head of King Edwin, who died in battle in 633, was apparently taken to York according to Bede and placed in the porticus (side chapel) of the church of York in the later seventh century. St Wilfrid (d.709), St Egbert (d.729) and St Wihtberht were all buried at Ripon (Yorks) at some point in the early eighth century. The remains of King Edwin were discovered by a priest called Trimma in the later seventh century and taken to Whitby (Yorks) where they were buried (presumably minus his head!). Edwin's daughter, Queen Eanflaed (d.704), and her husband King Oswy (d.670) were also buried at Whitby (known then as *Streanaeshalch*) in the later seventh century, as was their daughter Abbess Ælflaed (d.714). Bishop Cedd of the East Saxons was buried at the monastery he founded at Lastingham (Yorks) in 664, at first outside, but he was later reburied inside a stone church dedicated to Mary, to the right of the altar, according to Bede. Bishop John of York was buried in the porticus of his monastery at Beverley (then known as *Inderawuda*) (Yorks) in 721. King Æthelred and Queen Osthryth of Mercia were buried at Bardney (Lincs) in the early eighth century. There is a later tradition that Merewalh, king of the Magonsætan, was buried at Repton (Derbs) in the later seventh century. By the ninth century some of the churches in the region had received numerous Episcopal or royal burials. Kings Eadberht (d.758) and Osbald (d.799), and archbishops Egbert (d.766) and Eanbald (d.796) were buried at York. Various members of the

Mercian royal families were buried at Repton (Derbs), including King Æthelbald (d.757), King Wiglaf (c.839), and his grandson Wystan (d.849).

It seems likely that the aristocracy also sought to provide burial for their kindred in and around churches. According to Bede's *Life of St Cuthbert*, a *praefectus* (a royal official) sought to ensure burial for his wife in 'holy ground' in the late seventh century and this was not implausibly near to a church, since it was said to be near sacred shrines and relics, and it was seemingly a consecrated cemetery. Also according to Bede, in addition to the abbesses and members of the royal family buried at Whitby, also buried there were many other noble folk. Whether the leading members of lay society were normally buried at or near major religious communities is unclear. Members of the aristocracy were certainly founding their own churches by the early eighth century. This is made clear by Bede's famous complaint in a letter to Bishop Egbert of York in 734 that they were founding churches of dubious quality and learning in order to acquire land from the king:

> those who are totally ignorant of the monastic life have received under their control . . . many places in the name of monasteries . . . having usurped for themselves estates and villages . . . they gratify their own desires alone, laymen in charge of monks; nay, rather, it is not monks that they collect there, but whomsoever they may perchance find wandering anywhere, expelled from true monasteries for the fault of disobedience, or whom they can allure out of the monasteries, or, indeed, those of their own followers whom they can persuade to promise to them the obedience of a monk and receive the tonsure

We should not assume that because Bede was critical of such churches that they did not provide adequate pastoral care and meet high ecclesiastical standards. Such churches

2 Grave marker from York Minster. Late seventh- to early ninth-century. The inscription reads: '+ Here [beneath this?] turf [or tomb?] rest the [remains?] of Wulfhere'. After CASSS volume III, copyright University of Durham, Tom Middlemass

The geography of death

3 Sarcophagus from St Alkmund, Derby. A fragment of the lid of this ninth-century sarcophagus also survives. It was discovered buried beneath the medieval floor of the church in 1967-8. It is not clear whether this sarcophagus was made for St Alkmund, or for Ealdorman Æthelwulf of Berkshire. Phil Sidebottom

4 Carved panel from Wirksworth (Derbs). This panel was found reused as a coffin lid beneath the floor of the church in 1821. Phil Sidebottom

5 Fragments of carved panel from South Kyme (Lincs). There has been debate about whether this panel was from a shrine or an altar. Photo Paul Everson and David Stocker. Copyright Department of Archaeology, University of Durham

clearly met the needs of some members of society, and may have become foci for burial of their patrons and their families, if not for anyone else.

In addition to the documentary evidence, there is also architectural and sculptural evidence that suggests that many churches served as burial grounds in the region from the eighth century onwards. This evidence includes grave covers, such as the highly decorated examples from Kirkdale (**1**), and various forms of grave markers, such as those carrying inscriptions excavated at York Minster (**2**) and Whitby. An elaborate sarcophagus was excavated at Derby, St Alkmund (Derbs) (**3**), and elaborately carved panels found at Wirksworth (Derbs) (**4**), Hovingham (Yorks) (**colour plate 1**) and South Kyme (Lincs) (**5**) may have formerly been panels from sarcophagi or shrines. Crypts may also have been used for burial, and they survive at Ripon and Repton, as do mausolea such as a sunken two-celled example from Repton (see below, p.23). Many eighth- and ninth-century stone crosses have been found in or near churches in the region, and while none of these has ever been found *in situ* in a funerary context, it is not implausible that some of them had a funerary or commemorative function (see below pp.126-8), although, obviously, we do not know whether crosses were invariably erected at the site where the individual commemorated was buried.

Archaeological evidence enables us to identify many more burial sites of the seventh to ninth centuries. It also reveals that during that time many burial grounds came into and went out of use, even some associated with churches, as did churches themselves. A

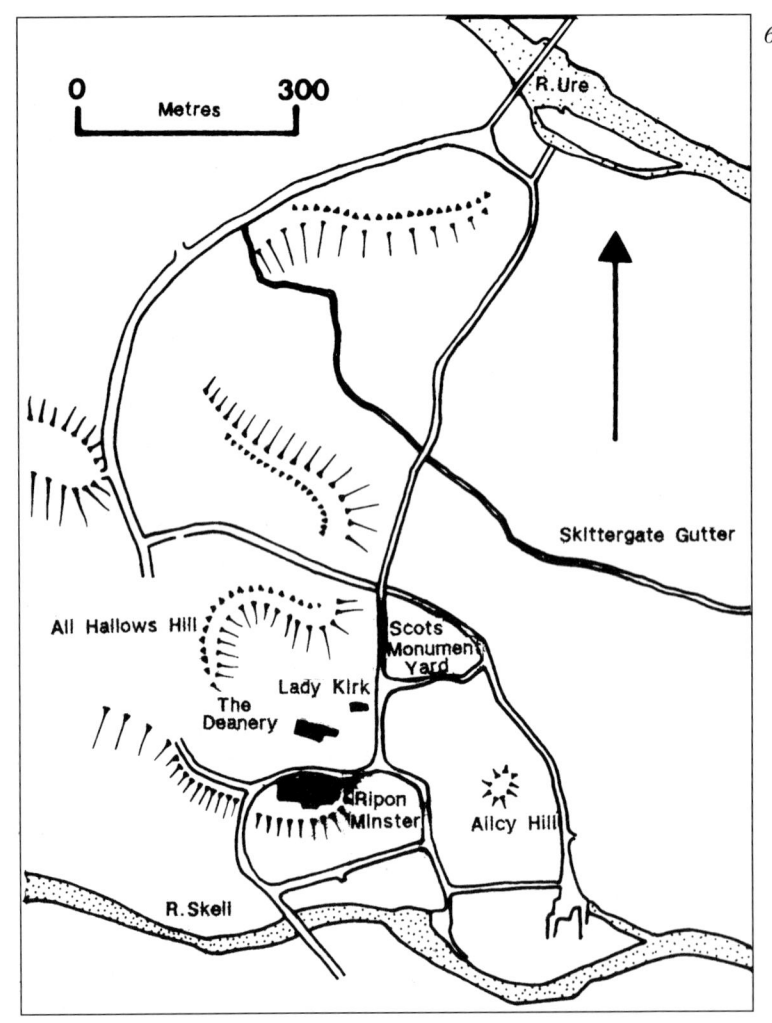

6 *Location of Anglo-Saxon cemeteries at Ripon (Yorks). After Hall and Whyman 1996, Alex Norman*

number of early religious communities are characterized by the presence of numerous ecclesiastical and burial foci, often placed in striking topographical settings. At Ripon, for example, there are several sites on prominences within *c*.2-300m of St Peter's church that have produced evidence for burial (**6**). First, St Peter's itself with its seventh-century crypt was where St Wilfrid was buried in the early eighth century, on the south side of the altar according to Bede. Second, a cemetery at Ailcy Hill which appears, on the basis of radiocarbon dates taken from the skeletal remains, to have been in use between the sixth/seventh centuries and the tenth century (the published dates are 550-660, 660-810, 680-880, 660-830, 780-990 cal. AD). Second, a cemetery associated with a two-celled church, the Ladykirk, which is ostensibly undated but which has produced fragments of sculpture of eighth- and ninth-century date. Some of the burials were associated with the church, but others were cut by it, demonstrating that burial preceded the construction of the church. Burials which may be broadly contemporary have also been excavated on the other side of St Marygate from the Ladykirk, in the Deanery Garden, and at All Hallows

Hill, although no secure dating evidence has been recovered. The various burial grounds have particular characteristics, which suggest that they may have provided burial for distinctive parts of the local population (see below, pp.99-100). The archaeological evidence also suggests that the religious community founded at Ripon by the later seventh century took over a site that had an existing burial ground at Ailcy Hill. The earliest complete west-east aligned burials had disturbed earlier burials, apparently aligned north-south. The change in orientation appears to have been accompanied by a change in the population that was being buried there. The earlier burials were of men, women and children who were presumably members of the local community, whereas the later burials seem to consist only of adult males and this may be an indication that only members of the religious community were then being buried at Ailcy Hill.

At Repton a similar pattern emerges of multiple ecclesiastical and burial foci located in a striking setting, in this case on a bluff overlooking the River Trent (**7**). There is, as at Ripon, evidence for transitions in burial practices, and for fluctuations in the use of burial sites. For example, about 30 burials have been excavated which preceded the construction of the crypt. The crypt seals a layer which contains a coin of *c*.715 and is separated from the burials by a number of pebble surfaces, followed by a timber building, and so the burials would appear to be of seventh-century date (although it should be noted that one of the burials which possibly belongs to this group had a coin in its hand of *c*.725 date). These burials seem to have been associated with a church, to judge from the presence of imported vessel glass and window glass. Following the construction of the crypt, burials took place to the south and east through the eighth and ninth centuries, and from the tenth century to the north. The crypt was later incorporated into a church. There was a two-celled sunken structure to the west of the church, which was probably a mausoleum. It had seemingly fallen into disrepair by the later ninth century, as the excavation of it revealed fallen pieces of moulded stucco, window glass and roof lead. It was subsequently used to inter the disarticulated remains of some 250 or more individuals. It is uncertain whether this was the result of a single act (perhaps associated with the visit of a Viking army in 873-4, as some have suggested) or the product of gradual accretion since radiocarbon dates have been recovered which range from the eighth to tenth centuries (see below, pp.100-3). Burial subsequently occurred over and around the mound covering the mausoleum. The cutting of a V-shaped ditch, *c*.10m wide and *c*.4m deep, disturbed burial near to the crypt. This ditch was filled back in after 30 to 35 years. The ditch has been associated with the activities of the Viking army that over-wintered at Repton in 873-4, although the purpose that it was intended to serve is unclear, given that it appears that the army had involved itself in internecine warfare in Mercia, and may have allied itself with one faction (see below, p.102).

At Whitby, recent (and on-going) excavations of the cemetery at Abbey Lands Farm, *c*.200m south of the medieval Abbey church, have added considerably to the picture provided by both documentary evidence and the poorly recorded excavations of the 1920s, and subsequent limited excavation of 1958. Over 100 burials have so far been excavated, although the cemetery clearly extended beyond the excavated area. Dating is difficult, but a few associated finds suggest that the cemetery was in use some time between the seventh and ninth centuries. However, the presence of Roman pottery and a Roman gaming-piece has

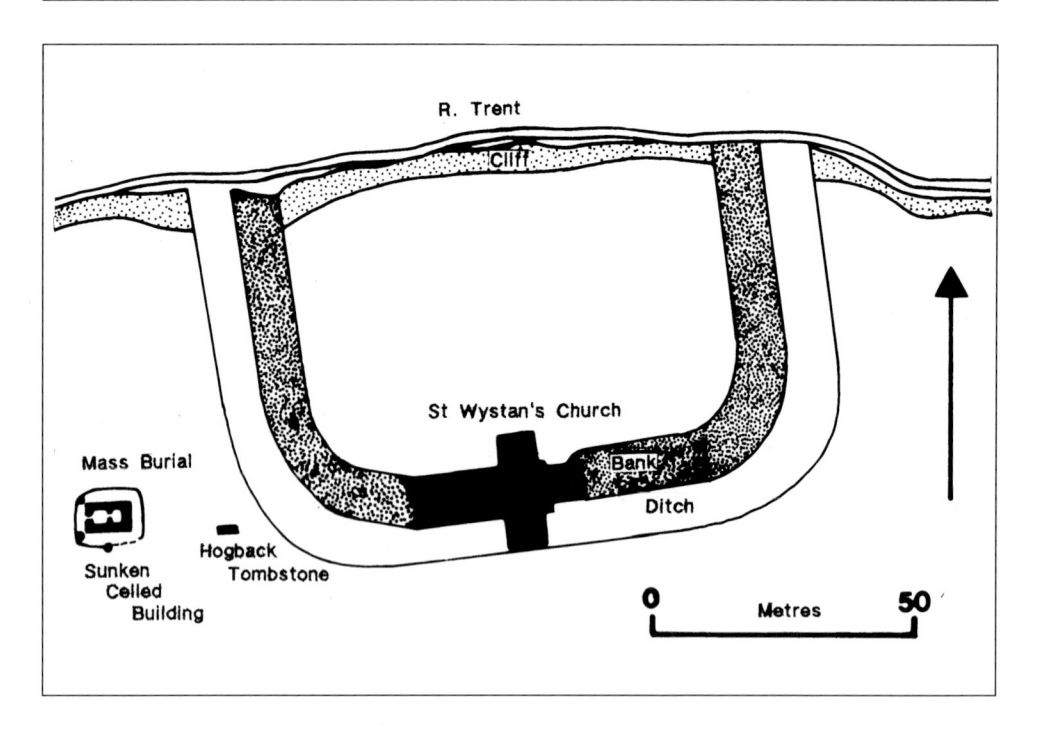

7 *Church and mausoleum at Repton (Derbs). This plan shows the location of recent excavation and geophysical survey at Repton.* After Biddle and Kjølbye-Biddle 1992, Alex Norman

encouraged speculation that there may have been a cemetery on the headland during the Roman period, although only future excavation or radiocarbon dates will enable us to determine whether this was, indeed, the case. The cemetery appears to have been divided into two parts by a wall running north-south. The alignments of the burials on either side of the wall are slightly different, and there is more intercutting of graves on the east side of the wall and to the north. It has been suggested that the cemetery was once defined by a boundary wall, but was extended at a later date. Previous excavations and the survival of Anglo-Saxon funerary sculpture suggest that there may also been early medieval burials to the north of the medieval Abbey church, although the reliability of the 1920s excavations is open to question.

Recent excavations at Flixborough (Lincs) have revealed a so-called 'high status' site occupied from the seventh century into the post-Conquest period. One building contained four burials and had a fifth immediately outside, and this may have been a church or chapel (**colour plate 2**). The presence of a church is certainly suggested by some of the artefacts discovered at the site. These include items suggestive of literacy, such as styli, book-mounts, an alphabet ring, and an inscribed lead-plaque, which had possibly been attached to a reliquary (**colour plate 3**), and there is also evidence for glazed windows, which at such a date is likely to have come from an ecclesiastical context. Burial also took place in a small inhumation cemetery close to the settlement area, of which eleven graves have been excavated. The graves were aligned west-east, there were no grave goods and they included both male and female adult burials. The burials have been dated to the eighth or ninth centuries on the basis of the juxtaposition with the settlement and the presence of iron coffin-fittings, although it is possible that they are later in date. The practice of burial at these two sites appears to have been short-lived, and it is not clear where the inhabitants of Flixborough continued to bury their dead, although the site of the later parish church is a possibility. That the site underwent a change of function is suggested by the fact that a hearth was inserted into the eastern end of the building interpreted as a church some time before the mid-ninth century when the building was demolished. It should also be noted that the artefacts associated with an ecclesiastical foundation are found at Flixborough only from the eighth and ninth centuries.

There is, then, some evidence to suggest that there were two or more cemeteries associated with some churches of seventh-, eighth- or ninth-century foundation. Sometimes these cemeteries can be distinguished not just by their location but also on the basis of the demographic characteristics of the population buried in them, the nature of the burials (whether in coffins, sarcophagi, or placed directly in the ground), or the location of the burials (in a church or mausoleum, within or some distance from the church). Some churches appear to have had separate burial grounds for the laity and for members of the religious community, with the cemetery for the latter consisting of predominantly or solely male burials (where it is a male religious house).

In some cases, cemeteries, or parts of cemeteries, were in use for a relatively short period of time, and there is evidence for the periodic reorganization of cemeteries throughout the Anglo-Saxon period. Other examples may be added to those discussed above. At Crayke (Yorks), for example, Anglo-Saxon burials have been excavated outside the limits of the nineteenth-century graveyard (**8**). This cemetery, or at least part of it, seems to have been abandoned in the post-Conquest period as it was covered with a layer that included late medieval pottery. Radiocarbon dates (AD 770-1020) suggest that the abandoned part of the cemetery had probably been in use between the eighth and early eleventh centuries. Finds of later medieval pottery suggest that the area was no longer used for burial much after the eleventh century. We know that the religious community was founded around 685 by St Cuthbert, who was granted land at Crayke to use as a dwelling place on his journeys from Lindisfarne to York. However, it is not certain that the excavated burials were those of members of the monastic community. There were adult male and female burials in this part of the cemetery and it may have been a lay cemetery, although it is possible that there were women within the religious community. This is suggested by the fact that in the later ninth century the community was headed by someone who is said to have been called *Geve*, which is a female name. If this is correct this may indicate that both monks and nuns occupied Crayke. It is, as yet, unknown whether there was another cemetery associated with the religious community established at Crayke, but by analogy with the other sites we have considered it is not implausible that there should have been more than one burial site. The excavated burials were not in alignment with the later medieval church at Crayke and, given that burials near churches commonly follow the same alignment, it may either be the case that the church was later rebuilt on a different alignment, or that the church associated with the burials was located elsewhere in Crayke. In this respect the discovery of fragments of eighth- or ninth-century sculpture further down the hill near Crayke Hall may be significant.

The geography of death

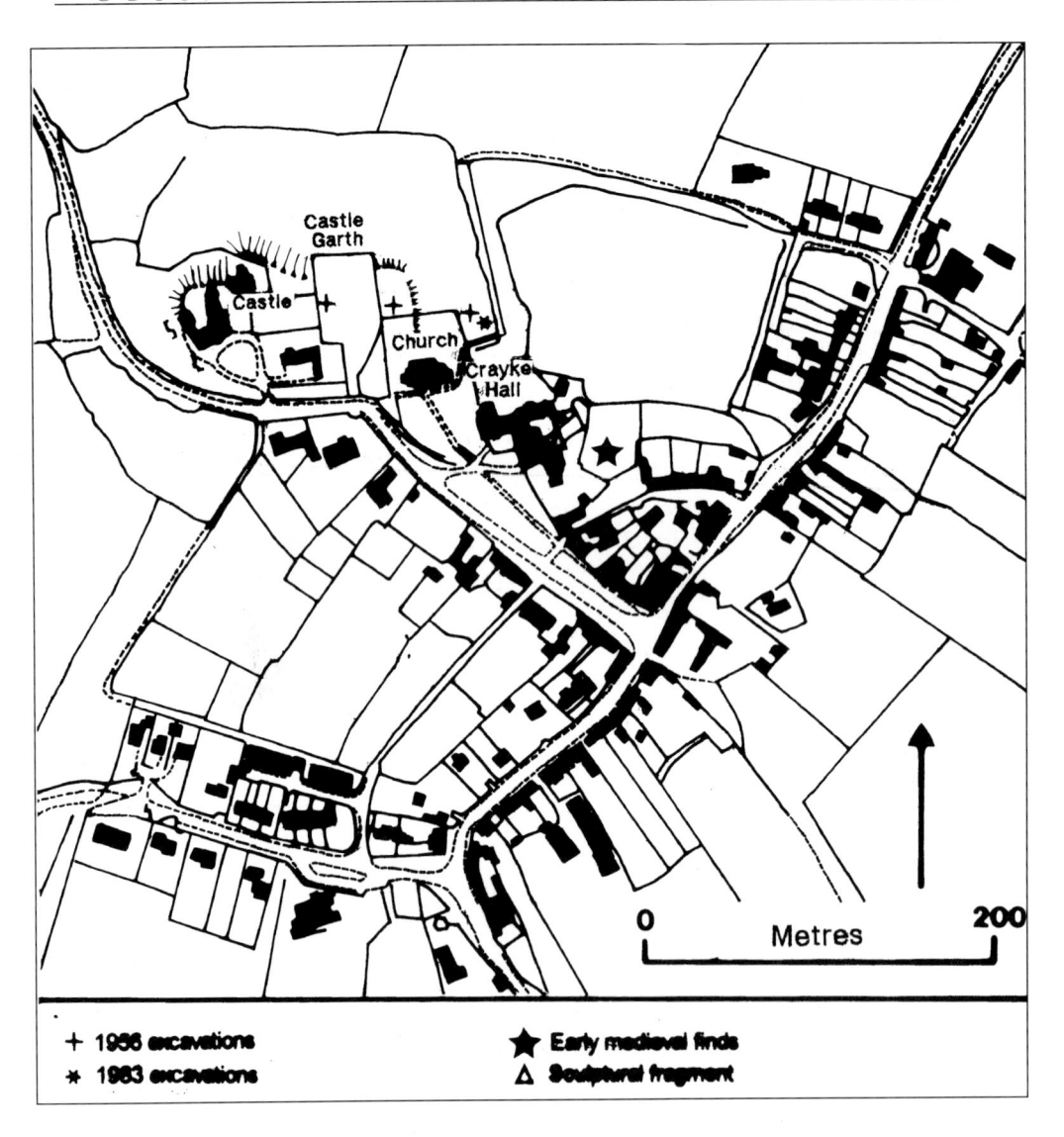

8 Cemetery at Crayke (Yorks). This plan shows the location of excavation and the find-spot of pieces of Anglo-Saxon sculpture. After Adams 1990, Alex Norman

At Addingham (Yorks) a number of mid- to later Anglo-Saxon burials have been excavated to the west of the present parish churchyard, near a church which was associated from at least the end of the ninth century with the archbishops of York (**9**). There were no grave goods, coffins or other datable features, but radiocarbon techniques have dated the cemetery (AD 880-990, 670-790, 670-860, 720-900 at I). This cemetery appears to have gone out of use in the eleventh or twelfth century, when the manorial centre at Addingham spread over the former burial ground, and burial was confined to, or moved to, an area much closer to the parish church. The burials at Addingham were probably

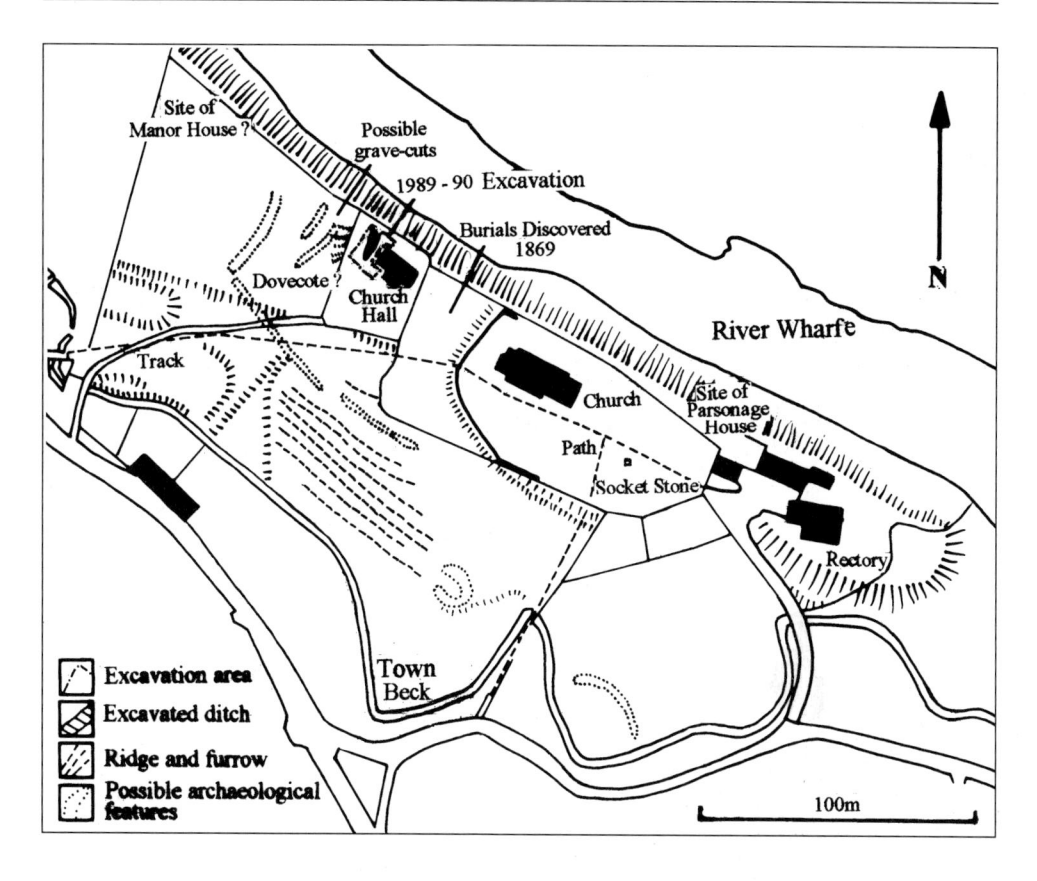

9 Burials at Addingham (Yorks). This plan shows the location of the most recent excavations, and other archaeological features found in the vicinity. After Adams 1996, Alex Norman

those of a lay community, as they included adult males and females and infants. It is possible, given the short life of this cemetery, that rather than there being one continuous area of ground devoted to burial, that there may have been discrete cemeteries opened for burial at different periods, or perhaps for different sectors of the population during the same period.

At Kirkdale (Yorks) recent excavations have uncovered a series of graves to the north of the churchyard. The area was subsequently cultivated and has produced *c.*500 sherds of eleventh- and twelfth-century pottery, suggesting that it was no longer used for burial at that date. The present church and churchyard are clearly the remnants of a once larger religious complex about which little is known, as it is not documented in the Anglo-Saxon period. Finds from the site include carved stone grave covers (*see* **1**) and high status metal (*see* **48**) and glass artefacts, and they suggest that this was a major religious centre in the eighth and ninth centuries. Burials excavated near to the church were on a similar alignment to the burials excavated in the north field, but different from the alignment of the existing church, suggesting that the church had been rebuilt on a slightly different alignment. The site was clearly reorganized at some point, probably in the eleventh century. Indeed, there is a sundial at Kirkdale that recorded that the church was rebuilt from its dilapidated state in the mid-eleventh century:

> Orm, son of Gamal, bought St Gregory's minster when it was completely ruined and collapsed, and he had it constructed recently from the ground to Christ and St Gregory, in the days of King Edward [the Confessor] and in the days of Earl Tosti. And Hawardmade me and Brand the priest.

By this time, if not long after, the burial ground to the north of the church had gone out of use.

Excavations outside the western boundary of the parish churchyard of All Saints at Pontefract (Yorks) have revealed a large burial ground of seventh- to ninth- or tenth-century date, according to unpublished radiocarbon dates. Little is known about the early history of Pontefract, although it may have been an important estate centre or vill at the time of King Eadred's visit to meet the Archbishop of York and the Northumbrian councillors in 947 (it was then known as Tanshelf). Symeon of Durham, writing in the early twelfth century, refers to Pontefract as 'Kirkebi' (an Old Norse name meaning 'settlement of the church'), a name that suggests that it was the site of a relatively important church in the tenth century when such a name must have been coined. The burials were, indeed, associated with an Anglo-Saxon church, but it has not been possible to date it closely (**10, 11**). It appears that the later parish church of All Saints was either accompanied by or preceded by another church. Whatever type of church this was, the cemetery associated with it included adult males and females and infants, suggesting that it was a lay cemetery. This burial ground at Pontefract appears to have extended up the hill towards the location of the Norman castle, and it may have been truncated by the construction of the castle, since a number of burials have been excavated that preceded the castle's Norman chapel. The eastern part of the cemetery appears to have been encroached upon by urban development of the eleventh and twelfth centuries.

It is increasingly apparent that the cemeteries of early medieval religious communities either went out of use, or contracted in size in the later Anglo-Saxon period or in the period

10 Anglo-Saxon church and cemetery at Pontefract (Yorks). West Yorkshire Archaeological Service

immediately following the Norman Conquest. Changes to the local settlement pattern doubtless explain many of these examples of shrunken or abandoned cemeteries. It may also be, however, that in some of these cases the church had undergone a change in status, from that of a sizeable religious community, to that of, effectively, a parish church, meaning that there was no longer any need to provide a burial ground for members of the religious house. In others, the lay population for which the church provided burial may have declined in size, perhaps as a result of the foundation of other churches in the vicinity that were permitted burial rights. We also know that some cemeteries were disturbed or obliterated as churches were built and extended during the seventh to ninth centuries, as we have seen at Repton, Ripon and Pontefract. In the tenth and eleventh centuries, even more examples of burials disturbed by ecclesiastical building campaigns can be found. For example, at Stow (Lincs) recent excavations in the angle between the nave and the north transept have shown that the porticus of the later Anglo-Saxon church disturbed a number of graves which seem to have been associated with an earlier church.

11 Burial truncated by walls of the church at Pontefract (Yorks). West Yorkshire Archaeological Service

Non-churchyard burial

Not everyone was buried in or near churches between the seventh and ninth centuries. The most visible and well-studied examples of non-churchyard burial from the seventh century are found in barrows. There are many in the Peak District of Derbyshire and in the Yorkshire Wolds. Some of these barrow burials, such as those at Benty Grange, Cow Low (Derbs), Caenby (Lincs) and Painsthorpe Wold (Yorks), included elaborate assemblages of grave goods (see below, pp.93-4) (**colour plate 4**). Such elaborate barrow burials have been interpreted by some archaeologists as a defiant pagan reaction to the new Christian religion. Yet there is nothing that is *prima facie* un-Christian about either burial in a barrow or with grave goods (see below, p.94). They were clearly in use within a broadly Christian milieu, and these barrows may represent, rather, an aristocratic alternative to churchyard burial. Both forms of burial are proclamations of status. Those who chose elaborate burial in barrows may have done so because they did not have strong family ties to any particular minster church, which would have obliged their kin to take them there and the religious communities to accept them.

The use of prehistoric barrows and enclosures and newly-made barrows for burial in the seventh and eighth century has been identified at many sites, but not all are as elaborate as those described above, and many included unaccompanied burials, or burials with only occasional grave goods, in particular small knives. Little attention has been paid to these, and they have tended to be assigned earlier rather than later dates. This is not necessarily the case, and it is worth noting that many of the artefacts found in such burials (such as knives) are largely undecorated and, thus, undatable. A recently excavated cemetery accompanied by evidence for buildings at Thwing (Yorks) is located within a series of Bronze Age enclosures. The burials are west-east aligned, without grave goods, some had coffins, and there is evidence for grave markers. The cemetery has been dated to the seventh to tenth centuries, on the basis of the coffins, radiocarbon dates and associated settlement evidence (see below, p.95). Unelaborate burials associated with prehistoric features have also been found at Garton Slack (Green Lane crossing site, and at the site known as Garton Slack I), Cottam (Kemp Howe), Fimber, Painsthorpe Wold, Uncleby (Yorks), and Hurdlow (Derbs). At Ash Hill, Swinhope (Lincs) two skeletons were found in a barrow previously used in the Neolithic for burial, and they have produced radiocarbon dates ranging between the late ninth and early eleventh century (cal AD 885-1010).

Many of the well-known elaborate barrow burials may have been accompanied by a series of adjacent, unelaborate burials. At Painsthorpe Wold, for example, the burial mentioned above was accompanied by other unelaborate burials. At Calver Low (Derbs) the tumulus seen in the mid-nineteenth century by Thomas Bateman was not excavated and so we do not know what sort of burial it may have contained, but nearby there were five burials, of which four were unaccompanied by grave goods and the other contained only a small knife. The excavations of the nineteenth century generally concentrated on the barrows themselves and their rich contents, and this may have skewed our understanding of the setting, and hence the significance, of barrow burials.

A number of churches built in the tenth or eleventh century have been shown to have been preceded by burial grounds, for which there is no evidence of an earlier associated church, and this may provide evidence of other non-churchyard burials prior to the tenth century. At Barton-upon-Humber (Lincs) burial at the site of St Peter's must have begun in the later ninth century and includes a series of burials, many of which were in wooden coffins (*see* **32**). Before the foundations of the tenth-century church were dug, over twenty burials were exhumed. At Barrow-upon-Humber (Lincs) another late Anglo-Saxon church was clearly preceded by a series of burials, as the footings cut through some of the burials. The stone linings of two burials are typical of later Anglo-Saxon burials, and disturbed soil above some of the burials has produced two coins of *c*.870. A series of radiocarbon dates acquired from the skeletal material have centred on a date around *c*.900. Of course, either or both of the cemeteries which preceded the tenth-century churches could have been associated with a yet-to-be-discovered church nearby, or have been satellite burial grounds of some other church, as the two excavated churches were not necessarily the only churches in the vicinity. It is conceivable that these burial sites were in some way connected to the religious community founded in the vicinity by St Chad in the late 660s *æt Bæruwe*, assuming of course, that it survived into the ninth century.

The church built at Kellington (Yorks) in the later eleventh century was positioned over an earlier cemetery, in which at least one of the burials was aligned north-south (**colour plate 5**). At Holton-le-Clay (Lincs) traces of middle Saxon domestic settlement were overlain by a late Anglo-Saxon cemetery, which was then built over in the later eleventh century when the church was constructed. There may, however, have been a church by the later tenth century given the survival of a fragment of a tenth-century carved stone grave slab built into the tower, since such pieces of sculpture are commonly found in association with contemporary churches.

Burial at or near churches was not universal prior to the tenth century. Burial in or near prehistoric barrows and enclosures, and the occasional newly erected barrow, was not uncommon in the seventh century and recent research has suggested that such settings may have continued as a location for burial much later. Some churches built during the later Anglo-Saxon centuries were clearly built over existing cemeteries, and it may be that these were cemeteries unassociated with a church prior to the tenth or eleventh century. On the other hand, such an interpretation depends on an absence of evidence for an earlier church, and it would not be wise to press the case.

Saints' cults

The relics of saints were an important feature of the funerary landscape of Anglo-Saxon society. Cults and religious communities were intimately linked, and cults provided a focal point for pilgrimage and patronage. They conferred prestige, they were central to local pastoral work and they were important to regional traditions and identities. They also eventually became a part of the English cultural tradition, in which the whole nation could share by the eleventh century. Cults also attracted the burial of the wealthy and the influential in society, who wanted the benefits that burial near to the saints (*ad sanctos*) conferred. A number of saints' cults and the resting-places of many saints are recorded in the region, in saints' *Lives*, the writing of Bede, and in an Old English list of saints' resting-places (called the *Secgan be þam Godes sanctum þe on Engla lande ærost reston*) which survives in two eleventh-century manuscripts, but the first part of which was compiled in the ninth century. From the latter source we know that saints were venerated at the following churches by the end of the ninth century, although many of these relics were to be removed from these churches in the tenth or early eleventh century. Bishop John (d.721) rested at Beverley, and the remains of Bishop Wilfrid (d.709), Bishop Ecgbert (d.729) and Wihtberht, probably one of Ecgbert's companions who went to Frisia to preach in the late seventh century, were at Ripon. Hygbald, possibly a late seventh-century abbot in Lindsey mentioned in passing by Bede, rested at Hibaldstow (literally 'Hygbald's holy place') (Lincs), and Eadburh, whose identity is uncertain, rested at Southwell (Notts). Other saints who died in the seventh, eighth or ninth centuries listed by this source include Alkmund (Derby) (d.800), Wystan (Repton) (d.849), Guthlac (Crowland, Lincs) (d.714),

Osthryth and Æthelred (Bardney) who died in the late seventh and early eighth century respectively. The majority of King Oswald of Northumbria (d.642) was said to rest at Gloucester, while his head was with St. Cuthbert at Lindisfarne and his arm at Bamburgh (Northumb). However, Bede reveals that some or all of the remains of Oswald were brought in the later seventh century to the monastery at Bardney (Lincs), and his remains were removed to Gloucester in 909 during the wars against the Scandinavian raiders.

It is not clear why some individuals that we know to have been venerated at churches in northern England in the early medieval period are not included in this late Anglo-Saxon list of saints' resting-places. There is no mention of anyone we know to have been buried at Whitby or at York, for example. It may be because this list of saints' relics recorded only saints' cults that were still actively venerated at the time when the list was compiled. Support for this hypothesis comes from later lists of saints' resting-places, such as that contained in the *Chronicle of Hugh Candidus* of Peterborough (Cambs) of the mid-twelfth century, and two other lists of the fourteenth century, which, while similar to the Old English lists, have some omissions and some additions. It is as if they were 'living' documents, changed as interest in saints waxed and waned. The list of Hugh Candidus mentions that the saints Wulfrannus, Symphorianus (a Cornish saint) and Etritha rested at Grantham (Lincs), St Bertun (an eighth-century abbot) at Beverley, Hild (the first abbess) at Whitby, and Æthelburg at Hackness (who must be the Abbess Æthelburh referred to in the *Life of St Wilfrid* as a witness to the death of King Aldfrith in 705, and the Oedilburga commemorated on a cross-shaft in the church (*see* **45**)). Hugh may well have been drawing on a now lost list of northern saints, as it is unlikely that he added these, and many other, entries from his own research. Indeed, the form of many of the place-names he uses suggests that he was drawing on an Old English list. The lists of saints' resting-places also indicates that there was not thought to be a problem with venerating parts of saints, as the entries for St Oswald make clear.

It is particularly significant that the Anglo-Saxon lists of saints' resting-places survive in two eleventh-century manuscripts. Clearly other earlier, probably regional, lists pre-dated the surviving versions, and it may be that the saints of earlier Anglo-Saxon kingdoms were in the eleventh century drawn together to emphasize 'the saintly prestige of the country as a whole' (Rollason 1978, 83). William of Malmesbury writing in the early twelfth century drew a distinction between the Normans and the English on the basis of their possession of saints' relics, directly linking the English possession of relics with the power and prestige of the English nation.

Saints' cults were commonly politically very sensitive. For example, the monks at Bardney were less than happy to receive the remains of King Oswald of Northumbria on the recommendation of Queen Osthryth of Mercia, who was his niece. Oswald had previously conquered the province of Lindsey, and the monks left the cart bearing his remains outside overnight. They were only persuaded to take his remains by 'a sign from heaven', in the form of a pillar of light shining upwards from the cart. St Alkmund was a Northumbrian prince who had fled to Mercia and was allegedly murdered by the command of a Northumbrian king from a rival dynasty. The fact that his cult was fostered at Derby in Mercia implies the involvement of the Mercian royal house. The Mercians were in dispute with the Northumbrians in the early ninth century, and they may have promoted the cult of a murdered prince of Northumbria to try to undermine the Northumbrian king's position given his alleged involvement in the murder.

Both the Scandinavian raids and settlement of the ninth and tenth centuries, and the West Saxon conquest of the region in the tenth century, affected the landscape of sanctity in northern England. The remains of St Cuthbert were taken from their resting-place on Lindisfarne in 875 and the community moved around northern England for the next seven years, staying briefly at Crayke, before eventually settling at Chester-le-Street (Co. Durham). It has often been suggested that they were fleeing the Scandinavian raiders; however, while this may initially have been true, they did actually make efforts to come to terms with the raiders, and were instrumental in approaching one group and arranging the election of one of their number as king (below, p.177). West Saxon activity in the North was often accompanied by the removal of saints' relics from some of the major churches of the region, which will have had a major impact on patterns of pilgrimage, and commemoration of the dead, and on the prestige of the churches concerned. The removal of relics from churches was also an attack on their prosperity, since relics both attracted patronage and could be used to legitimate and protect landed possessions. The relics of St Oswald were taken by West Saxon initiative from Bardney into Mercia in 909, and Alfred's daughter Æthelflaed may have been behind the transfer of the relics of St Alkmund from Derby to Shrewsbury, and those of St Werburgh from Hanbury (Staffs) to Chester. According to William of Malmesbury, Glastonbury acquired the relics of many northern saints, including those of Hild of Whitby, Ceolfrith of Monkwearmouth-Jarrow and Aidan of Lindisfarne, and this transfer of relics was possibly associated with the military campaigns of King Edmund of Wessex in the 940s. The campaign of his successor, King Eadred, in 948, which resulted in the burning of the monastery at Ripon, may have been the occasion when the relics of St Wilfrid and the Ripon copy of Stephen's eighth-century *Life of St Wilfrid* were removed to Canterbury (Kent). In addition to the recorded removal of relics, one wonders what happened to the relics undoubtedly associated with the remains of shrines discovered at, for example, Wirksworth, South Kyme and Hovingham (*see* **4**, **5**, **colour plate 1**).

The Vikings

From the last decade of the eighth century Scandinavian raiders plagued England. It was not to be until nearly a century later, however, that the raiders began to settle in Northumbria, eastern Mercia and East Anglia. However, written sources have very little to reveal about how this settlement was effected or precisely where the newcomers settled. The Anglo-Saxon Chronicle simply tells us that the various leaders of the Scandinavian armies 'shared out the land' of the various kingdoms. Other types of evidence, such as that of place-names and archaeology, are not reliable guides to the Scandinavian settlements, and they do little more than to support broadly the impression given by the Chronicle that the Scandinavians settled in northern and eastern England. A discussion of where the Scandinavian settlers buried their dead is hampered not only by this lack of information on where they lived but also by the difficulty of identifying the burials of Scandinavians.

It has been traditional to identify Scandinavian burials on the basis of alien burial rites, that is burial in unusual settings (such as barrows), burial with grave goods, and cremation (**12**). Yet there are problems with this approach. Burial practices in northern England were clearly not uniform in the ninth century, and it is important to note that burial practice was not uniform in contemporary Scandinavia either. Cremation, inhumation with and without grave goods, ship burial, and burial under cairns and mounds were all practised in Scandinavia in the ninth century, often in the same region or even the same cemetery. Thus, the identification of burial by or of Scandinavians is not straightforward.

Nonetheless, there are a few burials from northern England that it is difficult to explain as anything other than those of Scandinavians. These include the cremations found at a few sites, such as Heath Wood, Ingleby (Derbs) (**colour plate 6**), and Hesket-in-the-Forest (Cumbria). Other burials traditionally identified as Scandinavian are inhumations with grave goods. Again, this interpretation may well be appropriate, even if the grave goods are commonly of Anglo-Saxon origin. It should be noted, however, that many of the supposed burials with grave goods have, in fact, been identified solely on the basis of the discovery of jewellery or weapons in churchyards, not actually *in situ* in a grave. In total, the apparently Scandinavian burials that have been identified in England come from around only 25 sites (**12**).

The traditional map of 'Viking' burials may be misleading, since there are many more sites of burial in the later ninth and tenth century than are normally included on the map. Many of these cemeteries may easily have witnessed the burial of Scandinavian settlers, but they have not previously been discussed in the context of Scandinavian burials because they are not considered diagnostic of Scandinavian burial. It is, in truth, an entirely circular argument. The traditional map also omits the evidence of funerary sculpture which is found at dozens of sites in the ninth and tenth century and which indicates the existence of burial grounds of that date. It is difficult to maintain that the Scandinavian newcomers had a major impact on the geography of burial. Although a few new sites may have been used, on the whole the settlers seem to have quickly made use of existing cemeteries. Even the examples of cremation and inhumation in mounds, of which a number of examples have been excavated in Cumbria, appear to make use of mounds previously used for burial, or to have continued an indigenous practice.

The tenth and eleventh centuries

The question of where individuals were to be buried became particularly acute by the later Anglo-Saxon period. Prior to this time burial in churchyards may have been limited only to the social elite and ecclesiastics at the major religious houses of the region, such as Ripon, Repton and Whitby. However, increasing numbers of churches were being founded by the tenth century and it is likely that they had or wished to acquire the right to bury. Certainly by the tenth century, regulations were being made in law-codes about ecclesiastical receipts such as tithe and soul-scot, and they stress the importance of such payments being made to the rightful church. For example, a law-code of the third decade of the tenth century instructed reeves to make sure that tithe, soul-scot, church-scot and

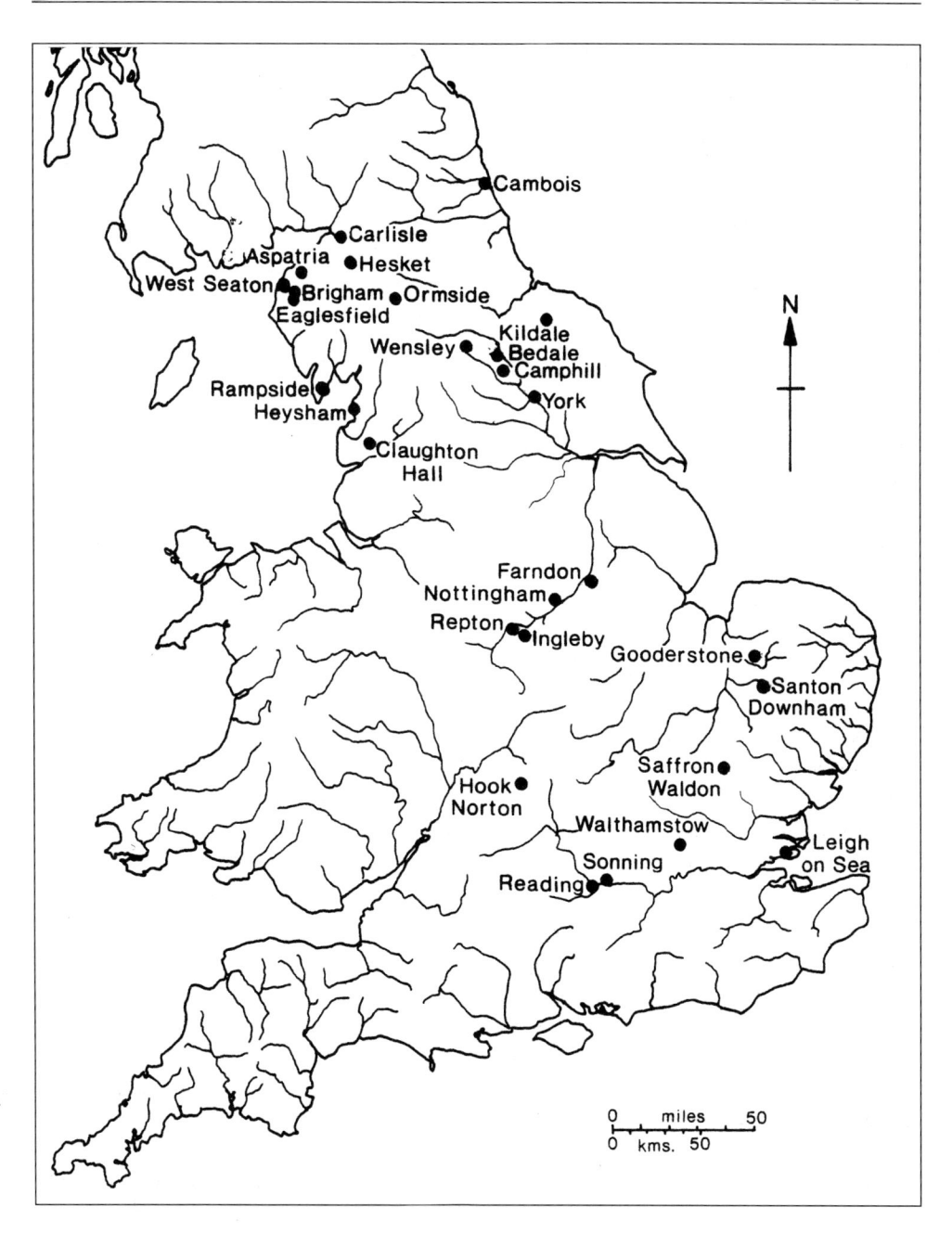

12 Map of 'Viking' burials in England. After Richards 1991, Colin Merrony

plough alms go to their lawful recipient, and a law-code of 1014 sought to ensure that soul-scot was to be paid for each corpse 'at the open grave'. Distinctions were also being drawn between churches with burial rights and churches without, and they suggest that this was also becoming an important test of status for churches. For example, a law-code issued by King Edgar (960-2) distinguishes between a church with a graveyard and one without, a factor that determined the amount of tithe to be paid by the thegn on whose land the church was located. In another code issued by Æthelred II in 1008 it is stated that 'if any body is buried elsewhere, outside the proper parish (*rihtscriftscire*), the payment for the soul is nevertheless to be paid to the minster to which it belonged'. There is little to suggest that burial in a cemetery at, or belonging to, a mother (or minster) church, or indeed any church, was either expected or demanded much before the tenth century, which is when the earliest surviving legislative control over burial location is found. It may be that it was only in the tenth century that the majority of people were for the first time told where they must bury their dead. This was also the time when certain individuals were forbidden from Christian burial in consecrated ground if they had been excommunicated or died without atoning for their sins, and the earliest surviving evidence for the consecration of churchyards also comes from the late tenth and eleventh centuries.

The homilist Ælfric of Eynsham commented *c*.1006 on the unholy behaviour that might break out when there was a dispute over where an individual was to be buried, and who was to receive the mortuary payment:

> Some priests are glad when men die and they flock to the corpse like greedy ravens when they see a carcass, in wood or in field; but it is fitting for a [priest] ... to attend the men who belong to his parish (*hyrnysse*) at his church; and he must never go into another's district to any corpse, unless he is invited.

The increasing concern to regulate burial location in the tenth century encouraged the Church to distinguish who was permitted burial in a churchyard and who was not. A law-code issued by King Edmund (939-46) stipulated that ecclesiastics who had failed to observe celibacy or who had had intercourse with a nun, and murderers and adulterers were not to be permitted burial in consecrated ground. The legislation of Æthelred II (978-1016) also prevented individuals who had committed violent burglary or murder and those who had a lack of legal surety from burial in consecrated ground. Later Anglo-Saxon law-codes also stipulate the range of crimes that would result in capital punishment, and given that this excluded them from burial in consecrated ground there must have been many execution cemeteries spread across the country. One Anglo-Saxon execution site that has so far been identified in our region is at Walkington Wold (Yorks). Twelve skeletons cut into a Bronze Age barrow have been excavated, of which ten had been decapitated, and one had its hands tied.

These law-codes were undoubtedly responding to a situation that was emerging and it is presumably not coincidental that the archaeological record reveals that the tenth century witnessed a proliferation of church foundations. In northern England they seem typically to have had an associated graveyard at their foundation. This has been revealed both by excavation and the survival of funerary sculpture. It must be significant that the regions where they are most common are characterized by few mother churches with large parishes. It is not entirely clear whether the proliferation of tenth-century churches caused, or was the result of, the decline in the roles of mother churches. Whatever the case, the period witnessed the increasing use of local churchyards by the elite, and probably also their followers and tenants, to bury their dead and to memorialize themselves; and this, along with the corresponding legislative efforts to protect the rights of mother churches, may have been the factors that finally made churchyard burial the norm.

This is not to say, however, that the location or size of cemeteries remained stable from that date. Throughout the regions examined in this study numerous burials have been excavated that appear to belong to the later Anglo-Saxon period. Some are not associated with a surviving church, and others are located near to medieval churches but outside the limits of the current churchyard. The burials are typically aligned west-east, unaccompanied by grave goods or with only a few, in particular small knives, and they occasionally contain evidence for the presence of coffins. Examples from Lincolnshire include the 11 burials aligned west-east found at Whitton (**13**) *c*.50m from the church, and the skeletons found *c*.70m from the churchyard at Great Hale. Similar burials have been found outside the churchyard at Kilham (Yorks), and the remains of four or five individuals have been recovered at Belton from graves that, at least in two cases, were aligned west-east, and with evidence for possible coffin-fittings in one. At Fillingham around nine burials have been excavated, along with the charnel from many more (**14, colour plate 7**). intact burials were aligned west-east and contained no grave goods. The graves were stone-lined, which is a characteristic feature of later Anglo-Saxon burial practices, as we shall see (below, p.106). The burials were located around 200m from the parish church, the earliest evidence for which comes from the eleventh century, and this suggests that either there was once a church at the west end of the village, or that burial occurred in the later Anglo-Saxon period at a site remote from the local church. Of the four inhumation burials found at Swaby one was aligned west-east and the others approximately south-south-west to north-north-east. The only associated datable material was eleventh-century and later pottery, and a bone comb of Anglo-Saxon date. There are many other examples of such small scattered cemeteries, some near to churches and others seemingly not, and while not all may be Anglo-Saxon in date, many may well be and would repay further investigation.

The main problem facing a discussion of these scattered later Anglo-Saxon burial grounds is that of dating burials unassociated with a church and unaccompanied by datable artefacts. In many cases only radiocarbon dating can help. A particularly instructive case of how radiocarbon dates can change our view of such burial sites comes from just outside our region, at Seaham (Co. Durham). There have been documented discoveries of human bones from the vicinity of Seaham Hall from the eighteenth century, and these have been variously labelled as prehistoric, Roman, 'British' and Anglo-Saxon. More recent excavations uncovered a group of ten inhumations aligned west-east which were unaccompanied by grave goods. Radiocarbon dating suggested that the burials were likely to have been within the period spanning the mid-seventh to late ninth centuries. Greater attention to such sites would potentially add much to our picture of Anglo-Saxon burial

13 Burials from Whitton (Lincs). The remains of 11 individual burials were found in an area measuring 2.0 x 2.5m. Some of the skeletons were cut by later burials indicating that the cemetery had been in use for some time. The site is c.50m from the parish churchyard. Kevin Leahy

practices in the seventh to eleventh centuries, about which we know much less than the burial practices of the preceding centuries. Clearly, any of these sites could have been associated with a church, which future investigation may reveal. But what is certain from the evidence currently available is that cemeteries were not an inherently stable feature in the later Anglo-Saxon landscape.

The written, sculptural and archaeological evidence from the region reveals that burial did take place at, in or near to some churches from an early date, but this may not have been afforded to anyone other than the local elite. For some, burial at a distance from churches continued to be practised right through the Anglo-Saxon centuries. This, however, is a long way from demonstrating that the Church had no control over burial at such sites before the respective churches were built. Recent work in Oxfordshire has demonstrated that a large late Anglo-Saxon cemetery located a couple of miles away from the church at Bampton was on land that belonged to the church and was presumably controlled by it. Nonetheless, it is not until the tenth century that the Church can be seen to be showing an active interest in the burial practices of wider society. In northern England the impact of the Scandinavians may, ironically, have been to encourage the fashion for burial in churchyards and for local displays of status at a thegn's churchyard rather than in mother churches, the kudos of which had been undermined by attacks on their property and resources and by their loss of saints' relics. The Anglo-Saxon centuries

14 *Burial from Fillingham (Lincs). A burial in a stone-lined grave with stones set around the head was cut by a second burial, of which the vertebrae and part of the skull are just visible. This intercutting of graves, along with other evidence for the disturbance of burials, in the form of additional bones in graves, indicates that the cemetery was in use for some time. The lower part of the second burial was destroyed by modern disturbance.* Andrew Chamberlain

witnessed major transitions in burial arrangements. Large cemeteries of the fifth and sixth centuries, probably serving several communities, were replaced by a greater number of smaller cemeteries which appear to have served just one. By the tenth century in some parts of the region, particularly Lincolnshire, virtually every vill had its own cemetery, to judge from both the locations of excavated cemeteries and the distribution of funerary sculpture.

The Normans

The Norman Conquest of 1066, and the subsequent acquisition of huge tracts of land and patronage of the Church by the Norman aristocracy, had an important impact on burial location. It is not particularly useful to try to summarize the Norman impact on the Church — as, indeed, on any other aspect of society — as having been solely one of either continuity or of change. In many respects the Norman impact on the Church was gradual, with the replacement of ecclesiastical personnel with Norman or continental men, and the rebuilding of Anglo-Saxon churches in Norman or continental styles taking place over at least a fifty-year period. Unlike the earlier Scandinavian settlers, the Normans were Christian and did not have any radically different religious beliefs or burial practices. The main impact that the Normans had was to replace the greater aristocracy with a class of men whose interests — landed and spiritual — were divided between England and Normandy. Many of the first generation of major Norman lords chose to be buried back in Normandy, although lesser lords with few or no remaining interests in Normandy appear to have been buried in England from the start. The choice was important because it had financial implications, relating to patronage and bequests. Choice of burial location also had cultural implications because it helped to determine perceptions of lords as being either 'English' or 'Norman'.

The attitudes of the new Norman overlords to Anglo-Saxon saints also had a major impact on the Church and on funerary practices. The Norman ecclesiastics rejected many Anglo-Saxon saints and their cults, although others continued to receive patronage, once their authenticity had been checked. A number of saints had new *vitae* commissioned, including John of Beverley for whom Folcard of St Bertin was commissioned by Archbishop Ealdred of York to write a *vita* in the 1060s, and St Guthlac of Crowland who had a new *vita* written by Orderic Vitalis in the early twelfth century, at the behest of the prior of Crowland, Wulfwine. New saints were occasionally created in the wake of the Norman Conquest. For example, the cult of Earl Waltheof, the last English earl of Northampton who was executed in 1076 after his involvement in a revolt against William the Conqueror, was fostered at Crowland by the English brethren and their French abbot, Geoffrey of Orleans (1109-*c*.1124). There is no evidence that this cult had political connotations, as had earlier cults of murdered royal princes, or that it was used to foster anti-Norman feelings: rather, it seems to have been a local cult in which both the indigenous population and the newcomers could share. Indeed, Abbot Geoffrey rebuked the Norman monk Ouen of St Albans for his denigration of the cult. This cult appears to have served a socially integrative function.

The building of castles by the Normans had a major impact on the landscape. Although defended noble residences were not unknown in England (e.g. Goltho (Lincs)), the speed with which new ones were constructed, the replacement of earlier noble residences, and, in time, the emergence of new architectural forms transformed the landscape. This was, perhaps, most dramatically apparent in towns, where Norman castles not uncommonly caused the destruction of houses and other buildings, such as at Lincoln where 166 tenements were said to have been destroyed 'on account of the castle'. In some instances castles were built on top of late Anglo-Saxon cemeteries. This has been demonstrated at, for example, Norwich, Hereford, Worcester, Newcastle-upon-Tyne, Newark (Notts), York and Pontefract. At Newark recent excavations at the castle have uncovered a late Anglo-Saxon cemetery containing at least 70 burials and probably many more. All of the burials were aligned west-east and contained no grave goods, but a few of the burials had stones placed around the head (so-called 'ear-muffs') and several were outlined by stones, a typical feature of later Anglo-Saxon burial practices. Indeed, radiocarbon dates acquired later confirmed that the burials belong to the tenth or eleventh century. There is no evidence that there was an associated church — although a number of beam-slots suggest some sort of building activity on the site — and the parish church is about 300m away. The castle walls truncated some of the burials, and a ditch containing eleventh-century material cut others, and it appears that a palisaded bank and a ditch enclosed the earliest castle on the site, which preceded the first stone phase of the castle built by Bishop Alexander of Lincoln *c*.1130-40. The castle appears to have occupied a site at which burial had until recently taken place, or even was still taking place. We have already seen that the Norman castle at Pontefract truncated earlier burials, and burials have also been found beneath the outer walls of York castle. It may be an exaggeration to say that the Normans were making a statement about their newly-won authority by obliterating Anglo-Saxon cemeteries, since the primary aim was doubtless strategic, concerning the need to acquire the best sites in which to build a castle. Nonetheless, the result of Norman castle-building campaigns may have been to substantiate Norman authority by creating very decisive breaks with past traditions, including, perhaps, where urban communities buried their dead.

The Norman Conquest also led to a monastic renaissance in many parts of northern England. In the years after the conquest, Reinfred, a knight of William de Percy, was impressed by the ruins of the former monastery of *Streanaeshalch*, while visiting his lord at Whitby and he decided to enter the monastic life. Following a visit to Evesham (Worcs) he learned of the golden age of Northumbrian monasteries as described by Bede, from Aldwine, the prior of Winchcombe, and Ælfwig, a monk of Evesham, who later travelled north with Reinfred. They first went to Monkchester (Newcastle) and were then invited to Jarrow, where they were shown the ruins of the earlier monastery. In 1078 Reinfred restored *Streanaeshalch*. Other houses revived at this time included Durham and Monkwearmouth, and they represented a genuinely Anglo-Norman venture, which quickly enough attracted the burials of wealthy and influential laymen.

The twelfth century saw a host of new houses founded in England, influenced by the monastic reforms on the continent. William the Conqueror set the tone with his penitential foundation at Battle (Sussex). It has been estimated that at the time of the Norman Conquest there were around 50 monasteries in England, but that only a century later during the reign of Henry II there were over 500. Many of the new religious houses founded in the eleventh and twelfth centuries were chosen as places of burial by major lords, although they do not, on the whole, seem to have attracted burial for wider society. Choices about where the dead were to be buried have much to reveal about Anglo-Norman politics and about the attitudes of the newcomers to their newly conquered lands. In 1090 Robert de Lacy founded the Cluniac Priory of Pontefract outside his castle and was buried there in the 1120s. The *Historia Laceiorum* records that Robert's mother and father were also buried there, on either side of the altar, beneath marble slabs, implying that they had been moved there from an earlier resting place after Robert had founded the Priory. Robert clearly made a very public statement about his attachment to Pontefract.

Recent studies have suggested that less than a quarter of Norman lords chose to be buried back in Normandy in the late eleventh and early twelfth century, which appears to contradict traditional arguments that the Normans took a long time to acculturate to their new lands. Two, not very convincing, caveats may be expressed. First, it may be assumed that many Norman lords spent more of their time in England and thus increased their chances of dying and then being buried in England. However, it is clear that place of death regularly did not determine place of burial, and so burial in England must have been a deliberate choice by the deceased, or their family. Second, it might be argued that many monastic houses in England were in a sense an enclave of Normandy, being dependencies of Norman mother houses. However, most alien houses in England functioned independently, and had few contacts with their mother house. It seems to be the case, then, that in exercising the choices available to them most Norman families chose to bury their dead in England, suggesting a significant level of cultural and spiritual assimilation to their adopted land (Golding 1986).

Later medieval burial grounds

In the later Middle Ages (*c*.1200-1500), the rate of new parish church foundation slowed down, in large part as a result of the consolidation of canon law in the twelfth century which subjected the foundation of new churches to complex litigation which sought to preserve the rights of mother churches, their rights of burial, in particular, and the accompanying mortuary payments. Although the ecclesiastical system became more fossilized, new churches were still founded, although not all succeeded in achieving parochial status or burial rights, and others went out of use. The later Middle Ages witnessed numerous disputes about burial rights between mother churches and their chapelries or former daughter churches. Chapels without burial rights often had to make a very strong case in order to be allowed to bury their dead. One of the most bitter disputes in the region concerning an attempt made by the worshippers at a chapel to gain autonomy from the parish church occurred in the parish of Snaith (Yorks). The parishioners who used Carlton chapel attempted, with the support of a local landowner, Brian de Stapleton, to gain burial rights in 1391. Although the parishioners of Carlton approached the papacy they stood little chance against the combined efforts of Selby Abbey (Yorks), to which Snaith church was appropriated, and the people on whom they drew for support, John of Gaunt, the future Henry IV and the Archbishop of York.

The roles served by the various chapels within the parishes of the major mother churches of the region were very varied. For example, within the parish of Repton the chapels at Foremark and Ingleby did not have burial rights, whereas the chapel of Smisby was allowed to bury the local dead, and the parishioners who were served by the chapel at Measham (Leics) appealed to be allowed to bury the dead in 1278 on account of the great distance of the parish church which was nearly 10 miles away.

Churchyards continued to grow and contract in size, as we have seen that they did in the Anglo-Saxon centuries. Church building campaigns often saw areas of the churchyard taken over as the church was expanded, with burials being disturbed in the process. The rebuilding of the south aisle at Bakewell (Derbs) disturbed numerous graves, as can be seen from the incorporation of many grave covers into the fabric of the aisle (*see* **60, 61**). At Bolsover (Derbs) excavation has revealed that the thirteenth-century tower and a bell-casting pit cut through earlier burials. Scaffolding pits dug at Repton in the twelfth century during building work cut through earlier burials. Excavations at the York churches of St Andrew and St Helen-on-the-Walls, at Kellington and at St Mark's in Lincoln have revealed that successive stages of rebuilding of those churches saw the churches expand out over the churchyard, often cutting through burials. At the Gilbertine priory of St Andrew, York it has been shown that a series of burials successively cut and were cut by a path leading through the cemetery, suggesting changes in the use of that part of the churchyard. Elsewhere secular building activity can be shown to have disturbed burials. At St Mary Magdelene in Doncaster (Yorks) the churchyard was gradually encroached on from the fourteenth century following the transformation of the church into a chantry chapel, and in the sixteenth century a moot hall was built on top of it (**15**). A chapel and associated cemetery in Bakewell appears to have gone out of use in the later Middle Ages, or possibly a little later, in the wake of urban building activity. Some excavations, such as those at Kellington, appear to show that more care was taken in the Anglo-Saxon period than at a later date not to disturb burials when subsequent graves were cut or when building activity occurred. From the twelfth century less care was seemingly taken and this may indicate something about prevailing attitudes to the dead. Whether it reflects (as the excavators have suggested) the increasing dominance of the doctrine of Purgatory, with a greater concern with assisting the soul through Purgatory than with maintaining bodily unity in readiness for the Day of Judgement is difficult to say, and the fact that places of burial became more fixed in the landscape than they had been during the Anglo-Saxon centuries may have led to an inevitable disturbance of burials as time went by.

Later medieval changes to the geography of burial concerned not only which churches were allowed to bury the dead, but where in relation to particular churches burial might take place: inside or outside; in a side chapel or chantry chapel; near to a particular altar, and so on. Burial of the laity inside churches had been forbidden in the later Anglo-Saxon period (although it did sometimes occur, as the burial of Earl Siward in his church of St Olaf in York in 1055 reveals), but by the later Middle Ages was not uncommon. The Statutes of Chichester (1292) stipulated that there should be no burials in the church or chancel other than of lords of the village and patrons of the church and their wives, rectors and vicars. Later medieval wills provide valuable information about the preferences concerning burial location expressed by some members of society, those who were wealthy enough to leave wills. They generally stipulate at which church a person wished to be buried, and most of those of will-making status who stated a preference asked for burial within the church. The clergy were the group most likely to have been buried in the chancel. Also popular for burial were locations near to the various altars within a church. Christopher Daniell has recently undertaken an analysis of burial preferences expressed in wills from Yorkshire and Nottinghamshire dated to between 1389 and 1475, which were largely written by urban citizens. Although a preference was not always expressed and occupation was not always stated, from those wills that do provide this information it can be seen that the group who most commonly requested burial in the chancel were members of the clergy (**16**). A higher proportion of members of the laity asked for burial near to one of the altars. Accounts of churchwardens' income often leave records of a variety of fees payable for burial in certain positions in the nave and the churchyard, and they reveal that burial in or near the chancel and various altars was the most expensive, and therefore prestigious, option. The tombs, effigies and slabs that were placed over the burials in commemoration of the wealthy and socially prominent were

The geography of death

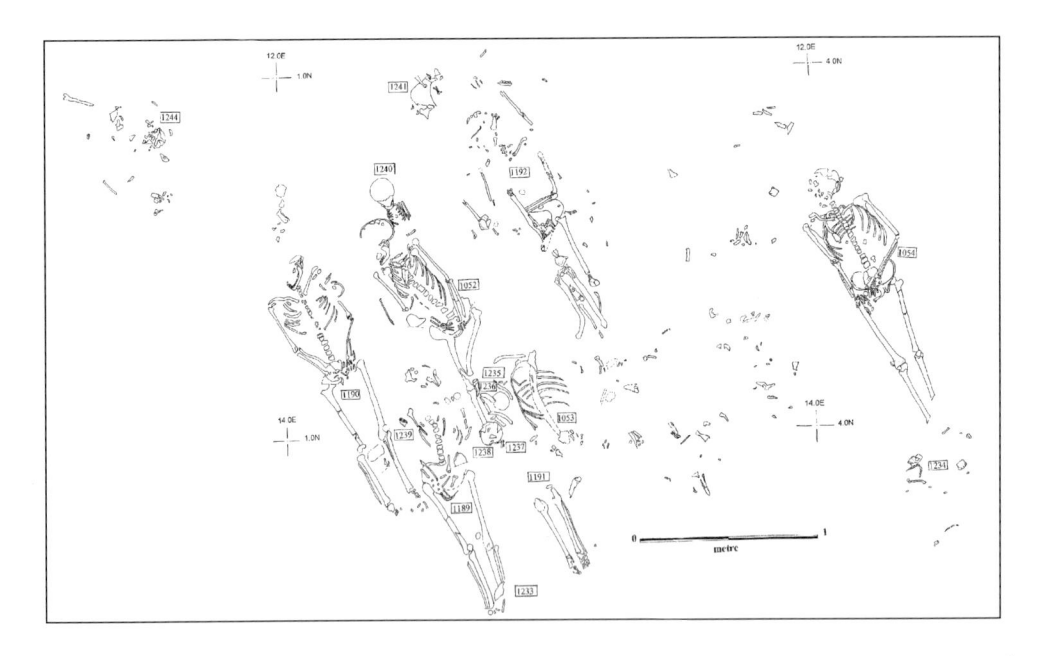

15 Burials from St Mary, Doncaster (Yorks). This site plan (looking west) shows the crowded nature of a medieval churchyard, with burials packed close together and intercutting. ARCUS

often used in wills to locate exactly where a person wished to be buried. For example, Richard Byll, a merchant of Hull (Yorks), asked in his will of 1451 to be buried in the chapel of Holy Trinity in the town 'near the tomb of William Procktour'.

Across the region there was not a common experience in the later Middle Ages concerning the burial of the dead. Many rural communities had a church which possessed burial rights, but many others did not, and people were forced to travel, sometimes great distances, in order to bury their dead. Excavations at Burnham (Lincs) and Bolton (Yorks) have indicated that these two chapels did not have full burial rights, given the absence of an associated cemetery, but that, nonetheless, a few burials may be found in such chapels, presumably of wealthy patrons, lords of the manor, or, in the case of Bolton, founders of the chantry in the church. In contrast there were some villages in the region that had more than one church — such as Waddingham, South Kelsey, Middle Rasen and Hemswell (Lincs) (**17**). Generally this was characteristic of villages divided into more than one manor, and burial location might be determined by which manor families and individuals were most closely associated with. Another contrast between the burial traditions of rural communities derived from the burial practices of their lords. Many rural communities did not have a resident lord or one who made use of the parish church for burial, whereas others had a church that was so dominated by the lord and his family that it was effectively a private chapel for the lord. Lords were often a very visible presence in churches: not only because of their attendance at services, but also because of displays of their heraldic devices and other symbols of status and office, and because of their appropriation of space within churches for their family monuments, in the form of effigies, tombs and brasses.

i) Requests for burial in the chancel (105 out of 126 state occupation of the testator):

Occupation	Number of requests
Rector	51
Vicar	23
Chaplain	9
Gentleman, Knight, Esquire	9
Widow, Lady, Daughter	5
Burgess, Citizen	4
Cleric	2
Canon	2
Grocer	1

ii) Requests for burial near to one of the altars in the church (81 out of 187 state occupation of the testator):

Occupation	Number of requests
Citizen, Merchant, Tradesman	26
Gentleman, Knight, Esquire, Lord	20
Chaplain	19
Widow, Wife, Daughter	10
Rector, Parson	6

16 Preferred place of burial as indicated in wills from Yorkshire and Nottinghamshire, 1389-1475. After Daniell 1997

Many of the towns in the region had more than one church, and were divided into many parishes. For example, Derby had six parish churches, Nottingham had three, and by the early twelfth century Lincoln had *c*.35. This multiplicity of parish churches, most with graveyards, in the towns of eastern England is in contrast to the situation in western England, and is doubtless related to the lack of strong mother churches monopolizing burial, which was a feature of such towns at Worcester, Hereford and Gloucester. Choice of burial in towns was determined by a number of factors. The parish in which the individual lived was commonly cited in wills as the preferred place of burial, but membership of religious or craft guilds often determined choice of burial place. However, while some guilds had their own chapels, on the whole most had a chapel which was located within parish churches, meaning that even if guild membership informed choices about burial location, in practice burial in a parish church followed.

Chantry chapels were another important feature of the later medieval funerary landscape, both in rural and urban locations. A chantry was a chapel established to provide prayers for the souls of the deceased: they were usually paid for by a bequest, and it was

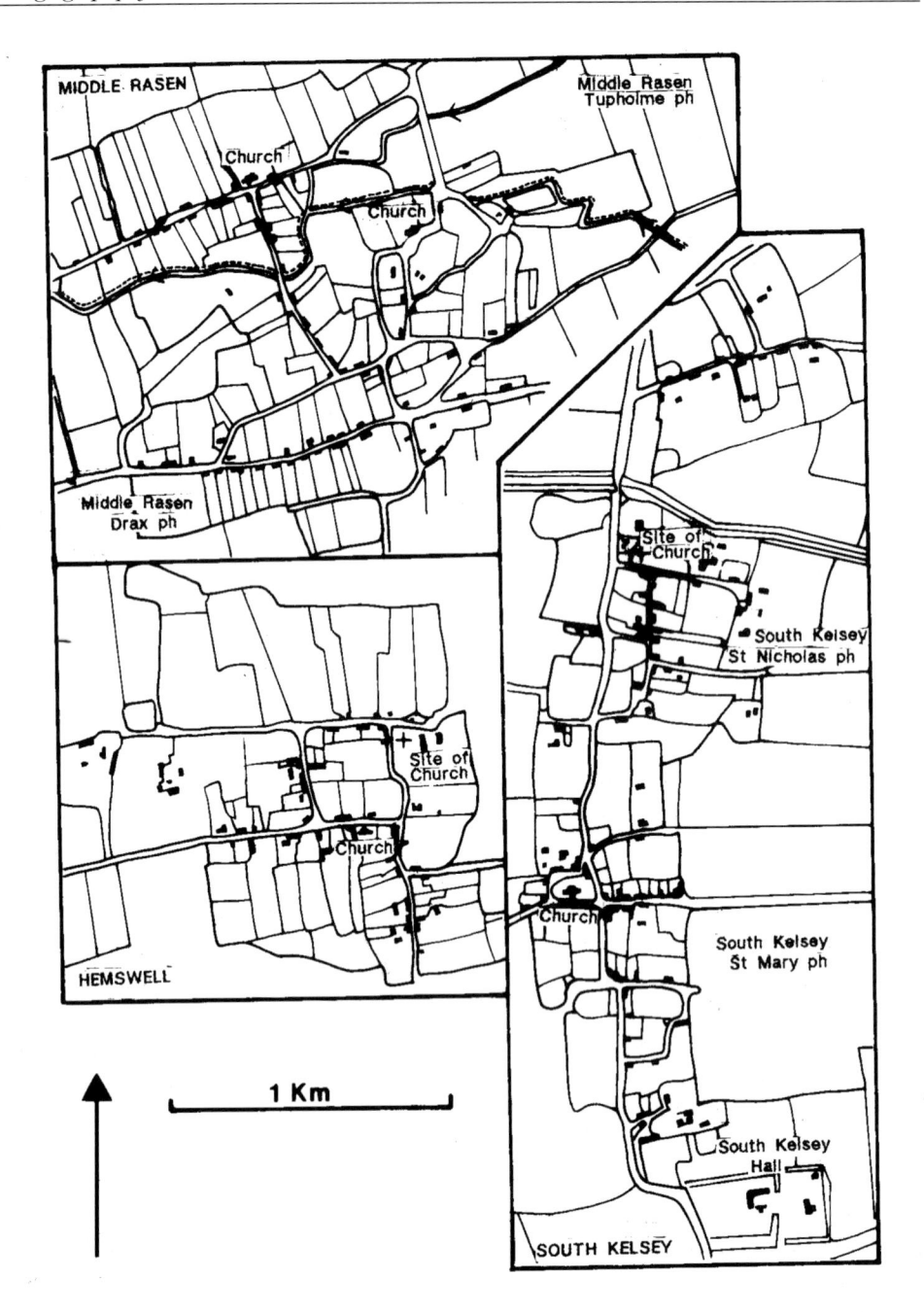

17 *Villages in Lincolnshire with more than one church.* After P. Everson, C. Taylor and C. Dunn, *Change and Continuity: Rural Settlement in North-West Lincolnshire* (London, 1991), Alex Norman

anticipated that the priest or priests paid for by the bequest would offer prayers in perpetuity. A chantry may be established for an individual, a family or a group. Often chantries were established within an existing parish church, where in addition to offering prayers, they also provided a focal point for burial. Other chantry chapels were separate buildings, such as that built after the battle of Towton (1461) by Richard III.

Excavation has revealed some evidence for zones within medieval churchyards, suggested by either the demographic characteristics of the population buried in them or by the nature of the burials (in coffins, in sarcophagi, or placed directly in the ground, for example). Often this can be shown to reveal something of the nature of the church itself. Churches of monastic communities appear to have had separate burial grounds for members of the community and for the laity, and the former consist of predominantly or solely male burials (where it is a male religious house). For example the cluster of adult male burials to the east of the church of the Gilbertine Priory of St Andrew in York may indicate the location of the monastic cemetery. Burials located elsewhere in and around the church include females and infants and appear to have been the burials of members of the laity. It is often suggested by archaeologists that the north side of churchyards was not favoured for burial in the Middle Ages because it had sinister connotations. However, there is little evidence from excavations to support this argument, and a more pressing factor determining the popularity of parts of the churchyard may have been the amount of land available for burial on all sides, and the main points of access through the churchyard and into the church. Some excavations have certainly suggested that there were higher proportions of males or females in some areas of a churchyard, but the significance of this for discussions of, say, gendered differences in funerary treatment is not as clear cut as some have suggested, and it hardly speaks of a dichotomous distinction in the mortuary treatment of men and women. The extensive excavations of the tenth- and eleventh-century churchyard at Raunds (Northants), for example, revealed a higher proportion of adult female burials on the north side of the churchyard, but not an overwhelming female presence. The crowded southern part of the churchyard is where the elaborate funerary monuments were found. If this may be taken to indicate that the south side of the churchyard was a more popular place for burial, and was associated with more prestigious burials, a major factor may have been the fact that the main pathway through the churchyard was on the south side of the church, rather than any notions of the sinister connotations of the north side. It may be appropriate to say that adult males were more likely to be buried in prestigious places within both churches and churchyards, but that some women were also afforded this right, and some men were also excluded. It has recently been suggested that there was a cluster of later medieval female burials on the north side of the church of St Mary Magdelene, Doncaster (Yorks), but this observation suffers from the potential unrepresentativeness of the sample from a partially excavated churchyard. Many excavations in crowded and disturbed churchyards result in the recovery of skeletons in such a condition that sexing cannot be adequately attempted. In sum, there is no evidence to suggest that men and women were routinely buried in different ways in the medieval period.

A number of excavations have revealed that there were sometimes zones for infant burials in medieval churchyards. At some churches this has been shown to be close to the walls of the church. It appears to have been more common in the Anglo-Saxon centuries, but less so at a later date. However, a cluster of juvenile burials has been found outside what was the east end of the chancel prior to the thirteenth century at Kellington, and a cluster of infant burials has been excavated on the north side of the tower at Bolsover, although not all were necessarily medieval. Two points have to be considered when trying to attach any significance to such patterns. The first is that infant skeletons survive less well than those of adults, and thus the apparent restriction of infant burials to certain zones may not have been as rigid as appears. Second, there is often surviving skeletal evidence for infant burials dispersed among the adult burials. One interpretation that has been offered for the clustering of infant burials along the walls of churches is that it was thought that the water running off the roof of the church would serve to bless the infant burials. This is not implausible, but it seems unlikely that this was a universal belief, and the communities who buried their dead in different churchyards may have had a variety of, now irrecoverable, reasons for burying the dead in the places that they did.

Burial in both towns and villages was not limited to parish churches, and also took place near to monasteries. Clearly monks and their lay brothers were most commonly buried in monastic cemeteries, but many secular lords chose to be buried at monasteries, often entering the monastery towards the end of their life. This choice was doubtless informed by the intercessory powers of the monks who could be expected to remember the lords who patronized them in their prayers. Many lords left money in their wills or gave money earlier in their life by charter in order to ensure burial in the desired place for themselves and their relatives in monasteries. For example, in the early twelfth century the death of Jordan, the nephew of Roger de Buisli who had founded Blyth Abbey (Notts), saw his elder son ceremonially place on the high altar a deed granting land to the abbey in return for the burial of his father. Lay burials are also both documented, and have recently been excavated, at the Gilbertine Priory of St Andrew in York, and at the Augustinian Friary in Hull, and are discussed in subsequent chapters. The presence of elderly members of the aristocracy and gentry within monasteries was not always harmonious, as they often demanded and expected special favours, such as Dame Margaret Darcy who entered the nunnery at Heynings (Lincs) in 1393 and requested a private room 'on account of the nobility of her race'.

Burial in churchyards was not invariably continuous. Bloodshed within a churchyard meant that burial could not continue until the churchyard had been reconsecrated. Sometimes this might result in a lengthy cessation of burial. For example, the churchyard at Beverley Minster did not receive burials for two years prior to 2 November 1306 when it was reconciled. Another, unusual, interruption to normal burial practices lasted between 1208 and 1214 when Pope Innocent III placed an Interdict on England, which was effectively to call a general strike of the clergy following a dispute over the election of a new Archbishop of Canterbury. In addition to this act depriving the laity of normal ecclesiastical services, it also, in theory, meant that they could not be buried in consecrated ground. There is some evidence for burials taking place outside consecrated ground, but on the whole there is little comment in written sources on the practical impact of the Interdict for the laity. It may be that the Interdict was interpreted in diverse ways on the matter of burial, as we know that it was where baptism, marriage and the celebration of mass were concerned.

Some new burial grounds came into use following the outbreak of plague. At Newark (Notts) a new churchyard was licensed on 15 May 1349 because it was said that so many people had died from the plague in recent times that the churchyard was no longer big enough to bury the dead of the town. As an order from Archbishop William Zouche of York to the vicar of Newark put it:

> The mortality of the plague which has been afflicting various parts of the world began to attack the townspeople of Newark some time ago now, . . . and is daily gaining in strength there, with the result that the burial ground of the church, because it is small and has no room to expand, is not adequate for the burial of the dead.

New burial grounds were also consecrated by the archbishop between June and August 1349 in Yorkshire at Egton in the parish of Lythe, Cleasby in the parish of Stanwick, Wilton (Leatham parish), Seamer (Rudby parish), Brotton (Skelton prish), Barton (Gilling parish), and Easby (Stokesley parish). The chapel of St.Oswald at Fulfor was permitted to perfom burial but only on the understanding that when the pestilence had ceased to afflict society the parishioners should revert to burying their dead at the church of St. Olaf in the suburbs of York. They failed to conform to this demand, however, and in 1353 Archbishop John Thoresby accused the residents of Fulford of 'taking a fooolish delight in novelty'. No black death cemeteries hve been excavated in northern England, but in London an excavation at one of the two emergency cemeteries established in the city , at East Smithfield, discovered both ordinary burials laid out in rows and two mass burial trenches and a mass burial pit, containing the remains of some 266 individuals. Despite the great number of burials, the individuals in the mass burials were placed in the grave carefully, up to five deep, suggesting that an attempt was made to provide orderly burial even during such terrible times. By contrast, the plague pits at Hereford were much less orderly.

The Black Death had a profound impact on medieval society. From its first outbreak in England during the winter of 1348-9, and through successive outbreaks during the later fourteenth and fifteenth centuries, hundreds of thousands died. The population of England may have declined by as much as a third during the second half of the fourteenth century. This clearly had an impact on burial practices. While on the one hand it placed great pressures on the ecclesiastical system to provide suitable burial for many more people in some years than was normally the case, on the other hand, and in the long term, the massive population decline saw many churches and their churchyards become redundant.

Battles also sometimes saw the dead buried in new places, in this case where they fell. The most extensively excavated battle cemetery from the region is from Towton (Yorks), where Lancastrian and Yorkist armies met on 29 March 1461 and fought one of the bloodiest battles of the Wars of the Roses. Contemporary estimates concerning the numbers of men that died vary from between 9,000 and nearly 30,000, although these figures are probably greatly exaggerated as the chroniclers attempted to show just how devastating a defeat the Lancastrians had experienced. Recent excavations on the site of the battle have revealed numerous skeletons of adult males, aged between 17 and 50. Many of the skeletons show signs of weapon injuries, both ones from a previous encounter that had healed, and others suffered shortly before death (**colour plate 9**).

Hospitals were also often places of burial, both for the people they cared for, and the religious communities who ran them. Burials including a chalice and paten, which are indications of priestly burial, have been found at the hospital of St Giles, Brough Bridge (Yorks) and at the hospital of St Leonard, Chesterfield (Derbs) (*see* **35** & **36**). Hospitals sometimes also took on the role of burying ostracized groups, such as felons. There were several types of later medieval hospital, including leper hospitals (which accounted for 25.8% of hospitals documented in the later Middle Ages), almshouses (55.6%), hospices for poor wayfarers and pilgrims (10.2%), and institutions for the sick poor (8.4%). Lepers were in some sense considered to be already dead, or dead to the world, when they entered the leper hospital, and they underwent a ceremony that was reminiscent of a funeral (see below, p.72). Hospitals were commonly located on the outskirts of towns. In part this was because they were usually relatively late foundations in the life of the town and there was little room left within the towns where they could be built — indeed, a rare intra-mural exception is St Leonard's York, which was an Anglo-Saxon foundation. However, there may have been other reasons for the common suburban locations of hospitals. Given that they catered for poor travellers and pilgrims then a location on the access routes into towns was a logical place for them to be founded. In the case of lepers, however, the social stigma attached to this condition may have been a major impediment to the building of leper hospitals within towns. Roberta Gilchrist (1992) has suggested that leper hospitals may have been deliberately located in liminal positions within the urban landscape because of the social liminality of lepers. Nonetheless, this did not mean that leper hospitals were hidden away. On the contrary they were highly visible to those entering and leaving the towns, and patronage of hospitals was an important part of the spiritual undertakings of the wealthier members of society, who hoped to assist the fate of their souls through charitable gifts and displays of extreme piety towards individuals who were regarded as undergoing Purgatory on earth. This may explain the visits by Bishop Hugh of Lincoln to kiss the sores of lepers.

Some of those individuals buried in a recently excavated cemetery in the Spittelgate district of Grantham (Lincs) had leprosy, and this would appear to have been the cemetery of the hospital of St Leonard documented in Grantham from the thirteenth century, but not previously located (**18**, **19**). Although there is no documentary evidence that this hospital housed lepers, the recent archaeological finds appear to confirm it. The dedication to St Leonard is another hint as this is the second most common dedication for leper hospitals in later medieval England, and, as with other later medieval hospitals, it is situated outside the main urban area of Grantham. Around 49 burials were excavated, although prior to the excavation contractors destroyed another *c*.20. The cemetery may have been larger, as a number of other burials from the vicinity were discovered in the nineteenth century. In addition to the adult burials, there were also infants buried in this cemetery, but it is unknown whether they were being cared for in some way in the hospital or whether they were buried there because their parents were cared for in the hospital. The children do not show any signs of leprosy, although it can take many years for leprosy to develop to such a stage that it leaves an indication on the skeleton.

Burial grounds for other ostracized groups are occasionally found, which were kept distinct from other cemeteries. Excommunicates and criminals were forbidden from burial in a churchyard and had to make other arrangements. Individuals executed just outside Lincoln at Canwick Hill were given burial by the brethren of St Katharine's Priory, who were paid to do this by the Master of the Hospitaller Preceptory of Maltby, on the common near to the gallows, and their names were entered in the book of the Fraternity of St John the Baptist. Those who were executed normally had to rely on friends and family, rather than the Church, to ensure that they were buried. Later medieval sources are a little inconsistent on the subject of who was not to be permitted churchyard burial, but they appear to have included usurers, excommunicates, the indicted and strangers to the parish (according to the Statutes of Salisbury of 1217-19), the concubines of clergy (Statutes of Winchester, 1224), and those who married without banns (Statutes of London, 1245-59). The Church often railed against those who took part in tournaments and threatened to forbid them from burial in a churchyard if they died during a tournament, although in practice this seems but rarely to have been effected. Suicides were not mentioned in official statutes during the later Middle Ages, although they had been forbidden from burial in consecrated ground in the later Anglo-Saxon period. Suicide because of madness did not prevent burial in a churchyard, and it may be that a jury rarely convicted a person of suicide rather than madness or misadventure to enable them to be buried in a churchyard.

Jews were another group excluded from burial in a Christian churchyard, and they had their own cemeteries, of which the one at Jewbury, York has been extensively excavated. A community of Jews was first established in York in the 1170s and the Jews were expelled, along with all the Jews in England, in 1290. It has been estimated that there were on average *c*.200 Jews in York during this time. The cemetery is not documented until *c*.1230, although the chronicler Roger of Howden recorded that the provincial Jews were permitted to buy land outside the walls of the cities where they lived from 1177 to use for cemeteries, so it may have been founded earlier. Alternatively, the York Jews may initially have buried their dead in London. Jews normally established their cemeteries outside towns, because of a requirement for them to be located away from inhabited buildings. The Jewish cemeteries identified at Oxford, Winchester, Northampton and London were all located outside the walls of the town. The Jews of Lincoln had their own cemetery by 1290, but it is not known when or where it was founded. It is possible that the Jews based in Lincoln, Stamford (Lincs) and Northampton initially made use of the York cemetery, before they acquired their own. After 1290 the Jewish cemeteries in England were sold off by the Crown to wealthy urban citizens who subsequently developed the land.

Although burial in the later Middle Ages was largely restricted to the churchyards of parish churches and monasteries, hospitals and recognized execution sites, a few examples of burial in other locations have been identified in the region. Excavation has occasionally revealed infant burials within settlements, in buildings or the crofts of the houses. An infant burial was excavated in a building at Riplingham (Yorks). It is difficult to say whether this was a secretive act, perhaps done in the wake of an act of infanticide or because of the death of the child before it had been baptized, for example. In some cases it cannot have been an attempt to conceal the birth of a baby since the child was several months old.

The geography of death

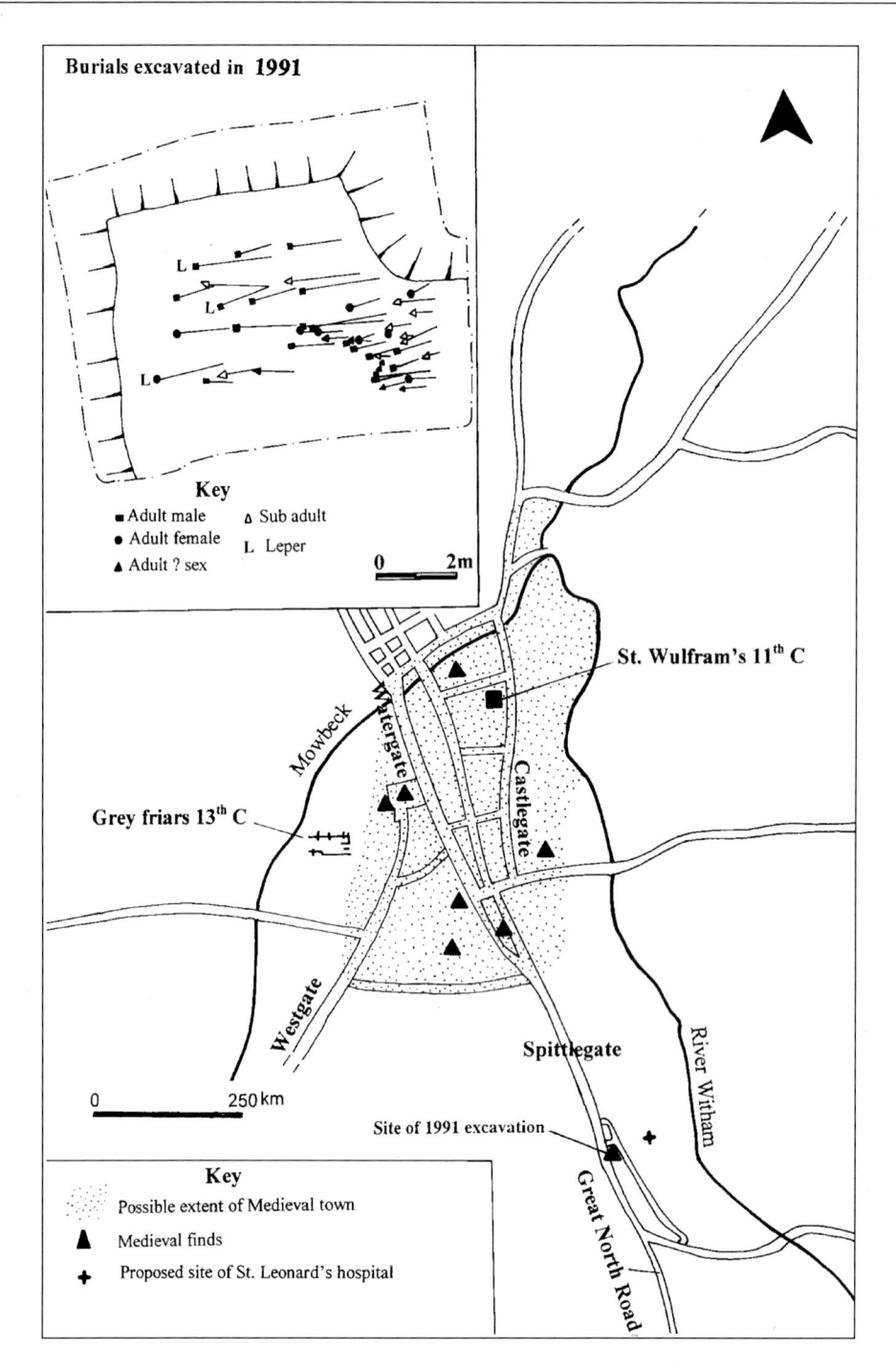

18 *The location of the hospital of St Leonard, Grantham (Lincs). The existence of the hospital was known from documentary sources, but its location was not known until the recent excavation of skeletons showing evidence for leprosy (see inset). It is not untypical for leper hospitals to be located on the edge of urban areas.* Jo Mincher

The geography of death

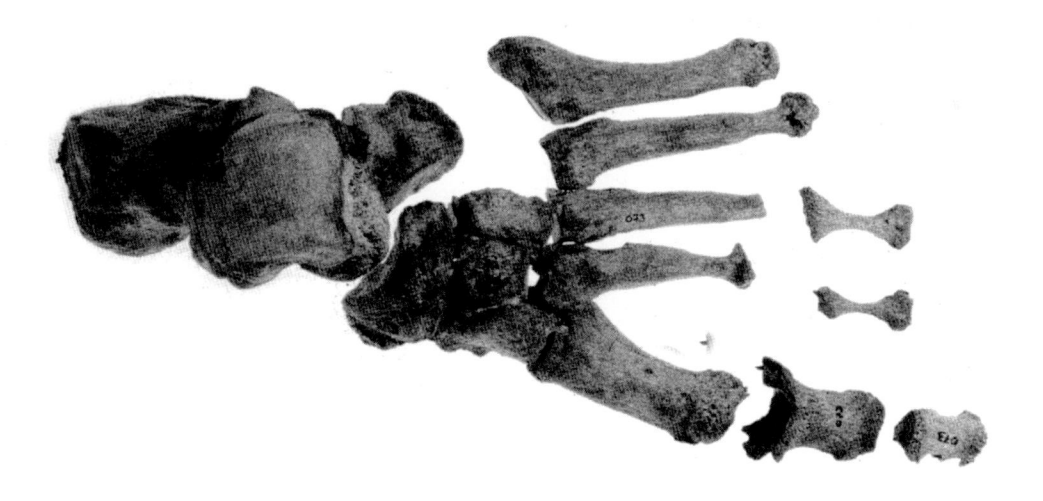

19 Skeleton showing signs of leprosy from the hospital of St Leonard, Grantham (Lincs). The bones of the left foot of a female skeleton. Leprosy has caused the metatarsals to become narrowed towards their distal ends, and the phalanges are narrowed in the middle. The disease has also damaged the joint of the big toe at the ball of the foot. Andrew Chamberlain

Saints

The number of saints in the region continued to grow during the later Middle Ages, although not all saints were officially sanctioned in Rome. William Fitzherbert, archbishop of York (d.1154), was canonized in 1227 after miracles were reported as having occurred at his tomb. His cult was very strong at York, and in 1227 his relics were translated to a new shrine. A window in the Minster depicts a pilgrim making an offering at the tomb of St William in the hope of, or in gratitude for, a miracle. Between 1300 and 1540 there were only three new officially sanctioned English saints, of whom one, John of Bridlington (d.1379), was located in our region. He was the prior of the Augustinian priory at Bridlington who led a life of fervent prayer. Miracles were reported at his tomb, and he was canonized in 1401. Others in the region who came to be regarded as saints include Richard Scrope, the archbishop of York whose opposition to the 'usurping' king, Henry IV, saw him beheaded and later invoked by the Yorkist factions, and John Dalderby, the bishop of Lincoln who was credited with numerous miracles after his death. The cult of the recluse and spiritual adviser to the nuns of Hampole (Yorks), Richard Rolle, was venerated in the north-east. A collection of miracles, which he is said to have performed, was prepared in the expectation that he would eventually be canonized. In 1383 a wanderer in the town of Leicester invoked Richard Rolle to help in the recovery of an apparently drowned child, which helped to demonstrate his sanctity. Some individuals appear to have regarded themselves as would-be saints during their lifetime, such as the Carthusian monk Richard Methley of Mount Grace Priory (Yorks).

Saints were commonly moved at a later date from the places in which they were initially laid to rest. The translation of saints to new locations, often in the same church, commonly led to the saint being worshipped in two locations. When St Hugh of Lincoln (d.1200) was translated within Lincoln Cathedral in 1280 two new shrines were created because, although his body was discovered intact, as soon as his body was moved the head came apart from the body. St Hugh was then translated in two parts. This was considered miraculous because it turned out that the receptacle that had been prepared for Hugh's body was only large enough for the body without the head. Thereafter there were two shrines: the Shrine of the Head, and the Shrine of the Body.

Conclusions

It is clear that there was much variety in the geography of burial between *c.*600 and 1500. It was not simply the case that there was a constant expansion of the number and size of churchyards. Many churches and churchyards both came into and went out of use at various times through the Anglo-Saxon and medieval centuries. As such, the region is comparable to most other parts of England. There are, however, some contrasts with other regions. The region studied in this book yields a lot of information about later Anglo-Saxon burial practices because of the great wealth of stone sculpture of this date serving funerary and commemorative functions. This allows us to see a range of sites where burial was taking place, which would otherwise not be known to us in the absence of excavation of cemeteries or relevant documentary evidence. The small, scattered mid- to later Anglo-Saxon cemeteries identified in the region have not been extensively discussed in other regions, although recent work on Oxfordshire (Blair 1994, 72-3) suggests that they may be a widespread phenomenon. Evidence to suggest that later medieval churchyards were sometimes smaller than, or in a different location from, Anglo-Saxon cemeteries has also been noted in other regions.

Important mother churches, with large parishes, dominated many parts of the region in the Anglo-Saxon and later medieval periods and burial was often restricted to the mother church or to one or two chapels. This pattern has been identified in many other parts of the country. However, Lincolnshire provides a contrast, as it is characterized by much smaller parishes, and by a proliferation of churches during the tenth and eleventh centuries that had associated graveyards. The density of churches in later Anglo-Saxon Lincolnshire has much in common with the situation in East Anglia. Only a few villages in the study region had more than one medieval church; again, Lincolnshire proves to be the exception. In this respect, Lincolnshire is again most like East Anglia, and the common factor would appear to be the complex manorial history of these regions, where many villages were divided into two or more manors, and this, in addition to population density, may explain the prevalence of villages with more than one church, and, often, more than one burial ground. The large number of urban churches in the region studied in this volume is comparable to the situation in other parts of eastern England, but contrasts with the western Midlands, as we have seen, where many towns were dominated by a mother church which monopolized burial rights.

There are a few respects in which the study area is lacking in evidence. There are few known Anglo-Saxon execution sites in comparison with southern England. Few hospitals have been excavated in the region. Nonetheless, the region provides a good study area for exploring the range and diversity of burial practices in the Anglo-Saxon and medieval centuries. In the following chapter we shall examine the different ways in which people prepared both themselves and others for their death.

3 Preparation for burial and beyond: deathbeds, wills and funerals

In order to understand medieval attitudes to death and to the dead it is important to place death and burial in their social and religious context. Death and burial in the Middle Ages were not simply regarded as specific events; rather they were understood as processes, and in order to develop our insights into the content and the significance of these processes we need, in addition to analysing the archaeological evidence, to draw on documentary sources that describe them.

The Middle Ages were pervaded by the expectation that death should be prepared for. This preparation took a number of forms. Individuals were expected to put their worldly affairs in order, and this commonly took the form of a will both for the wealthy and, by the end of the Middle Ages, for the peasantry. However, it is important to remember that much would have been set in order prior to the composition of a will, and, therefore, wills do not necessarily reveal all of a person's worldly affairs. The soul also had to be provided for, and wills often make provision for the soul by commending it to God, Jesus, the Virgin or to one or more saints, and by asking both ecclesiastics and laymen to say prayers for the soul of the deceased. Money was often left specifically to ensure that priests, monks, friends, family and so on would say intercessory prayers. Pilgrimage and the promotion and patronage of the cults of saints were also understood to have intercessory benefits throughout the Middle Ages. The soul could also be helped on its way to heaven by charitable acts undertaken before death, and this became of increasing concern following the development of the notion of Purgatory during the twelfth century (it was officially recognized and defined in 1274), which introduced the idea of the soul undergoing a journey on the way to Heaven which could be assisted both during one's lifetime and afterwards, through the prayers of others. In the later Middle Ages the foundation of a chantry chapel, to provide a priest to say prayers and to perform masses for the soul, became an option for the wealthy, and for the less wealthy guilds performed a similar function, and were, in effect, collective chantry chapels.

For those who were powerful and influential, suitable provision for the moment of death might also be made, and evidence for this can be found throughout the Middle Ages. Within royal, aristocratic, or monastic households the deathbed arrangements were an important and highly formalized stage in the preparation of the dying for the moment of death, and might involve the presence of physicians, monks, priests, family, friends and servants. Finally, the funeral was the process which took the deceased to the grave and involved a series of events, including processions, church services and prayers, and the committal of the body to the earth. All of these events in preparation for death and burial are found throughout the Middle Ages, although the importance placed on each, and the amount of evidence available, varies at different times and in diverse social contexts.

Anglo-Saxon saints and their preparation for death and burial

Our knowledge of the processes of preparation for death and burial in the Anglo-Saxon period is largely limited to royal, aristocratic, episcopal and monastic contexts. The deaths of future saints are often especially well documented, not least because securing a good death was an essential part of the stages by which sainthood was achieved. For example, Bishop Wilfrid (d.709) who was abbot of the monasteries of Ripon (Yorks) and Hexham (Northumb) made extensive plans for setting his affairs in order as his death approached, which are described in detail in the monk Stephen's near contemporary *Life of Saint Wilfrid*. As soon as Wilfrid became ill in 708 his household at Hexham began to pray for him, asking that the Lord would grant him an extension of life so that 'he could speak to them, and dispose of his monasteries and divide his possessions, and not leave us as it were orphans, without any abbots'. As news of his illness spread his abbots and anchorites journeyed to his bedside, and their prayers were answered as the bishop lived long enough to arrange his affairs. He effectively made a verbal will. He ordered his treasurer to open up his treasury at Ripon, which contained gold, silver and precious stones, some of which he had intended to take to Rome, and asked that messengers be sent to take this treasure to Rome on his behalf. Of the rest of the treasures, part was to be given to the poor 'for the redemption of my soul', part to the new abbots of Ripon and Hexham so that 'they may be able to purchase the friendship of kings and bishops', and part to his followers who had suffered with him in exile. He appointed his successors, and then headed south to set in order the affairs of monasteries in Mercia at the request of King Ceolred of Mercia. Wilfrid's death occurred at a monastery in Oundle (Northants), and his final illness was met with prayers and singing day and night. Once he had died his body was washed by the monks and clothed in robes; it was then placed on a carriage and the monks set off for Ripon, singing prayers. Wilfrid almost immediately began to perform miracles. A cross was erected at Oundle where the water used to bathe the body had been emptied and here many marvels were performed. A nun with a withered hand was cured after washing her arm in the water used to wash the robe in which Wilfrid was clothed after his death. Wilfrid also intervened to prevent some nobles from burning the building at Oundle in which he had died even though the rest of the monastery was burned. Wilfrid quickly proved capable of avenging any wrongs done to him after his death.

Bede records that Hild, the first abbess of Whitby (Yorks) (d.680), also secured the good death necessary for a saint. She suffered a debilitating illness during the last seven years of her life during which time she continued in her work and prayers. During this time 'she never ceased to give thanks to her Maker and to instruct the flock committed to her charge both in public and in private', and at the point of her death she instructed her nuns to carry on and to keep the peace of the gospel. A good death was not the only means by which someone might achieve sanctity, and the visions of Hild's death experienced by a nun in a distant part of the monastery and by another nun at Whitby's daughter house of Hackness (Yorks) were important in confirming Hild's sanctity. According to his biographer, St Guthlac (d.714) was also aware that he was going to die, and was able to make plans for his burial, including instructing the monk Beccel to wrap his body in a linen cloth. Guthlac performed miracles both during his lifetime and after his death.

Would-be saints were expected to conform to an ideal, and it is this that renders the descriptions of the final days of such individuals very similar. Indeed, Felix seems to have been borrowing from Bede's prose *Life of St Cuthbert* in his descriptions of Guthlac's death.

Preparation for death and burial among the laity

Saints' *Lives*, and other ecclesiastical works, particularly Bede's *Ecclesiastical History* (c.730), are important sources for the lives and deaths not only of ecclesiastics, but also of members of the laity. Saints' *Lives* were not simply biographies of particular holy individuals but were also models of a holy life presented for others to follow. The lessons contained in saints' *Lives* and in the writings of Bede are mostly aimed at monks and hermits, yet the miracles, in particular, contained in them seem also to have been of relevance to laymen, albeit those of high status. Both Bede's *Ecclesiastical History* and the eighth-century *Life of St Guthlac* written by the monk Felix were dedicated to laymen, and contain visions of the afterlife that would have been of interest both to ecclesiastics and to a lay audience. For example, according to Felix the future St Guthlac was taken to the edge of hell by demons and shown what to expect there. He saw:

> the smoking caverns of the glowing infernal regions . . . [and] not only could he see there the fiery abyss swelling with surging flames, but even the sulphurous eddies of flame mixed with icy hail seemed almost to touch the stars without drops of spray; and evil spirits running about amid the black caverns and gloomy abysses tortured the souls of the wicked, victims of a wretched fate, with various kinds of torments.

The Irish monk Fursa was taken from his body to see various images of the afterlife, a story that Bede says he included in his *Ecclesiastical History* because he ' thought it might be helpful to many to include it in this history'. The poem *De Abbatibus* written somewhere in the north of England in the early ninth century by the monk Æthelwulf includes the story of a man, Merhtheof, who had died and been presented before God for judgement. God had sent him to gain forgiveness from his first wife for having broken his vow to her by marrying again. After initially deciding to condemn him to Hell — where he would be 'swallowed up amid the dark flames' — the wife changed her mind. Merhtheof was sent back to earth to make amends for his sins, which he did by becoming a monk, and which eventually enabled him to die 'in a purified state'. Such a story would have been relevant to laymen in revealing that they could atone for their sins, among other ways, by entering a monastery.

A number of tales told in saints' *Lives* and in other written sources both suggest a lay audience, and reveal something of the potential concerns of the laity about their fate after death. There are indications that the dead were not considered to be absent, but rather to be in a reciprocal relationship with the living. The dead — especially saints — could offer intercession for the living, while the living could make funerary arrangements and offer prayers for the dead. For example, Bede reports a vision experienced by Dryhthelm, who was a layman at the time, who was escorted by an angel on a tour of the afterlife. He was shown a valley where the souls of men were being tormented by raging fire on one side and hail and snow on the other. This was, said the angel, 'the place in which those souls have to be tried and chastened who delayed to confess and make restitution for the sins they had committed until they were on the point of death'. Dryhthelm was told that the souls of the dead could also be helped by 'the prayers, alms and fasting of the living, and especially by the offering of masses, and are therefore set free before the Day of Judgement'. Another vision described by Bede was experienced by a Mercian noble who had fallen ill and decided not to do penance until he had become well again — 'for he did not wish his friends to accuse him of doing in fear of death what he had refused to do when he was well'. In the vision he was approached by two youths who showed him a small book that listed the good things he had done in his life, following which spirits arrived with an enormous book recording all of the evil deeds he had performed. The two youths willingly handed him over to the evil spirits since his evil deeds far outweighed his good deeds. Bede comments that this event occurred for the benefit of others, who would understand from this story the dangers of putting off doing penance.

Bede also places a parable in the mouth of a noble at the court of the Northumbrian king, Edwin, *c*.627, which reveals the importance of Christianity as a surer guarantor of life after death than the pagan belief system:

> Your Majesty, when we compare the present life of man on earth with that time of which we have no knowledge, it seems to me like the swift flight of a single sparrow through the banqueting-hall where you are sitting at dinner on a winter's day with your thegns and counsellors. In the midst there is a comforting fire to warm the hall; outside, the storms of winter rain or snow are raging. This sparrow flies swiftly in through one door of the hall, and out through another. While he is inside, he is safe from the winter storms; but after a few moments of comfort, he vanishes from sight into the wintry world from which he came. Even so, man appears on earth for a little while; but out of what went before this life or of what follows, we know nothing. Therefore, if this new teaching has brought any more certain knowledge, it seems only right that we should follow it.

At a later date the homilist Ælfric of Eynsham (*c*.950-*c*.1010) discussed at great length the fate of individuals between death and the Last Judgement, and emphasizes the punishments and rewards that the soul may expect according to a person's actions on earth. He also stressed the value of intercession by men and saints for the souls of the dead, and that in Heaven our friends await our coming and are anxious for our souls. In doing so, Ælfric draws attention to the reciprocal relationship between the living and the dead.

It is apparent that there was information available for the laity about their possible fate in the afterlife, and this presumably reflects something of their concerns. However, it is difficult to know how widely these stories would have been known, and it may be that if there was an intended lay audience it consisted only of kings and their immediate circles. We have to remember that whatever their wider currency, texts such as the *Life of St*

Guthlac — written about a Mercian noble who early in his life had engaged in the pursuits characteristic of his noble class — were not exclusively, or even primarily, intended for a lay audience. Nonetheless, the strong moralizing and didactic tones of much Anglo-Saxon literature, even when about holy figures and saints, must have had resonance for the laity, who would have empathized at the very least with the early lives among the laity of many of the characters concerned. The worlds of the laity and of churchmen were not so far removed from each other, and kings and nobles dominated both.

On the other hand, the solution recommended by early texts to the potential dangers of the afterlife may not have been especially appealing to the laity. In the Anglo-Saxon Church the administration of penance was both solemn and terrifying, and effectively removed the penitent from their previous life. It was very different from the auricular confession of the later Middle Ages, and it generally involved a long period, sometimes permanent, of penitential endeavour. For example, after his vision of the afterlife recounted by Bede, Dryhthelm abandoned his wife and family, took the tonsure and devoted the rest of his life to penitential observance in a monastery. In the writings of Archbishop Theodore of Canterbury (668-90) it is apparent that penance might vary according to the sin that had been committed — from fifteen days for drunkenness, to fifteen years for homosexual practices, to a lifetime for homicide, adultery and theft. Moreover, the teachings of the Church on marriage and sexual activity, and the restrictions it placed on the sexually active taking communion, may have been unappealing to the laity, and they certainly would have often made it impossible for members of the laity to celebrate communion even if there were a church in the vicinity to which they could go.

There has been much debate about whether the Anglo-Saxon Church, in particular prior to the tenth century, concerned itself with pastoral care or with ministering to the lower social orders. Early written sources indicate that pastoral care was envisaged as preaching and teaching; baptism; visiting the sick; receiving the faithful into the church on Sundays and major feast days; the prohibition of clearly pagan activities (such as sacrifice to pagan gods, incantation, divination and the taking of auguries); penance and confession; seeking out those who had not recently received clerical ministrations; and an obligation to leave behind a priest 'for the offices of the church' if a minster was moved. While this suggests that pastoral care extended to a wide section of society, it is not, in fact, clear that these ideals were consistently met. The available documentary sources suggest that where the laity were the intended audience of texts it was, in fact, kings and nobles who were envisaged and it is they who figure prominently as the people who experience visions, are cured by miracles, are damned for bad behaviour and so on. Where members of the lower classes appear it is arguable that they often do so only to reinforce the lordly status of another character. Such an example concerns the baby boy of peasant stock who was resuscitated by Bishop Wilfrid, and whom Wilfrid demanded should return to serve him when he was seven. St Cuthbert performed miracles on two ordinary villagers, but the story Bede tells is there to contrast with the bishops of his own day: St Cuthbert performed the miracles while preaching in remote areas, in contrast to bishops of Bede's day who, he complains, did not visit such areas at all. In such sources it is always difficult to tell where reality ends and literary and spiritual excursus begins, but on the whole early Anglo-Saxon texts did not feel it necessary to say much about the lower orders.

The preparations made by people further down the social scale for death are much less well documented. It is not unreasonable to believe that the messages about death and the afterlife recorded in the written sources filtered through, to a greater or lesser extent, to the wider body of the laity, through their attendance at church services, for example, where such messages might be conveyed both through sermons and through the elaborate architecture of churches. We know that Anglo-Saxon stone sculpture depicted a range of ecclesiastical messages, and that these may have been very visible, as they may often have been painted. There is also some limited evidence to suggest that Anglo-Saxon churches were painted or adorned with painted panels. Bede tells us that Benedict Biscop (d.689), the first abbot of Monkwearmouth-Jarrow, brought pictures to ornament the church:

> These comprised an image of the Blessed Ever-Virgin Mother of God Mary, together with others of the Twelve Apostles . . . images of the Gospel stories . . . images of the Apocalypse of Blessed John . . . Thus those coming into the church, *even all those who were illiterate*, whichever way they might look might contemplate the lovely sight of Christ and his Saints . . . or reflect upon the grace of our Lord's incarnation . . . or, having as if before his eyes the critical moment of the last judgement, might remember to examine himself more strictly [my italics]

At a later date, Archbishop Ealdred of York (1060-69) is recorded as having enlarged the church at Beverley and having covered the ceiling with a painting. Whatever the level of religious instruction the masses were given, we do know that saints' cults attracted wide interest and were perceived as having benefits for the wider community. This is revealed by such stories as Bede's account of the people of modest standing who benefited from the miracles wrought at the cross erected by Oswald, king of Northumbria and future saint, prior to a battle at 'heavenfield' (somewhere in northern England), and at the spot where Oswald was killed against King Penda of Mercia, at Oswestry (Shrops). The laity may also have undertaken pilgrimages — this is implied by the miracles that are reported as having taken place at both 'heavenfield' and Oswestry. The people who went to those places both expected miracles to be performed and also took away things from the site — such as fragments of the cross, and the soil from around the cross — in order to cure the sick.

Complaints in the writings of later Anglo-Saxon ecclesiastics about so-called 'superstitious' practices reveal that pre-Christian ritual practices and beliefs were still ingrained within secular society. In particular, belief in the value of the worship of trees, stones and wells is commented upon. For example, the monk Ælfric in one of his treatises on healing condemned the practices that some people engaged in when they experienced physical suffering:

> Let he who is unhealthy pray for his health from the Lord, and patiently endure the strokes . . . let him not buy the body's health through any devil's craft with his soul . . . No Christian man is allowed to fetch his health from any stone, nor from any tree, unless it is the holy-cross sign, nor from any place, unless it is the holy house of God.

This suggests that the belief system of the lower orders was not shaped solely by the Church and that any preparations that they made for death, or to ward off death for that matter, were not solely Christian in origin.

Saints were important for the laity in Anglo-Saxon society. A study of the fates of saints reveals the continuing role that the dead might play in Anglo-Saxon society through the miracles they performed, the prophecies they made and the condemnations they exercised. Saints' cults did not just happen, however, rather they were actively fostered and promoted. For example, St Guthlac was translated into a monument at Crowland around which King Æthelbald of Mercia had constructed 'wonderful structures and ornamentations', and where he founded a monastery. The discovery that Guthlac's body was incorrupt was a sign of his sanctity. The relics of the Northumbrian king St Oswald (d.642) were brought to Bardney (Lincs) in the later seventh century under the auspices of the patrons of the monastery there, King Æthelred and Queen Osthryth of Mercia. It is also notable that the resting-places of many saints were royal or episcopal vills, such as Repton (Derbs), and this may be another indication of the active fostering of saints' cults for the benefit of the living. Cults were useful to the living because they afforded important protection to the possessions of religious communities, they attracted continuing patronage of the church where they rested, they became focal points for pilgrimage, which also had potential financial benefits, and devotion to a saint's relics was a means by which the living could ensure the passage of their soul to Heaven through the intercessory role of the saint. Determining where saints were finally to be laid to rest was an important element in the success of a saint's cult, and was a decision that the would-be saint was often involved in making. Saints were important in the political landscape, and their bodies were sometimes divided. Saints were also often translated from their initial resting-place, as the political balance in a region changed. The relics of a number of saints were removed from northern England and taken to churches further south during the tenth and early eleventh century in the wake of the Scandinavian raids and settlement of this time and following the growing power of the royal house of Wessex. Thus, the role of the saintly dead was likely to change over time, and the initial decisions that were taken about where saints were to rest might be overturned by subsequent generations.

Anglo-Saxon wills

Anglo-Saxon wills have much to reveal about the preparations of the nobility for death. Surviving wills are mostly from the tenth and eleventh centuries. There are indications in wills that suggest that they were sometimes read out loud, which hints at there having been many more verbal wills than the surviving corpus of written wills indicates. A striking feature of Anglo-Saxon wills concerns the details given about the heriot, which was a fee paid in kind upon death to the king, or other lord. According to wills, these payments regularly consisted of sword, spears, shields, horses, and money. These are all items that had commonly been buried as grave goods at a much earlier date. It may suggest that although the dead had long since ceased to be buried with grave goods, such artefacts still had a role in the mortuary processes (see below, pp.108-9).

Wills of this period also dispose of large amounts of land and a wide range of artefacts. Wulfric Spott (*c*.1004), for example, bequeathed large amounts of land in Derbyshire, Staffordshire and 'between the Ribble and the Mersey', and he also left to his goddaughter 'the brooch which was her grandmother's'. A will made by Ulf and Madselin, who were major landholders in Lincolnshire, some time between 1066 and 1068 provides some insights into the processes by which wealthy individuals prepared for their death. Ulf and Madselin were about to go to Jerusalem, presumably on pilgrimage, and they distributed their land in the will. They gave lands at Skillington (Lincs), Hoby (Leics) and Morton (Yorks) to Archbishop Ealdred of York, who was to hold them on a mortgage of eight marks of gold: if they returned home the gold would be returned to the bishop, if not, the bishop was 'to supply for their soul's sake as much as the land is worth above that gold'. Land at Carlton (Lincs) was given to Peterborough Abbey 'for the redemption of their souls', and an estate at Overton (Leics) was to be sold and the money 'employed for the souls of both of us'.

Archaeological evidence for preparation for death

The large corpus of Anglo-Saxon stone sculpture from the region also reveals some of the decisions that had to be made about the fate of the deceased. Some of these decisions, such as what types of sculpture to commission, what it should display and how it should be decorated, may have been decided during the lifetime of an individual. Although there is no clear evidence that this was the case, the care taken to prepare for death, according to wills, saints' *Lives* and other documentary sources, suggest that it is not unlikely that the person who was to be commemorated by a piece of stone sculpture might have had some say in its commissioning — although whether their wishes were always carried out is another matter. In contrast, inscriptions on sculpture at Thornhill (Yorks) reveal that sculpture was sometimes commissioned by other people for the deceased (**20, 21**).

Excavation of a variety of types of cemetery suggests that the funeral accorded different individuals might vary. Some individuals in the seventh century, and occasionally perhaps later, were interred in barrows, some of which were newly created. This involved a great deal of time and effort to prepare the site for burial, and many such burials were also lavishly provided with grave goods. This appears to contrast sharply with seventh-century burials in 'ordinary' row-grave cemeteries, where grave goods were, on the whole, much less common and lavish. However, some individuals were buried in comparatively unelaborated fashion near to the barrow burials, and their status may have been signalled as much by the proximity of their burial to the elaborate barrow burials as by the form that their grave took. Thus, we have to be careful to consider the location as well as the form of burials when assessing their comparability and differences. The lavish seventh-century burials in barrows have quite a standardized form, with grave goods of similar type being found across the country. This has been related to the emergence of more established aristocratic families than had existed in the fifth and sixth centuries, which were expressing their status in a region-wide, if not nation-wide, fashion. During the following centuries this standardization of elite burials was increasingly notable in above-ground display. As a result, what went in the ground became increasingly unimportant, and wealth was used to negotiate status in more long-lasting and visible media than grave display. Most communities had their own burial ground by the eleventh century, and what went into graves became increasingly diverse, and varied from cemetery to cemetery. It appears to have been possible for people to exercise more individualized choice about how they prepared the dead for burial.

Cemeteries of the eighth to eleventh centuries, which vary greatly in size, location and the types of individuals being buried there, reveal that burial commonly required a certain amount of preparation. Many cemeteries, including those in towns, near major religious communities and in relatively remote locations, included a large number of burials in wooden coffins. Of these, many had relatively elaborate fittings, including locks in some cases (*see* **30**). Other graves contained stone coffins, or were lined with stone, which suggests a high level of investment in the grave, as, indeed, does the provision of grave-markers above many graves. While these may have been largely for the wealthier members of society, the fact that evidence for grave-markers in wood (e.g. at Thwing (Yorks)), as well as in stone, has been excavated suggests that it was not only those able to afford stone grave monuments who were able to have their grave marked above ground. It should, however, be observed that wooden markers may have been not a sign of lesser wealth so much as a deliberately more humble choice on the part of the wealthy. Indeed, in general, we cannot assume that the more austere graves indicate that less care had been taken or that less wealth was available for the burial. The positive embracing of austerity by the pious may skew the relationship between wealth and forward planning on the one hand, and the nature of the grave prepared on the other. Although from the eighth century burials were not as elaborate as they had been in the fifth to seventh centuries, this does not necessarily mean that funerals had ceased to be either important or elaborate by the later Anglo-Saxon centuries (see also chapter 4).

From archaeological evidence it is sometimes possible to say something about the post-mortem treatment of the body. The shrouding of a body in readiness for burial is

20 *Cross-shaft with inscription from Thornhill (Yorks)*. Phil Sidebottom

1 Carved panel from Hovingham (Yorks). This now rather worn stone depicts scenes from the life of the Virgin. This panel may have come from a shrine or sarcophagus, but it has also been suggested that it may have been an altar panel

2 Burial near chapel from Flixborough (Lincs). Humber Field Archaeology

3 Inscribed lead plaque from Flixborough (Lincs). Humber Field Archaeology

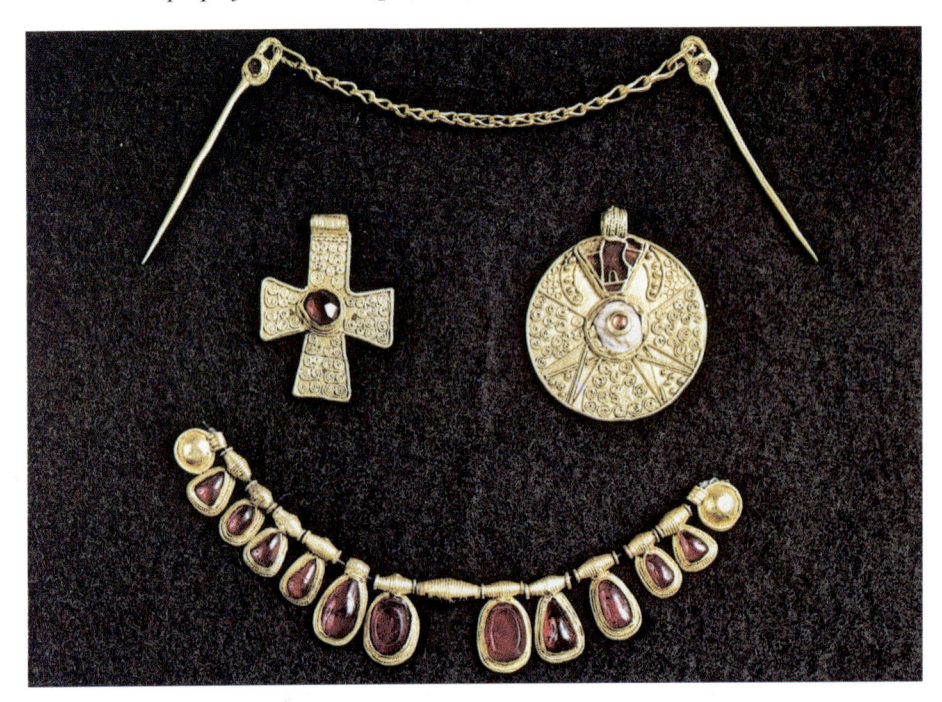

4 Grave goods from barrows in Derbyshire and Yorkshire. The pins are from Cow Low (Derbs), the pendant is from Womersley (Yorks) and the necklace from Brassington (Derbs). Sheffield City Museum

5 *A burial aligned south-north cut by a later burial aligned west-east at Kellington (Yorks).* Andrew Chamberlain

6 *Burial mounds at Heath Wood, Ingleby (Derbs). Mound 50 in the foreground, with mound 56 behind.* Julian D. Richards

7 *Burials at Fillingham (Lincs). These stone-lined graves, and the stones set around the skulls are characteristic of burials of tenth- and eleventh-century date. The skeletons lie right on top of the bedrock.* Peter Cleghorn

8 *Burials at Wigber Low (Derbs). This large double grave contained a knife, sword, spearhead, socketed blade, iron buckle, the bronze fittings of a probable satchel and the ribs from a side of beef.* John Collis

9   *Skull excavated at Towton (Yorks). This skull has blade wounds and puncture.* Published with the permission of Shannon Novak and the editors of *Blood Red Roses: the Archaeology of a Mass Grave from the Battle of Towton AD 1461*, Oxbow Books, Oxford 2000

10 *The visit of Christ to Hell from a fifteenth-century wall painting from Pickering (Yorks). Note that he is leading the sinners from Hell, chief among whom are Adam and Eve.* Author

11 Wall painting at Blyth (Notts), depicting the Last Judgement. This section of the wall painting shows the dead rising from their coffins. Jim Williams

12 *A devil listening to gossiping women on a wall painting from Melbourne (Derbs). Such an image of devils writing down the gossip of women is also found on a corbel in the nave of the church at Sleaford (Lincs). Late medieval commentators often commented on the uncontrolled chattering of women, and the images at Melbourne and Sleaford were reminders of the dangers and the sinfulness of such behaviour.* Author

13 *Peasants labouring on the land in window glass from Dewsbury (Yorks).* Jim Williams

14 Painted panel from Newark (Notts). A rare example of a scene from the Dance of Death, from the early sixteenth century. Jim Williams

15 Tomb in the churchyard at Loversall (Yorks). This unusual fifteenth-century tomb depicts various types of window tracery. Jim Williams

16 *The blessing of Joan Fitz Payn from the Gray-Fitz Payn Book of Hours. Inside the large initial D Christ blesses Joan Fitz Payn, who kneels before him wearing an heraldic mantle. The heraldic shields on the page announce family alliances, as well as providing a decorative border.*
Fitzwilliam Museum

Quia repleta est malis anima mea: & uita mea in inferno appropinquauit. Estimatus sum cum descendentibus in lacum: factus sum sicut homo sine adiutorio inter mortuos liber. Sicut uulnerati dormientes in sepulcris: quorum non est memor amplius & ipsi de manu tua repulsi sunt. Posuerunt me in lacu inferiori: in tenebrosis & in umbra mortis. Super me confirmatus est furor tuus: & omnes fluctus tuos induxisti super me. Longe fecisti notos meos a me: po

17 Coffin and depiction of Hell from the Luttrell Psalter. An old man looks down into a hellmouth, below which is a corpse in a coffin. British Library

18 Sir Geoffrey Luttrell preparing to go off to battle from the Luttrell Psalter. British Library

19 *Window glass from St Mary Magdalene, Newark (Notts). The surviving window has been created out of fragments of several fourteenth- and fifteenth-century windows. In addition to scenes from the Life of the Virgin, the story of Adam and Eve, the Life of Christ and the Seven Deadly Sins, the window also has depictions of patrons of the church. In this panel two women who were presumably patrons are shown praying. Behind them stands a man holding a church, who had presumably also made some sort of donation to the church.* Jim Williams

20 *Window from All Saints, North Street, York. The subject of this window is Richard Rolle's version of the Last Days, described in his poem the* Pricke of Conscience. *The English inscription records that 'on the fourteenth day all that lives shall die: child, man and woman'.* Royal Commission for Historic Monuments

21 *Members of the Fitzherbert family praying in a window glass at Norbury (Derbs).* Jim Williams

22 *St Anne teaching the Virgin to read on a window from Norbury (Derbs) (central panel). Members of the Fitzherbert family are depicted praying in the lower panels.* Jim Williams

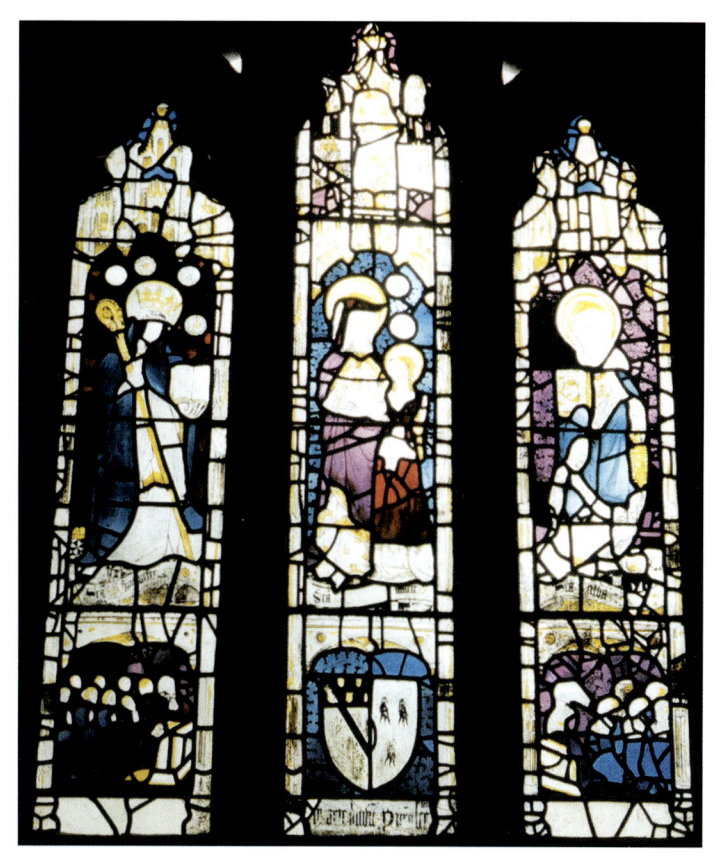

23 *The Seven Corporal Acts of Mercy from a wall painting at Pickering (Yorks). The scenes shown here depict, from left to right: sheltering the stranger, clothing the naked, visiting prisoners, tending to the sick and burying the dead.* Author

24 Wooden tomb of Sir Roger Rockley at Worsborough (Yorks). This cadaver is depicted immediately below the lifelike figure of the lord in his armour. Jim Williams

25 Excavation of a skeleton in progress at Grantham (Lincs). Andrew Chamberlain

often revealed by the presence of shroud pins, or stains on the skeleton, caused by the presence of shroud pins (see below, p.103). Narrow graves are often an indication that the individual was clothed or shrouded when they were placed in the ground, rather than placed in a coffin. Tightly packed bones are another indication of shrouding. It appears to be the case that from the eighth century it was more common for individuals to be prepared for burial by being wrapped in a shroud than for them to have been clothed. There is little documentary evidence for this, but contemporary continental sources seem to suggest that the dead were specially dressed for burial in robes that may have been reminiscent of baptismal robes (Samson 1999).

As we saw in the previous chapter, there were a variety of types of burial ground in the middle and later Anglo-Saxon centuries, and it appears that there was a certain amount of choice to be exercised about where an individual was to be buried. It is, however, difficult to know how far there was a free choice, and how far particular burial grounds were restricted to particular social or religious groups. At Ripon, for example, there appear to have been several cemeteries between the seventh and ninth centuries, and while some areas for burial may have been limited to members of the religious community based at Ripon, others were presumably available to members of the laity. A similar situation may have obtained at other religious communities, such as Repton, Crayke, Addingham, Whitby (Yorks) and Flixborough (Lincs). For some individuals, such as executed felons and excommunicates, there were, however, limited choices to be made about where they were to be buried, since they were forbidden burial in consecrated ground. Even the burials of especially holy individuals and would-be saints could not necessarily be easily achieved in the preferred location, as we have seen (above, p.32).

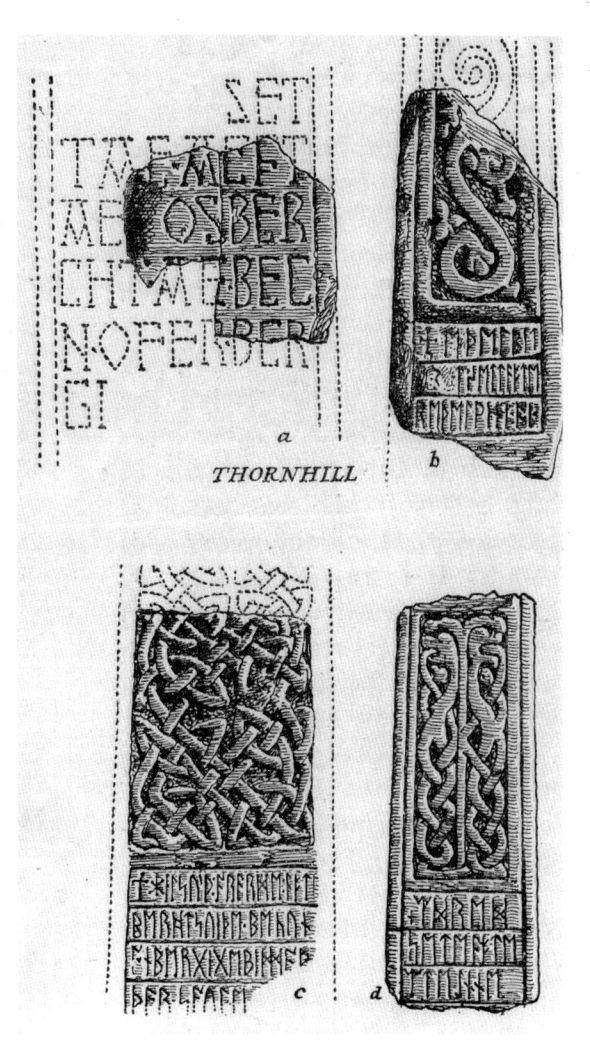

21 Stone sculpture with inscriptions from Thornhill (Yorks): a is a grave-slab, and b, c, d are cross-shafts. After Collingwood 1915

At Addingham excavation has revealed that individuals were sometimes removed from their initial grave and placed in another grave alongside another burial. This indicates a high level of planning and preparation for burials, and that the dead did not cease to be of concern. It also shows that the dead were not necessarily left to rest in peace. The empty graves where bodies appear to have been removed were located in the western part of the excavated cemetery, and it has been suggested that they were moved closer to some focal point to the east. It may be that whatever choices were initially made about where to bury someone were later superseded as it became possible to achieve for them a more prestigious burial place. At Pontefract (Yorks) evidence has been found for the careful rearrangement of skeletons to make way for later burials in the same grave. In one grave the bones of the previous occupant were neatly stacked around the coffin of the later burial (**22**). The long-since dead eventually had to give way to the more recent dead.

22 *Burial disturbed by later burial from Pontefract (Yorks). The bones from the earlier burial had been neatly stacked up around the coffin of the later burial.* West Yorkshire Archaeological Service

Preparation for death and burial in the later Middle Ages

From the eleventh century there is much more evidence available about the processes by which people prepared for their death, and the arrangements made for burial. There was an understanding in the later Middle Ages that the fate of the soul after death could to some extent be determined by things that a person did during their lifetime. This became increasingly important from the twelfth century following the beginnings of the formalization of the concept of Purgatory, with the doctrine of Purgatory finally being promulgated at the second Council of Lyons in 1274. While Heaven and Hell were places where the soul would eventually rest permanently, Purgatory was a place where the soul would rest for an undefined time, during which the purgatorial flames and torments would cleanse the soul of sin in order to reach Heaven. The doctrine of Purgatory offered some insights into what would happen to the soul after death, something that prior to the twelfth century had not been clear. To assist the soul through Purgatory to reach Heaven a number of measures might be taken. Living a good life was clearly important, but it was also necessary to do penance for sins committed, and for prayers and masses to be said for the soul after death. If a person was wealthy enough it was possible to put in place arrangements to ensure post-mortem commemoration and prayers. It is, however, important to note that we know far more about intentions for there to be post-mortem prayer, than about what actually happened. As we shall see, the wishes of the deceased were not always carried out.

Discussions of Purgatory offered by priests, and the iconography of Purgatory, depicted it as a terrible place, closer to Hell than to Heaven, where the soul was incarcerated. The imagery of prison was often used to depict Purgatory. Nonetheless, it was made clear that the soul could be freed by the intercession of the living. When combined with other influences, such as that from popular ghost stories, about the torments of the soul and the need for assistance from the living, the laity was placed under considerable pressure both to take proper precautions for their own soul and to assist the souls of others.

Churches were full of the images of the fate that awaited people after death. Although there was agreement within the medieval Church that the soul would eventually end up in Heaven or in Hell, there was debate about where the soul would reside between death and the final destination. One belief was that the souls of the virtuous would rest in the bosom of Abraham, which is depicted on the Percy tomb in Beverley Minster (Yorks) (**23**). The soul was commonly depicted as being weighed or judged in some way, whether in Abraham's bosom or by St Michael. On a fifteenth-century alabaster tomb at Harewood (Yorks) St Michael is shown with weighing scales, the common iconographic representation of this saint. There seems to have been a divergence of opinion about what the soul actually looked like, and this visual diversity was also found in theological debate. Iconographic evidence suggests that some thought that the soul was a child, which was released by the body after death, whereas others depicted it as an adult with a continuing life. Depictions of the Day of Judgement, such as those on wall

23 The Percy tomb from Beverley Minster (Yorks). This fourteenth-century monument shows a concern with the fate of the soul. On this side the soul of the deceased is shown resting in a napkin held by angels above the patriarch's lap.

24 Depiction of Hell from the west front of Lincoln Cathedral. After Bilson 1907

paintings at Blyth (Notts) and Corby Glen (Lincs), were probably not uncommon in later medieval art although few survive (**colour plate 11**). Images of Hell are often found in sculpture. For example, on the west front of Lincoln Cathedral two angels are shown tending a dying man and preparing to meet his soul, while below a devil is pushing three souls down into the mouth of Hell (**24**). A tympanum (now in York Museum) shows three devils gathered around a dying man, ready to seize his soul, and a sculpture (possibly formerly from York Minster) depicts the hell cauldron and the tortured fat of the damned (**25**). Images in the east window of York Minster and in a window in St Michael, Spurriergate in York depict the fall from Heaven of the angels who became devils, and in the window at St Michael's they are shown being transformed into hideous creatures as they fall to Hell. A fifteenth-century wall painting from Pickering (Yorks) depicts Christ visiting Hell after his death on the cross and before his resurrection, ministering to those who had died without knowing him (**colour plate 10**). At the mouth of Hell he is met by Adam, holding an apple, and Eve, a stark reminder of the fate of sinners. These particular sinners, it is worth noting, commonly stand in later medieval iconography for the peasantry.

Intercessory images abound in the fabric and fittings of later medieval churches, on wall paintings, window glass, wooden carving (e.g. misericords, rood screens), alabaster

25 Depiction of Hell on a tympanum from York. After Bilson 1907

panels and various types of funerary monument. They feature not only Christ but also other biblical figures and saints who were believed to have intercessory powers. These may have been particularly popular images for patrons. We should also remember that images such as these were not just relevant to the wealthy who paid for them and to the literate, and the importance of these visual messages on the laity should not be underestimated. The poor and the illiterate would have seen these forms of artistic patronage and, in addition to it reminding them of their position in the social hierarchy, they would also have drawn on this imagery to understand what the fate of their soul might be and how they could do things to help it. The iconography displayed in churches was an important means by which the laity understood the message of the Bible and the teachings of their priests, as the images reinforced the verbal messages that were conveyed in church. This visual information was not necessarily simply passively absorbed. Church services were very visual in content and were mobile, involving the priest moving around the church blessing various altars. On certain feast days the attributes of the saint being commemorated would be commented upon. The sorts of images that were available to all members of the community included the need to carry out acts of charity to save the soul, the horrors of Hell and of Purgatory, and the importance of hard physical work in the grand order of things was impressed by depictions of Adam and Eve at their toils. Even if they could do no more for their souls than to attend church services, believe in the teachings of the Church, live a just life and repent their sins, the importance of doing this, and the implications of not doing so, were everywhere apparent to lay society.

Ecclesiastical iconography was made real and relevant to those who saw it, not least because it was constantly updated. Many of the images displayed in churches would have been of the wealthy and the socially prominent. Even saints and biblical figures were commonly depicted in the fashionable dress of the wealthy of the day. In contrast, images of Adam and Eve toiling at their labours normally depicted them as peasants. Other images that may have had wide resonance include the gossiping women being overheard by the devil in a wall painting at Melbourne (Derbs) (**colour plate 12**) and on a corbel on the nave arcade at Sleaford (Lincs) who were clearly wearing clothing of the day, and the fashionably dressed blasphemers being tempted by devils in a wall painting at Corby

Glen. Medieval ecclesiastical art also served to reinforce the social order, and, for example, depicted manual labour as part of the divine order of the world, part of the way things must be in order for God's will to be carried out on earth. A window at Dewsbury (Yorks) (**colour plate 13**) shows peasants labouring on the land, and these were depicted alongside images of Christ and saints and the heraldic arms of local lords. Each social group had its part to play in the divine order, and the expectation was that everyone would eventually be rewarded in the next world. As Thomas Brinton, bishop of Rochester (1373-89), put it, 'the rich have been created for the benefit of the poor and the poor for the benefit of the rich', and 'Since servitude was introduced into the world by sin, justice demands that masters should rule over servants and that servants should be subject to their masters'. This notion was both offered in sermons and also depicted in the visual elaboration of churches. While the preparation for death and for burial by the poorer members of society is less well known than the measures taken by the wealthy, it may be inferred from the visual messages with which they were commonly confronted. They were regularly confronted with what they needed to do, and with the implications of failing to meet these requirements.

In theory, death would be the great leveller for all social classes. The fourteenth-century Dominican preacher John Bromyard commented that in the grave there would be no difference between kings and beggars, masters and servants. However, in reality it is apparent that the wealthy hoped, and probably expected, that the social hierarchy would be maintained. This is made apparent by their elaborate funerary monuments, which clearly display their wealth, and by depictions of wealthy patrons in window glass, and also in their personal devotional books, often shown receiving the personal attention of saints and other Biblical figures. This was one of the great sources of consternation for many theologians, as the rituals of death ran counter to their pronouncements on the fate that would await those who had both adhered to the teachings of the Church and played their part in the world that God had created. In many ways, there was a clash of ideology between the clergy and lay elite where preparation for death and expectations for the afterlife were concerned.

Approaching and identifying death

Identifying when death was nigh was considered important in the Middle Ages because it gave people time to put their worldly and spiritual affairs in order before they died — 'Lord, make me to know my end and the number of my days, so that I may know what I am lacking' (Psalm 39:4). A fourteenth-century account of the signs of impending death states that death is nigh when the eye mists, hearing fails, the nose goes cold, the tongue curls back, the face falls in, the lips blacken, the mouth gapes, spittle runs, hair stands on end, the heart trembles, the hands shake and the feet go stiff. Such accounts were as much moralizing accounts as they were medical texts, and they warned of the need to make spiritual preparation for death. Indeed, the final lines of this account of the signs of the approach of death are 'All too late, all too late/ When the bier is at the gate'. Medieval commentators were also concerned to distinguish between different types of death —

natural and unnatural, good and bad. Such distinctions had legal significance, and they were also important in determining both the fate of the soul of the deceased and whether they would achieve sanctity, for which the right kind of death was essential. A number of manuscripts survive from the fourteenth and fifteenth centuries of texts which were manuals explaining how to ensure an appropriate death, known as the *Ars Moriendi*. These manuals offered guidance about what death meant for Christians, the temptations that the dying face in their last hours (crisis of faith, despair, impatience, complacence, concern about their worldly goods), the questions that should be asked of the dying (to ascertain whether they are glad to die in the faith of Christ and that they repent of their sins), the things that the dying should do (pray, cry with the heart, weep, commend their soul to God), and the things that should be said, and the prayers that should be offered, by others to the dying. These manuals are not medical texts, but spiritual guides, and their concern is with the soul. As one of these manuals states:

> Though bodily death be most dreadful of all fearful things . . . yet spiritual death of the soul is as much more horrible and detestable, as the soul is more worthy and precious than the body.

A number of tests were established for identifying death, including the use of feathers and mirrors under the nostrils or mouth, the mixture of milk and urine or the placing of mugwort under the head. While these may have had a medical basis, the use of these tests as literary motifs also had moral implications, as they both reminded people that death eventually came to all and they also served to warn people of the need to make sure that someone was dead before making arrangements for replacing them in the living world. There were a number of popularly known stories about individuals who 'came back to life', and about families and friends who had been too hasty to move on. Such stories were essentially derived from the Bible, and from the story of Lazarus who spent three days in Hell before Christ raised him back to life. Yet, even if such tales about the return to life of the dead were ultimately literary motifs, that is not to say that they did not have a significant impact on medieval people and their attitudes to the dead.

There is some evidence to suggest that death might not necessarily be accurately diagnosed in the Middle Ages. Inaccurate diagnosis may lie behind some later medieval tales of individuals who are said to have recovered from death. Given, however, that such recoveries tended to be attributed to miraculous interventions, rather than to misdiagnosis, there may have been little general fear about premature burial. Nonetheless, fear of premature burial is sometimes hinted at. This fear may have lain behind the request in the will of Sir Thomas Cumberworth of Somerby (Lincs) of 1450-1 that his body should be taken to the church of Somerby and left there for 24 hours before burial.

When death was near, the priest would be called to administer the last rites. This involved hearing confession and granting absolution. Then the sacrament of extreme unction would be administered, which involved making the sign of the cross on the eyes, ears, nostrils, mouth, hands, feet and back and asking for forgiveness for the sins committed through each part of the body. Finally, a consecrated wafer would be given to the dying person. The last rites could be administered again if the person recovered, although there was a popular belief that a person who recovered after the last rites should henceforth lead a penitential life, abstaining from sexual intercourse and from eating meat. As death approached windows were often opened in order that the soul could easily make its departure. This, however, was the ideal, and the reality for many people may have been rather different. In particular, after the outbreak of plague in England in 1348 there was often a shortage of priests to perform the last rites, and emergency measures had to be brought into effect that, allowed, for example, the dying to make final confession to a layperson if no priest was available.

The impending death of a monk was unlike other deaths in that, in theory, monks were already dead to the world. Upon entering a monastery the monk was entering 'a place of protracted transition' (Finucane 1981, 44), and was escaping from the dangers of this world to the protection of God, in the same way that the dead were taken from the dangers of this world. Monks were also socially dead to the world, in as much as they were no longer able to own or inherit property, and any will that the monk had previously written took effect immediately he entered a monastery. Thus monks, in effect, underwent two deaths — one ritual, and one physical — that were prepared for in different ways. For the ritual death a monk would wear his hood up for three days and speak to no one, and then at the end of this time the abbot would lower the hood and the monk would be resurrected into a new existence. As the moment of bodily death approached the monk would be laid on a bed of ashes to symbolize humility and penitence. As Walter Daniel says of the final earthly moments of Abbot Aelred of Rievaulx Abbey (Yorks) (d.1167):

> When we realized he was at the point of death, he was laid, as is the monastic custom, on a haircloth strewn with ashes, and there, amid the great gathering of his sons . . . he gave up his spotless spirit into the hands of his Father and fell asleep in Christ

When bodily death occurred the monk would receive all the benefits of the many prayers that would be offered by the other monks in the monastery.

The death of lepers was also different from that of other members of the laity, and the treatment of lepers bore some similarities with the ritual death of monks. Lepers underwent a ceremony that ritually separated them from the living community. The leper was led into church by a priest chanting the seven penitential psalms of the funeral service, and was then instructed to kneel under a black cloth spread between two trestles that were surrounded with candles, as if it were a bier. After a mass, confession and communion the leper was led into the churchyard and a spadeful of earth was thrown over his feet. From that moment lepers were, in a similar way to monks, 'dead to the world' without legal rights in the living community. As we have already seen (above, p.50), lepers were regarded as living in Purgatory, and as suffering for the souls of the living. When physical death eventually came, lepers had to be buried at the leper hospital, thus forever remaining separated from the rest of society.

The moment of death

It was widely considered desirable that people should not die alone. Artistic depictions of the deathbed generally show several people, usually including a priest, gathered at the bedside of the dying person. For example, an early fifteenth-century window from All Saints, North Street in York depicts Death waiting for the passing of a man and a woman while three mourners look on (**colour plate 20**). The implications of this window were there for all to see, not least because the window and its inscription echoed the version of the Last Days described in the poem *The Pricke of Conscience* by the fourteenth-century spiritual writer Richard Rolle. The English inscription explains that on the fourteenth day all that lives shall die, child, man and woman. Ecclesiastics had some of the most crowded deathbeds. Aelred of Rievaulx, for example, was visited by members of the monastery, the abbots of Byland Abbey and Fountains Abbey (Yorks), and his doctor Walter Daniel. In noble households, death was marked by a series of rituals in which the household played a major part. The deathbed was commonly attended by a great number of people, including family, friends, priests, physicians and members of the household.

In practice, however, not everyone enjoyed the accompanied death that was advocated in manuals on the craft of dying. The records of coroner's courts remind us that many people died violently or unexpectedly as a result of accidents or murder, and they did not enjoy the benefits of being able to prepare for their death during their final moments. It is difficult to judge what may have been the experiences of death of the peasantry. However, the treatment of the elderly and the infirm may provide some insights. There is little evidence to suggest that the elderly and those who were no longer able to work were routinely left to their own devices. Maintenance agreements made for elderly tenants when they passed on their land, commonly to their children or other relatives, indicate that they were normally provided with both food and somewhere to live. We also know that where infirmity and poverty prevented a peasant from working, there was some social mechanism to prevent them from starving. Often this involved the lord retrieving land from the peasant but putting in place measures to ensure that the peasant had some means of supporting him or herself. For example, in 1326 Adam Febgrays of Toynton (Lincs) appeared before the manorial court because he had not paid his dues to the lord. The lord's bailiff had entered his lands, harvested them, and delivered his crops, along with a brass pot, to the lord. Adam's 'infirmity and poverty' saw him relinquish his lands to the lord and ask for alms from the lord. The lord took Adam's lands, but he ordered estate labourers to plant two-and-a-half acres which Adam could make use of. Archaeological and documentary evidence reveals that often there was more than one living unit within the property boundaries of rural settlements, catering for different family groups, for elderly retired peasants as well as for sub-tenants. There is also evidence for the transformation of buildings formerly used for agricultural purposes into living accommodation. The holdings of peasants were, then, commonly crowded with people, certainly prior to the mid-fourteenth century when a major demographic decline set in. The medieval peasant community provided a level of mutual support and assistance at difficult times, and in this context it appears that the elderly and the infirm were generally well provided for. Other than in some cases of murder and death by misadventure, few people, in practice, probably died alone.

Great emphasis was placed on making suitable preparations for death in the later Middle Ages, yet this does not necessarily mean that the dying or those approaching the end of their life were always treated with reverence by their friends, family or wider society. A number of literary images from the later Middle Ages indicate that the elderly were often associated with evil in popular perception, and with the loss of worldly goods, friends and health. For example, an early fourteenth-century poem associates old age with the loss of hair, eyesight, good fortune and love and the development of a series of repulsive mannerisms, such as stumbling when walking, and spitting when speaking. Nonetheless, on the whole in both aristocratic and peasant society, careful and formal arrangements were generally made for the elderly and infirm.

Preparation of the body

Documentary sources provide some insights into the ways in which the body might be prepared for burial. It seems to have been common for the body to be kept in the home either until the day of, or the evening before, the funeral. For example, the will of Robert de Crosse of York (1395) requested that a night watch, or wake, was held while his body remained in the house overnight. As at an earlier date (above p.65), it seems to have been more common for a person to be wrapped in a shroud rather than in clothes in preparation for burial, and the dressing of the body seems not uncommonly to have been carried out by women. The shroud clearly carried a symbolic quality. There was little biblical precedent for the preparation of the body for burial, but that that there was involved a shroud (such as that in which Lazarus was wrapped). The shroud may have reflected something of the state of the individual. As the fifteenth-century sermon-writer John Mirk wrote, the shroud showed that a person was 'clean shriven and cleansed of his sins by contrition of heart and by absolution'. The shroud may also have echoed baptismal robes and been a reminder of the faith of the deceased.

In contrast, ecclesiastics were often prepared for burial in their ecclesiastical robes (below pp.113-14). Sometimes particularly elaborate arrangements were made. When the tomb of Archbishop Godfrey de Ludham of York (1258-65) was opened in 1969, quite a lot of body tissue remained, and this suggests that he had been embalmed, although the lead lining of the coffin was also important in preserving the body. The right leg was still rounded and the thigh was 5" in diameter, and much of the face remained intact, as did the fingernails. The dressing and embalming of the body was also sometimes undertaken for members of the laity. For example, when Queen Eleanor died in 1290 at Harby (Notts) her body was transferred to the Gilbertine house of St Catherine to the south of Lincoln where it was dressed and embalmed, in preparation for its journey to London.

Signs of sanctity

Knowledge that one's death was looming was regarded as a sign of sanctity. Abbot Aelred of Rievaulx Abbey who died in 1167 had apparently known for some time that he was about to die, and had announced his imminent departure on Christmas Eve 1166:

> Brothers, to be with Christ is by far the best. And how much longer, anyway, shall I be able to endure this excruciating affliction of the flesh? Therefore, I wish and crave that God, if it please him, may swiftly free me from this prison and bring me to a place of ease, where I may dwell with him in the place of his wondrous tabernacle.

Over the next few days he was able to talk to the monks and to his doctor and future chronicler, Walter Daniel, and to set his affairs, and those of the abbey, in order. He then received the last rites from the Abbot of Byland, and died on 12 January 1167. Although he did not predict the precise moment of his death, according to Walter Daniel he did appear in a vision to one of the monks of his monastery to convey this information, hence demonstrating his saintly qualities. Bishop Hugh of Lincoln (d.1200), who later became St Hugh, was also aware of his impending death and was able to give instructions about his funeral (see below, p.91). He asked to be dressed in the Episcopal robes he had worn at his consecration.

Prospective saints often experienced visions during their last hours and chroniclers of those moments write about them as if the dying person had entered into a liminal state which permitted them to communicate with voices, and to experience visions, from the beyond. As he was dying, St Hugh commented on the future for England and France, and Aelred of Rievaulx in his fevered state was thought by Walter Daniel to be talking with angels. Another common feature of the deaths of the holy was the discovery that their bodies were white immediately after death. Aelred of Rievaulx was 'as white as snow or milk', as was Hugh of Lincoln. The model for this aspect of their death was undoubtedly the death of Martin of Tours (France) (d.397) who was 'the archetypal hermit-monk turned ecclesiastical statesman' (Crouch 1997, 161).

Accounts of the idealized deaths of saints were intended to demonstrate the virtue and sanctity of the deceased, and they need not have been accurate representations of what actually happened — and in some instances, most certainly were not. However, at the same time from the twelfth century there was a new departure in descriptions of ecclesiastical deaths. They became increasingly 'realistic' in their quality, and the passive submission in the face of death that had characterized the deaths of future saints in the Anglo-Saxon period, was replaced by a greater desire to live on, and irritation with the signs of impending death. Aelred of Rievaulx's biographer, Walter Daniel, looked for physical evidence for the approach of death, such as sweating, watering eyes, twitching nostrils, a grey pallor and lips compressed between the teeth, rather than relying on some form of divine revelation. Daniel's interest in the physical signs of death may have stemmed from the fact that he appears to have been Aelred's physician, yet that is not all that marks out the description of Aelred's death as different from earlier holy deaths. Daniel described the suffering of Aelred, who did not die passively, and he seems to have disappointed his biographer by asking Christ to spare him further suffering and to 'release me that I may go to him soon, him whom I see before me, the king of glory'. Similarly, Bishop Hugh of Lincoln became argumentative with his household and complained about his failing health as his death approached. The calm and idealized death became less common in descriptions of deathbed scenes from the twelfth century, both for would-be saints and for laymen. Some have seen in this the birth of the concept of 'individualism' — that is the conception of what it was to be an individual, separate from others — and it has been suggested that until there had been this development in intellectual thought it was not conceivable that anyone would write about the personal, unique experiences of death. However, this interpretation has been questioned by many historians who have pointed to evidence from centuries prior to the twelfth which suggests that concern for the 'individual' was not unknown in earlier centuries; for example, the commemoration of individuals, confession of sins, prayers offered for individuals in order to assist their soul to Heaven and the awareness of the post-mortem implications of sin. It is difficult, therefore, to link new styles of writing about death in the twelfth century to the emergence of individualism, which now appears more like a gradual and growing sense of awareness than the result of a specific moment of discovery. We should be careful, then, not to confuse changes in styles of writing and in forms of artistic representation with real changes in perceptions, and in emotional and psychological reactions to death.

Wills

Wills were generally written by the wealthier members of society, although peasant wills survive in some numbers from the later fifteenth century. Wills were usually deathbed statements, so they present only a limited perspective on the ways in which an individual prepared for both the fate of their soul and the distribution of their worldly goods. Wills generally ignore ante-mortem gifts and donations; in other words, they may have little to reveal about forward planning already made. They are not even necessarily very reliable indicators of the wealth of a person, since they often ignore landed estates. Their real value lies in the hints they give about aspirations and preparation for the afterlife. Did they express hope or fear, and what do they reveal about pious beliefs? These questions are not easy to answer because a lack of interest in spiritual matters in a will need not indicate a lack of spirituality, or shallow spirituality, but rather may reflect the fact that the writer had already made arrangements for their worldly affairs and for their soul, and they felt comfortable with these provisions. Nevertheless, wills do provide important, if limited, insights into the ways in which people made provisions for their souls in the later Middle Ages.

Some of the most common instructions left in wills concerning the soul of the deceased involved bequests for prayers, either from priests or from friends and family. For example, the will of Richard Welby of Moulton (Lincs) from 1465 asked for intercessory services to be said at Moulton church, and at the Charterhouses at London, Sheen (Surrey), Hull and Mount Grace (Yorks), and money was left to ensure that this occurred. Other wills, such as that of Richard Archer of Lincoln in 1453, asked for the name of the deceased to be entered into the bede-roll of the parish, and many left money for candles to be lit in their memory. Bequests are also often made for the up-keep of church fabric, to friaries, leper houses, almshouses and to the poor, fulfilling the requirement to undertake charitable works for the good of the soul (see below, pp.170-1). Occasionally testators left money so that someone could go on pilgrimage on their behalf. Margaret Aske of Aughton (Yorks) asked for someone 'to go on pilgrimage to St Ninian's in Scotland at my expense, and offer there for my soul a gold ring with a diamond set in it'.

Despite the claims often made in wills that they are the personal statements of the dying, they were not necessarily as individual as might be thought. As a person approached the point of death they may have been under pressure from potential recipients of their possessions or from members of the clergy to write a will. Where the person concerned was not literate they would need someone who was literate to write their will for them. The will of Hull merchant John Dalton in 1487 states that Dalton had written the will himself, as do the wills of his brother Thomas Dalton (1497), and the merchants Robert Harryson (1520) and Henry Walker (1521), yet all four contain exactly the same formulae suggesting that even if they had written them themselves, the three later wills were influenced by the earlier will. In this instance, family and professional links may begin to explain the duplication of formulae in the wills. Despite the pious and seemingly personal statements made in wills, they were essentially literary constructs, and often quite formulaic. They need reveal little about the intentions and beliefs of the person in whose name they were written. Moreover, wills only tell us about what was intended, not about what actually happened once the testator had died.

One of the requests made most consistently in wills concerned where the person was to be buried. Sometimes the will simply indicated which church was to be the place of burial, but other times more specific instructions were given. For example, of the 355 extant wills left by inhabitants of Hull between 1400 and 1529, over 200 asked to be buried inside the church of Holy Trinity and 64 asked for burial inside St Mary Lowgate, the parish churches (strictly chapels) in later medieval Hull. The comparatively small number of churches in Hull was the result of the late foundation of the town, in the reign of Edward I in 1290. A lot of money was left in Hull wills for the funeral, including payments to the priest, money to pay some of the poor to be present, expenditure on candles and crosses to surround the hearse, and payments for the presence of the college of twelve clerics, called the Priests of the Table, who lived in the churchyard of Holy Trinity. Only one testator specifically rejected such extravagance. In 1434 John Fitlyng asked for only what was necessary for the praise of God and requested that all extravagance and appearances of vainglory should be rejected. He also left money for the sick and poor, in amounts that were said to be in honour of the five wounds of Christ, the Virgin Mary and the Holy Trinity. This will provides, as Peter Heath (1984, 218) has put it, 'a revealing commentary upon his fellow burgesses'.

Wills commonly made bequests to members of the family, friends and servants, to various churches and ecclesiastics, and to various poor and needy people. These bequests were partly a final settlement of a person's worldly affairs and partly an attempt to ensure that sufficient intercessory prayers were said for the soul. Charitable good works were also thought to aid the soul on its way to Heaven (below pp.169-71). The patronage of churches was an important means for the wealthy to ensure commemoration and prayers after death, but although in many cases this was achieved by a bequest left in a will, many lords also patronized churches during their lifetime and so wills provide only a partial insight into their activities. This patronage of churches had many benefits during one's lifetime, not the least of which was to impress on the parish community the importance of a lord and his family. Patronage of the church also commonly enabled a benefactor to negotiate their place of burial. Peasants also made wills. Unlike lords they were rarely in a position to dispose of large amounts of land, and much of their land was held on particular terms from a lord. However, peasants could dispose of their personal property as they wished.

Although we may use wills to understand something of the priorities of the will-making classes concerning the distribution of their worldly goods and the prayers and masses they wanted to ensure were said for their souls, it is difficult to use them as evidence for either anxiety or hope about the afterlife. The donations of money and goods made to various family members, friends, ecclesiastics and churches have perhaps more to reveal about the wealth of the will writer and their concerns to be commemorated in as wide a social context as possible. Some wills reveal that individuals chose which monuments they were to have and where they were to be erected. However, clauses in wills commissioning monuments for other family members who were already dead reveal that this was not invariably the case.

Preparation for death within the household

Wills also provide some hints that later medieval piety was not solely expressed through the formal setting of the Church. Bequests of devotional books and rosaries are reminders that much religious devotion was conducted within the home. Thirteen Hull wills refer to books, which are mainly devotional works. For example, in the will of John Bedford (1450) two breviaries are listed, and the will of his wife (1459) left primers to both Agnes Swan and John Swan, one of which is said to be the primer 'which I daily use'. In 1459 Elizabeth Bukk of Hull left three rosaries, one each to her daughter, her daughter-in-law and another young woman. Thomas Cumberworth left beads, clearly rosaries, to the Archbishop of York, the Abbot of 'Santasse', the heads of eleven other religious houses in the north of Lincolnshire, a number of nuns, several female relatives, Ralph, Lord Cromwell of Tatershall (Lincs), servants and friends. He also left a selection of devotional books to various members of the clergy. A fifteenth-century window in All Saints, North Street in York has much to reveal about the importance of literacy to the wealthier classes as part of their personal devotion. The window was donated by members of the mercantile Blackburn family and it depicts, alongside St Christopher and John the Baptist, St Anne teaching the Virgin Mary to read. Beneath this are images of Margaret Blackburn and her daughter-in-law reading. It is known that the Blackburn family favoured the Dominican order, and the Dominicans were advocates of the importance of education and literacy in devotion. This window may, thus, reflect the personal interest of the Blackburn family in private devotion through reading, and, perhaps, with female literacy in particular (Pedersen 2000).

Private devotion in the household was an important element of the spirituality of the wealthy, and the life of Sir Geoffrey Luttrell of Irnham (Lincs) (1276-1345) is instructive in this respect (**colour plates 17, 18**). Like many other men of his rank he left money in his will to a variety of churches, but he also left money to a number of individual clerks and chaplains, who may have formed his own personal religious staff. They included John Boothby ('my clerk'), the chaplains Robert of Wilford and John of Laford, and his confessor, brother William of Foderingeye. These bequests suggest that Geoffrey had a private chapel in the manor of Irnham. Some of these men may have been Dominican friars because Geoffrey clearly favoured them, as their depiction at the dining scene in his psalter reveals. By the fourteenth century the aristocracy and the gentry were increasingly removing themselves from the communal life of the parish and of the hall in their households, as can be seen from the proliferation of private, domestic rooms in castles and manor houses. Private contemplation, with the aid of devotional works and a priest, was increasingly becoming the norm for the wealthy. The illustrated manuscript known as the Luttrell Psalter commissioned by Sir Geoffrey has an emphasis on penance — the theme of water washing away sins runs through the manuscript — contrition and confession. Vices are everywhere to be seen, and some of the most hideous images are of unrepentant sinners. The importance of charity is emphasized on one folio as a rich man gives money to a cripple being wheeled on a cart. The importance of dying well is emphasized on another folio where a naked, worried old man looks down into a hell-mouth, below which is shown a corpse wrapped in a winding-sheet in a coffin (**colour plate 17**). Another image on the same folio shows a man suspended from a hook with another man pouring liquid into his mouth, and this is probably a symbol of gluttony. Another symbol of his sin is the knife sticking out from his pocket. A contemporary devotional lyric reports Christ's comments on courtly fashion, which speaks of knives sticking out from their waists for vainglory, in contrast to the spears that pierced his side. These images sit alongside the words of Psalm 87 which record the fate that sinners could expect:

> For my soul is filled with evils: and my life hath drawn nigh to hell. I am counted among them that go down to the pit: I am become as a man without help, free among the dead. Like the slain sleeping in the sepulchres, whom thou rememberest no more.

Aristocratic women also often possessed, commissioned and read books in the later Middle Ages. Private devotion with the aid of books was not limited to the men of the household, as we have seen in the case of Margaret Blackburn. So-called 'Books of Hours', which were effectively prayer books to guide the laity in the prayers they should offer at certain times of the day, seem to have been regarded as appropriate wedding gifts to young aristocratic women. The early fourteenth-century Books of Hours known as the Grey-Fitz Payn Hours appears to have been commissioned for Sir Richard de Grey of Codnor Castle (Derbs) as a wedding present for his wife, Joan Fitz Payn (**colour plate 16**). Books of Hours were often passed down through the female line in elite families.

Chantry chapels

Preparation for death was not simply a deathbed matter and might involve a range of measures taken during the lifetime. One such measure, which would be of benefit to the soul, was the foundation of a chantry chapel. A chantry chapel was one of the most personal statements of religious aspirations and beliefs, and they were founded to provide a priest or priests to say prayers and sing masses for the deceased. As the ordination for one chantry in Yorkshire put it:

> It is befitting to encourage with affectionate sympathy the sincere devotion of those who desire to give of their worldly goods to the increase of divine worship, the multiplication of the number of masses which are the more profitable to Christ's faithful people unto salvation, inasmuch as in the same the King of Heaven is placated by mystic gifts, and remedies for sins are more easily obtained by asking.

A number of chantries are known of from the thirteenth century, such as that founded for Bishop Hugh at Lincoln Cathedral *c.*1238, and that established at Harby (Notts) for Queen Eleanor by Edward I after her death there in 1290. The Dean of Lincoln was granted 100 marks for the endowment of the chantry at Harby, of which the prebendary of North Clifton (Notts) was to receive ten marks a year to pay the chantry priest, to provide him with a lodging and furniture for the altar. The majority of chantry foundations were made during the fourteenth and fifteenth century. Lincoln Cathedral, for example, had just one chantry at the end of the thirteenth century but by the early sixteenth century it had 36. Their popularity varied across the region, and while in some areas the majority were founded in the years after the outbreak of the plague in 1348, in other places, such as York, more chantry chapels were founded in the first half of the fourteenth century, a fact which may be accounted for less by a declining belief in their efficacy than by the severe economic decline which York experienced during the later half of the fourteenth and the fifteenth century.

A foundation charter for a chantry from the very end of our period provides a good statement of the function of a chantry. In 1510 a chantry was founded in St Mary's church at Badsworth (Yorks) for Isabella, wife of William Vavasour. The priest was to sing a requiem mass every week and a Placebo and Dirige at the altar of St Anne in the south arch of the church. He was to offer prayers for the soul of the founder and to exhort those present to do likewise. There was also to be an annual obit for Isabella, at which time money was to be distributed to the poor of the parish. The foundation charter also put measures in place to ensure the quality of the chantry priest. He was to be learned in plainsong and grammar, was to be a regular attendee at services in the parish church, and should refrain from going to alehouses and taverns and from playing illicit games. While it might be suspected that chantry foundations were purely for the benefit of a select few, the money that was left to maintain the chantry and its priest often also benefited the wider community as the priest was expected to be well qualified and to behave well, thus setting a good example to the parish priest, and was also often expected to join in parish services.

Large bequests were commonly left in order that the chantry chapel may be provided with a priest in perpetuity. However, in practice they did not always survive for very long, or else had to be supplemented by bequests from others. As has been mentioned, in York a severe economic decline saw the numbers of perpetual chantry foundations decline dramatically from the later fourteenth century, and increasingly those who could afford to provide for chantries put their money into shorter-term projects. For example, John Northby's will of 1430 bequeathed £100 to ten priests to say masses for two years. This decline in the number of chantry foundations need not mean, however, that there was a decline in belief in the efficacy of prayers for the soul, as some have suggested. The evidence of wills continues to reveal that for those who could afford it there remained the aspiration to provide for post-mortem prayers offered by a priest even if a chantry was not founded. A mayor of York, Robert Johnson, left money in his will of 1497 for daily prayers and masses to be said by a priest for seven years, and for the priest to stand at his graveside and say the psalm *de Profundis* and to caste holy water on the grave. They do not sound like the words of someone who had lost faith in the purpose of post-mortem prayers.

Some wealthy, and presumably also worried, individuals founded more than one chantry during their lifetime. One of the best-documented examples of multiple chantry foundation concerns William Wakebridge of Crich (Derbs). He founded two chantries in the parish church, dedicated to SS Nicholas and Catherine (1350) and to St Mary (1368). A chantry in the church at Annesley (Notts) was founded by John of Annesley in the 1360s, with William Wakebridge acting as a promoter of the chantry and benefiting from it. In 1368 William augmented the income of the chantarist at Normanton (Notts), which had been founded in 1346 as a chapel-of-ease within the parish of Southwell and had also acted as a chantry to its founder, Benedict of Normanton. The cartulary of Newstead Abbey (Notts) reveals that William gave land in Nottinghamshire to the abbey in 1352 as part of what was ultimately a failed attempt to found another chantry. William was also involved with others in founding a chantry at Bakewell (1365) and two chantries at Newark (1365). William Wakebridge was eventually buried in his chapel of SS Nicholas and Catherine at Crich. The reason for his avid foundation of chantry chapels may lie in the events of 1349 when eight members of his family died of the plague. His brother Nicholas died in May, followed by his sister-in-law Elizabeth (June), his brother Robert (July), his father, his sisters Joan and Margaret, his wife, and his brother John (August). Only one sister survived that year. William remarried almost immediately but he had no children, and his foundation of the chantries was probably spurred by the deaths of so many of his family in one year and by his lack of children. This is also doubtless why he made such elaborate arrangements for the perpetuation of his chantries.

Guilds

Not everyone was, of course, in a position to found a chantry and many took an alternative option of grouping together with others to form a religious guild (**26**). Guilds have been called 'cooperative chantries'. They were funded by the subscriptions of members, through money raised from feasts, festivals and processions, and sometimes through rents

26 Guildhall in York. Trinity Hall was founded by the fraternity of Our Lord Jesus Christ and the Blessed Virgin Mary c.1357-69, and was eventually taken over by the guild of the Merchant Taylors. The fraternity hall was on the first floor and a hospital was located in the ground floor undercroft. The hospital inmates both received charity from the fraternity members, and were also participants in the masses performed there, which would all contribute to easing the passage of the souls of fraternity members through Purgatory. Caroline Hamilton

on property. They were generally intended to provide a decent funeral for their members, and to offer prayers and celebrate masses for deceased members. Many guilds also provided support for members in need, and some guilds also regulated the conduct of particular trades in the places where they were located.

Guild regulations sometimes indicate what would happen when a member died. For example, the guild of St Mary, Chesterfield (Derbs) undertook to place 13 wax candles around the body and to keep them burning until the funeral. Each member of the guild would make a donation at the funeral for the soul of the departed. Similarly, the guild of the Resurrection of our Lord at Lincoln undertook to place a hearse around the body with thirteen wax candles burning in it, to make offerings and to say as many masses for the soul of the dead as there were brethren in the guild. It would also keep candles burning around the body until the body was buried. The guild of St Michael on the Hill in Lincoln took the banner of the guild to the house of the deceased member so that people would know that a dead member of the guild was inside, and this banner would be carried with a burning torch in front of the body to the church. The guild of St Katherine in Stamford (Lincs) undertook to ring bells in memory of the dead, and the regulations specify which services were to be said at the time of the death and immediately afterwards. Some guilds, such as those of Corpus Christi and St John the Baptist in Hull (Yorks), stated that their members must, under penalty, attend the funerals of other members.

The types of commemoration and post-mortem prayers that the deceased could expect are sometimes explained in guild regulations. The guild of St Helen in Beverley (Yorks) burned wax candles for the dead every Sunday and feast day, and at the morning mass on Christmas Day. The guild of St Mary in Chesterfield stipulated that each of the brethren was to leave money in their will to pay for masses, and annual services were to be said for previous aldermen and for Hugh of the Peak (presumably a founder or important benefactor). The guild of St Mary at Baston (Lincs) remembered the dead for a whole year with masses.

Guilds sometimes arranged for someone to go on pilgrimage to Jerusalem, Rome or Compostella in Spain on behalf of members of the guild. The guilds of St Benedict and St Anne in the parish of St Peter, Lincoln undertook to make contributions towards pilgrimages embarked upon by members, and to accompany the pilgrim to the edge of the city and to greet him on his return. The guild of the Blessed Virgin Mary in Boston (Lincs) had the right to grant Indulgences for sins (see below p.86). Its members were widely spread, including some in Cambridgeshire and Northamptonshire. Because of the large numbers of merchants and travellers in the town, two daily masses were sung: one at dawn and the other at nine o'clock in the evening, to enable those leaving early or arriving late to attend a mass.

The reasons why a guild had been founded are sometimes given in guild ordinances, and these are instructive for understanding the spiritual matters that were of concern to the founders of guilds. Often guilds were founded because of some perceived inadequacy with existing parochial arrangements or with the support available for a chantry. For example, at Stamford the guild of Holy Trinity was founded in 1365 following concern about the poverty of the existing rector, who became the chaplain of the guild. At Tydd (Lincs) two men founded a guild to augment normal parish services, and they joined together with others to provide money for a chaplain. The guild of Our Lady at Baslow was founded because of the distance of the mother church of the parish at Bakewell (Derbs). Some guilds were founded to take over chantry chapels for which funding had ceased. A monk had founded a chapel at Whaplode (Lincs) to pray for his soul, and when he died a group of men from Whaplode joined together to form a guild and kept the chaplain on as their priest. The guild of St James in the church of St Peter at Burgh (Lincs) was founded by five men who had been on pilgrimage to the church of St James at Compostella. They had encountered a bad storm on their return journey, which saw them vow to found a guild if they returned safely. The guild of St Mary at Dronfield (Derbs) did not hold regular services, and members came together only for funerals, revealing much about what was important to the brethren.

Other guilds seem to have developed out of personal donations to a church. For example, the guild of St John the Baptist in the parish church at Spalding (Lincs) was founded following the painting of an image of St John in the church in 1358 before which the painter, John de Roughton, and a few friends provided a light to burn. In 1383 John Torald joined together with others to make subscriptions to establish a guild there. The guild of the Holy Trinity, also in Spalding, began with the gift from a parishioner of a fully furnished altar in 1370. The guild of the Invention of the Holy Cross at Grantham (Lincs) developed from the carving of an image of Christ, the Virgin and John the Baptist and the donation of an altar by a parishioner, Roger de Wolsthorp, who turned it into a chantry. Other parishioners later turned it into a guild.

Guilds were not, however, founded solely for spiritual reasons. Membership of some guilds, such as the Tyler's guild of Lincoln, was demanded in order to be allowed to practice a particular craft. Other guilds, such as the guilds for archers and barbers in Lincoln, limited office holding in the guild to members who were involved in a particular trade. The guild for cordwainers in Lincoln demanded that cordwainers in the town who were not guild brothers had to pay 6d for candles. The Shepherd's guild at Holbeach (Lincs) was founded because local shepherds and herdsmen decided that the animals they looked after would be better cared for if they undertook some act of devotion. Some guilds provided practical help for members if they became sick, or if some personal misfortune had befallen them, such as if their house was burned or robbed. The members of the guild of St Mary at Chesterfield paid 2d each to brethren who had fallen into poverty through no fault of their own, and they helped those who were old, had lost a limb or contracted leprosy. The guild of All Saints at Crowland (Lincs) provided members who were sick or otherwise in need with 40d annually and a tunic and hood of russet. Brethren of the guild of St Margaret in Lincoln charged with an offence, such as theft or homicide, could expect fellow guild members to stand by them, and several other guilds offered help in the case of false imprisonment. Many guilds provided support for the poor, in the form of doles of food and accommodation, or even, in the case of guilds at Grainthorpe and Gedney (Lincs), through the invitation of 13 poor to the guild feast. The intention of this charity may have been similar to the charitable works that many individuals left money for in their wills, that is it was believed to be of benefit to the souls of guild brethren. The guild of Our Lady of the Assumption in the church of St Mary at Bridge in Stamford possessed a number of properties, which had been bequeathed to it in order both to maintain a daily mass and to repair the bridge, which may have served both a practical role and have counted as an act of Christian 'good works'.

The membership of some guilds reveals something of their social role in the community. For example, the guild of Holy Trinity, Grimsby (Lincs) was comprised of the urban elite. The very limited membership of twelve of the guild of the Blessed Virgin at Wigtoft (Lincs) also suggests that the guild members were limited to the very wealthy in that community. The York Corpus Christi guild, by contrast, had almost 17,000 members in the later fifteenth century including royalty, nobility, clergy, members of the urban governing class, labourers and the poor. The membership of such guilds suggests that the personal involvement of many members in the guild must have been minimal. Most guilds included female members, who commonly numbered around half of the lay membership, and on the whole there is little indication that women received lesser benefits from guild membership. One notable exception comes from the guild of St Mary at Dronfield, where twelve candles were to be placed around the body of male members but only six were to be placed around females. The officials of guilds seem to have been overwhelmingly men.

The social aspects of guilds have received much recent attention. Many guilds had elaborate annual festivals or processions, which served both to raise money for the guild and to provide a social outlet for members. The guild of St John the Baptist in Baston required the guild sisters to dance on the saint's day as they made their way in a procession to the church, and the guild of St Martin in Stamford held an annual bull baiting, with the bull later being sold off to raise money for the guild. The guild of St Helen at Beverley chose a beautiful boy to be Helen for the day of the annual feast. At Grantham the procession of the guild of Corpus Christi involved two priests carrying the body of the Lord accompanied by two boys carrying guild candles, followed by the members of the guild also carrying candles. There was then a feast and each married couple and single person in the guild brought a pauper to the feast who was fed there, and food was also given to the friars who accompanied the procession. The Corpus Christi guild at York established a processional order for its members, with a priest leading the way followed by the various craftspeople of the city, with the guild officers following behind. Many of these festivals were held on the feast day of the saint to whom the guild was dedicated. It is generally impossible to say why particular saints were chosen, but it may not be coincidence that they tended to be saints who had feast days during the summer. The quasi-religious form of the guild feasts occasioned much complaint from the clergy. It was typical for members of the guild to process to the feast in their common guild livery, which often involved hoods or complete gowns, and the halls where the feasts were held appear to have taken on a chapel-like appearance with candles and ecclesiastical imagery, while prayers were said and hymns were sung.

Indulgences

In addition to aiding the soul through Purgatory with post-mortem prayers and masses, there was also assistance for the soul that could be acquired during the lifetime. The indulgence was offered by the pope or his agents, and relaxed penance and the penalties and guilt of sin, and could bring remission from Purgatory. It was not intended to be a means by which medieval people traded-off their sins; they were also expected to continue to be contrite. Nonetheless, there may have been a perception that sins could be cancelled out by indulgences granted for contributions, both financial and spiritual, to the Church. Indulgences were granted for a variety of reasons, such as assistance in the building of churches (as was the case at Beverley Minster, for example) or bridges, support for almshouses, prisons and the poor, for reading certain books or attending certain services, pilgrimage to a shrine, and participation in crusades. Indulgences offered by bishops were initially limited to forty days per undertaking, although papal indulgences were for longer periods. From the later fourteenth century indulgences became ever more numerous and lengthy. Little was required for indulgences associated with the Image of Pity. The recitation of five Paternosters, five Aves and a Creed whilst contemplating the Image of Pity meant that the amount of time to be spent in Purgatory was reduced by between 26,000 and 33,000 years.

Although it is tempting to suggest that the ready availability of indulgences must have reduced their meaningfulness, in fact there seems to have been widespread belief in their value and efficacy. A number of guilds acquired the right to grant indulgences and used this as a means to attract new members. The guild of the Blessed Virgin Mary in Boston had the right to offer some of the most extensive indulgences in the country, and not surprisingly it had a large membership, which extended far beyond the bounds of the town. Many feasts celebrated by the guild had indulgences attached to them, and the guild calendar became extremely crowded. This led in 1480 to papal intervention to sort out a dispute which arose over disruption to the Feast of the Visitation of the Blessed Virgin Mary caused by the crowding of so many other feasts at the same time, meaning that some members of the guild could not attend the necessary observances in order to qualify for the indulgence. It was eventually decided that they would qualify if they observed the offices of the feast privately on the days when there were other feasts.

The cost of death

In the later Middle Ages death necessitated a series of payments: a heriot to a lord, payment to the priest for a funeral, additional payments to secure burial in more desirable locations in the church or churchyard, and mortuary payments. Records concerning these payments and reactions to them provide some useful insights into the attitudes of a wider cross-section of society than many of our other written sources permit. At Hornsea (Yorks) funerals were normally charged at 6d, with another 6d payable for commemoration on the octave, and at Torksey (Lincs) the levels of funeral payments were fixed by borough custom. However, payments at Scarborough (Yorks) for funerals varied, and burials usually also necessitated payments for wax for candles. Conflicts between parishioners and incumbents over the funerary demands made of them were not unknown, not least because parishioners were often uncertain as to what the payment might be. In the later thirteenth century there was a wave of anti-clericalism in some parts of Lincolnshire, prompted, in part, by resentment over the scale of fees for church services such as marriages and funerals. Some of the resentment was expressed through physical attacks on members of the clergy. The parochial chaplain and the clerk of Normanby le Wold were attacked in 1296, and Hugh the vicar of All Saints, Stamford was attacked in the market place in 1298. At Langtoft in 1296 there was an attempt to reduce the amount of offerings that had to be made to the church for, amongst other services, funerals, and there were similar efforts made in 1298 at St James's, Grimsby, at Grantham and at Moulton where parishioners attempted to remove funeral candles set around the bier when a corpse was carried to the cemetery in order to prevent the clergy from acquiring them as perquisites.

Another financial liability that had to be met at death was the mortuary payment, which was made to the church and was technically for any tithes that had been forgotten. However, it carried with it implications of heriot, which was a payment due to a lord on the death of his tenant, and often caused resentment, as could the fact that mortuaries varied from place to place. Sometimes it was a payment left specifically to the incumbent rather than the church itself. In rural areas it was often a beast, whereas in towns it was commonly the best robe or gown that was handed over. In the 1350s the abbey of St Mary's at York was claiming mortuaries of anvils, small boats, lead brewing vessels and other goods from the church of St Mary in Doncaster (Yorks) which the abbey held. In some places children and wives were exempt from paying mortuaries, but some of the mortuaries demanded would have placed a severe burden on families. It was not unknown for families to buy back their mortuaries, especially if they had included animals. For wealthier members of society, however, the mortuary was not simply a financial burden; it was also an opportunity to display their arms and armour. The will of Sir Brian Stapleton requested a gathering of his tenants and servants dressed in gowns of blue cloth where a man dressed in his arms would walk with his funeral cortège to Healaugh Priory (Yorks) (see also below, p.91). Thus, the mortuary payment was brought to the church in the most dramatic way possible. As Malcolm Vale (1976, 12) has commented, this display was a sign that while 'the knight may die . . . his arms live on'.

Black Death

The outbreak of plague in England in the winter of 1348-9, and subsequent outbreaks in the later half of the fourteenth and the fifteenth century, transformed the ability, and need, to prepare appropriately for death. It is difficult to estimate how many people died, but the population of England may have been one third to one half lower than its pre-plague levels by the end of the fourteenth century. The impact of the plague was very uneven, and some settlements were badly hit while others were barely affected.

A major factor in contemporary responses to the plague was the high mortality rate among the clergy, which seems to have been as high as 30 or 40% in some dioceses. For example, in the diocese of York 39% of parish incumbents died during the winter of 1348-9. The high clerical mortality affected wider society in two main ways. It often left them without pastoral care, and it demonstrated that not even the clergy were safe from the ravages of the plague, which must have had an impact on the faith of parishioners. In November 1349 Archbishop William Zouche of York sought papal permission to be allowed to ordain priests on days other than those laid down by canon law for ordinations, because of the high mortality among clergy. In 1344-6, 132 priests had been ordained annually, whereas in 1349-51 the high mortality among priests led to 402 annual ordinations. Dispensations were also acquired to ordain men who normally would not qualify for ordination, such as illegitimate men. In September 1349 Archbishop Zouche made an exception in admitting a canon regular from the monastery of St Oswald at Nostell to the vicarage of Tickhill (Yorks), even though the post was usually held by a secular priest, on account of the 'lack of secular priests, who have been carried from our midst by the plague of mortality which hangs over us'.

There were many contemporary complaints about the reluctance of the clergy to administer to their parishioners. For example, one Adam de Brantingham who was a chaplain in the parish of Hotham (Yorks) refused to take on the job of parish chaplain in 1362 even though there was a shortage of chaplains on account of the plague, and this decision was said to be 'the manifest peril of the parishioners' souls'. Yet, evidently, whatever the impact of the Black Death was on the mentalities of medieval people, it did not cause such a crisis of faith that individuals no longer wanted to enter into the priesthood. It is likely that a combination of career opportunities, concern about personal salvation and desire to provide spiritual service in the community continued to encourage men to enter the priesthood. Nonetheless, it tended to be the richer, especially urban, benefices that attracted new incumbents while many poor rural benefices remained empty. Contemporaries clearly often felt that the motive was material gain. In William Langland's *Piers Plowman* it is suggested that priests were eager to say masses because it was lucrative:

> Parsons and parish priests complained to the bishop
> That their parishes are poor since the pestilence-time,
> Asked for licence and leave to live in London,
> And sing masses there for simony [i.e. for money], for silver is sweet

This may not be a representative view, but it is notable that restrictions were placed on clerical wages in the aftermath of the outbreak of plague, which may suggest that the clergy were demanding higher wages, or at least that it was suspected that they might. We have to be careful, however, not to overemphasize archiepiscopal and other contemporary complaints about the supposed abuses of priests, as later medieval commentators not uncommonly become over-excitable where any hint of ecclesiastical misdemeanours was concerned.

The plague also appears to have hit monastic communities especially hard. An entry in the chronicle of Meaux Abbey (Yorks) captures the impact of the first outbreak of plague:

> This pestilence so prevailed in our monastery, as in other places, that in the month of August [1349] the abbot himself, twenty-two monks and six lay brethren died; of these, the abbot and five monks were lying unburied on one day, and then the others died, so that when the plague abated, out of fifty monks and lay brethren, only ten monks and no lay brethren were left. Thereafter, the rents and possessions of the monastery began to diminish, especially as the greater part of our tenants in various places died, and the abbot, prior, bursar and other seniors, when they died, left those surviving unacquainted with the property, possessions and common goods of the house

Nonetheless, monastic communities continued to recruit monks over the coming decades, and they remained major social and religious institutions, even if the monastic economy was hard hit through the loss of tenants. The episcopacy also seems to have managed to retain its standards after the outbreak of plague. So how far was the spirituality of the masses affected? And what impact did the plague have on the preparations that individuals made for their death? While it is not in doubt that the Black Death had a major impact on English society it is less clear that it prompted new developments in piety and devotion, or in preparation for death. Certainly a heightened sense of the dangers of a sudden and unexpected death may have emerged, but many developments that have in the past been ascribed to the plague (such as the foundation of chantry chapels and guilds, and the commissioning of particular types of funerary monuments) can, in fact, be shown to have had earlier origins (below, pp.164-5,181-4).

There was a contemporary perception among some of the clergy that the plague could be accounted for by the sins of the laity. In the summer of 1348, just before the plague arrived but at a time when many people in England had heard of its progress across Europe, Archbishop William Zouche of York announced to the clergy that they had to try to ward off the 'mortality, pestilence, and infection of the air now threatening England, whereof the sins of men are the cause'. He proposed that processions should be held every Wednesday and Friday in order to try to allay the plague. In 1361 Archbishop John Thoresby requested further processions, observing that 'the whirlwinds of war and . . . pestilences and other misfortunes' that had descended on England were the result of sin, adding that the situation could only be improved through the prayers and penance of the faithful. The circumstances of the later fourteenth century, with the horror of the plague exacerbated by the very changed social and economic situation that followed from the dramatic decline in the population, combined with a shortage of clergy in many places may have led some to question their faith and the efficacy of the Church. Complaints about superstitious practices in the later fourteenth century may indicate an increasing reliance on alternative practices. For example, in the later fourteenth century the blessing of bacon and eggs at the altar of the church of Nettleham (Lincs) which were then distributed as a holy offering among parishioners, and the prayers offered to a wayside cross at Rippingale (Lincs):

> A serious complaint has reached us that many of our subjects have made for themselves a pretended statue vulgarly known as Jurdon Cros, in the fields of Rippingale, and have begun to adore it, and to report that many miracles are done there. They are preaching and ringing bells and holding processions, for the deception of the people

However, as Colin Platt (1981, 70-1) has observed, it may not be that the laity were rejecting the Church so much as supplementing it, as it is difficult to know whether the laity would necessarily have seen a contradiction between such practices and 'the potent "magic" of the Eucharist'. Indeed, 'superstitious' practices were not invented in the wake of the plague, although they may have been fuelled by it.

We also have to remember that there were many other factors than the Black Death that affected contemporary perceptions of the Church. It is notable that in Lincolnshire, for example, the strongest evidence we have for anti-clericalism comes from the later thirteenth century rather than after the Black Death. The fourteenth century also witnessed other difficulties within the Church that may have affected the attitudes of both potential recruits to the priesthood and the wider laity. The fall of Acre in 1291 marked the end of the crusader states in the East and saw crusading turned into a defensive action, against Muslim expansion to the West, and a means of taming heretical groups within Europe. The wars between France and England in the fourteenth and early fifteenth centuries placed great financial burdens on the Church as a result of royal demands for taxation. The wars were also arguably a major factor in the increasing display of military and heraldic insignia in the fabric, fittings and monuments of churches. The removal of the papacy to Avignon (France) in 1309, following disorder in Rome, while a sensible strategy for the papacy, gave the impression that the Pope was the agent of the French king which was especially unfortunate in the light of the disputes between England and France and the later outbreak of open hostility. The so-called Great Schism of 1378 which saw two rival popes, one in Rome the other in France, did much to discredit the papacy and had major political and spiritual ramifications, since it caused nations to take sides in favour of one or the other pope, and even led to two English expeditions (to Flanders in 1383 and to Castile in 1386) being blessed as crusades by the pope in Rome, Urban VI, since they were against the allies of the French. It may not be coincidence that the first major outbreaks of heresy in England occurred at the time of the Great Schism. The extent to which the events of the fourteenth century led to a sense of pessimism within the Church is difficult to judge, but it does appear to have been a very different atmosphere from that pervading theological writing in the twelfth and early thirteenth centuries, at a time of reform, monastic expansion and the crusades.

It is difficult to say that the Black Death had a direct impact on ecclesiastical iconography, in particular on the way in which Death and the dead were portrayed. Images that reflected the need to be prepared for an untimely death appear to have become a little more common in ecclesiastical art after 1348, with an increase in intercessory images showing ways in which the soul could be saved, but this can hardly be described as an innovation in the wake of the Black Death. Equally images of what fate may await souls, whether in Heaven or in Hell, were not new either, as we have seen. Images of the Three Living and the Three Dead — a popular medieval legend in which three skeletal figures meet three living men and warn them of their fate (above, p.9) — may have increased in number following the outbreak of plague. Examples survive in wall paintings at Haddon Hall (Derbs), Wensley (Yorks) and Pickworth (Lincs). The invocation of the legend in inscriptions on funerary monuments also appears to have become more common from the later fourteenth century.

The figure of Death is less commonly portrayed in later medieval ecclesiastical art than are the implications of death, such as the Day of Judgement, and depictions of Heaven and Hell. Depictions of the Dance of Death became very popular in England during the fifteenth century, influenced by works produced on the continent which themselves had been influenced by popular pageants. No complete Dance of Death survives in England. One of the finest surviving fragments comes from the Markham chantry in St Mary Magdalene, Newark (Notts), which was made just at the end of our period in the early sixteenth century (**colour plate 14**). Only two panels survive. One depicts a young man taking money from his purse; the other depicts a grinning skeleton, pointing to the grave with one hand and in the other holding a carnation, a symbol of the shortness of life. It is probable that the other twenty-two panels in the chantry were also once filled with images of the Dance.

Funerals

Later medieval funerals were protracted affairs, and often very elaborate. Wills and accounts of chantry chapels and guilds sometimes provide insights into the nature of funerals, as they indicate what equipment was required for a funeral, including candles, a hearse and a cloth to cover it, not to mention the numerous people who may have been involved in the funeral cortège. Funeral pomp was common. One of the most elaborate funerals witnessed in the region was that of Bishop Hugh of Lincoln. The kings of England and Scotland and various bishops, abbots and nobles gathered at Lincoln, and assisted in the carrying of Hugh's coffin up the hill to the cathedral. It seems to have been common for the funerals of the wealthy to have been accompanied by displays of their arms and armour, which were then offered as mortuary gifts to the church where the burial took place. For example, Sir Walter Griffith (1481) and Henry Hertlington esquire (1466) both gave their best horses and armour to the churches at Burton Agnes and Burnsall (Yorks) respectively. In 1379 Sir Robert Swillington gave his coat-armour, helm, shield and sword to the church of Swillington (Yorks), and in 1394 Sir Brian Stapleton, a Knight of the Garter, gave instructions in his will that at his funeral at Healaugh Priory there should be 'a man armed with my arms, with my helm on his head, and that he shall be mounted and a man of good looks of whatever condition he is'.

In contrast, some wills specifically ask for there to be no such funerary ostentation. For example, in 1397 Sir Ralph Hastings asked for his body to be brought to Selby Abbey (Yorks) in a simple cart 'as soon as I end my last days in this miserable world'. Sir Thomas Boynton asked in 1402 that no expense should be made on the day of his burial 'on account of the repayment of my debts'. Lack of funds is unlikely to have been the overriding consideration for most of the will-making classes, and often it appears to have been a statement of their piety that determined the relative austerity of the funerals that they requested. Sir John Depeden of Healaugh (Yorks) asked for eight paupers dressed in black to attend his cortège and stipulated that there should not be a lavish gathering of his friends and neighbours, but rather that gifts should be given to the poor, servants and the sick.

Conclusion

Preparation for death could be a lengthy business, and it necessitated provisions both for the soul and for the worldly affairs of a person. To explore this issue we must rely to a large extent on documentary evidence. Nonetheless, archaeological evidence, including both excavated cemeteries and surviving monuments, wall paintings, window glass and manuscript illuminations enhance our understanding of the subject enormously. Although medieval churches contained numerous images of death, Hell and the implications of living a bad life, we should not suppose that churches were grim environments. Many of the images we have discussed offered positive messages, and promised rewards, in the form of salvation, in the next life for one's endeavours in this earthly life.

4 Graves

This chapter explores the form that burial actually took between c.650 and 1500. A striking feature of the various excavated burial grounds in the region from the seventh to fifteenth century is the variety of burial practices that are found, both between and within cemeteries. In addition to the few artefacts that are occasionally found in graves, the other main differences between burials concern the presence or absence of coffins, the types of coffins used, the orientation of the grave, and the ways in which the grave was prepared to receive the body. As we shall see, while there are many features common to graves of this period across the region, there is also much variation. This variation seems to have been as a result of a combination of factors, including social status or profession and wealth.

Grave goods in Anglo-Saxon burials

It has often been assumed that the Anglo-Saxon Church must have dictated how, as well as where, individuals could be buried. Yet, in fact, there is little evidence concerning the attitude of the Church to either burial rites or burial location. Certainly, the Church outlawed cremation, although this issue is not referred to in ecclesiastical sources nearly as often as is sometimes supposed. It is not clear, however, that burial with grave goods was regarded as un-Christian. Indeed, on the continent grave goods continued to be placed in burials long after communities became Christianized. We should not overlook the fact that there is no documentary evidence to suggest that the Church attempted to prevent the burial of grave goods, except for sacred items such as the Host. Nonetheless, some scholarly discussions appear to be underpinned by the notion that a gradual decline in grave goods represents a gradual 'Christianizing' influence on society. Consider, for example, the comment of Audrey Meaney and Sonia Hawkes (1970, 53) on the gradual decline of grave goods through the seventh century, that at first the Church was prepared to 'wink at' burial with grave goods, but that by the eighth century 'even dress-fasteners were now frowned on'. This sounds a little implausible, although, to be fair to these authors, the view is typical of interpretations of that era. Either grave goods are or are not acceptable to the Church and it is hard to see how a gradual reduction could have satisfied churchmen if they opposed them, or how a few grave goods could have rendered a person less pagan than someone buried with more grave goods.

It may be that other factors than Christianity influenced the decline in the use of grave goods that can be witnessed from the seventh century. The increasing availability of exchange networks for metal implements, especially weapons, and the desire to retain such items in circulation may account to some extent for the disappearance of weapons from burials during the seventh century. It may also be that changes in social structure led to new burial practices. It has, for example, recently been suggested that the development of more stable social structures and the emergence of hereditary elite groups by the seventh century lessened the need for elaborate funerary displays. At an earlier date such displays had been a product of social competition, and of the need for families competing for prominence in a community to display their status, but as the social hierarchy became more established the need to rely on what are very transient displays of power and status may have diminished. Indeed, it may be no coincidence that the seventh century saw increasing investment by the elite in, for example, the Church, in staking permanent claims to land, and in their estate centers. It was also a time when there is archaeological evidence for increasing differentiation of building types and for the delineation of property boundaries within settlements, suggesting that social differentiation was becoming increasingly inscribed in the landscape and in above-ground monuments.

However, any interpretation of the decline in the use of grave goods has to take account of two important factors. First, there continued to be some individuals who were unquestionably Christian who were interred with grave goods, notably abbots, bishops and priests who were often buried with their symbols of office, such as chalices and patens. The most famous early example of the burial of a certain Christian with artefacts concerns St Cuthbert who died in the later seventh century. When it was opened in 1827 his grave contained an ivory comb, a pectoral cross of gold set with garnets, a wooden travelling altar enclosed in silver plates, and fragments of rich textiles, which, with the exception of the textiles, appear to have been original to the later seventh-century grave. When the coffin had been opened in 1104 a gospel book, a chalice, paten and scissors were discovered and removed. Ecclesiastics appear to have maintained a tradition of clothed burial, which may have been connected with a belief in the need to be suitably robed when they were in Heaven. Indeed, St Cuthbert is said to have worn his shoes when buried 'in readiness to meet Christ'. Second, we must remember that archaeological preservation may militate against our ability to identify many aspects of funerary provision. In particular, evidence for clothing or for shrouds does not generally survive other than in the form of adornments (such as pins, clasps, fasteners and so on). What may, then, appear to be a burial on which little attention had been lavished, may have been the burial of someone specially dressed for the burial, sometimes in expensive garments to judge from contemporary continental sources (above, p.65). Indeed, there may be more continuity in burial rites from the earlier Anglo-Saxon centuries than we have previously allowed for, if we recognize that one of the most important facets of burial rite was the dressing of the body for burial. What we are able to study is altered by the way in which the body was dressed for burial, and the circumstances of archaeological survival.

The most elaborate assemblages of grave goods found in burials in the seventh century are typically found in barrows (see above, pp.00-00). For example, the finds from the barrow at Benty Grange (Derbs) include a hanging-bowl, a chain (perhaps from a cauldron), a six-pronged implement, a helmet and silver fittings from a cup, and those from the barrow at Cow Low (Derbs) include two garnet-set gold pins linked by a chain, a bronze-bound wooden box containing a palm cup and a bone comb, and a necklace of eight silver bullae, two gold beads and a drop-shaped glass cabochon pendant (**colour plate 4**). The barrows at Wigber Low (Derbs) have been excavated on several occasions and shown to include a series of burials accompanied by such items as knives, swords, buckles, spearheads, a gold disc pendant, and a beaver tooth pendant mounted in gold (**colour plate 8**). At Caenby (Lincs) the barrow contained an individual in a sitting position. The presence of fragments of wood to which decorated metal was attached may indicate either that there was a timber-lined chamber in the barrow, or else that the barrow contained a bed or an elaborate seat. Decorated silver foil may have come from drinking vessels. At Painsthorpe Wold (Yorks) a burial in a barrow was accompanied by a bronze annular brooch, a knife, two amethyst and nine glass beads, the remains of a bag and possible chatelaine and a work box. An unusual burial of seventh-century date has been excavated at Tattershall Thorpe (Lincs), where a single, seemingly isolated, burial was found on the banks of the river Bain accompanied by metalworking equipment. The artefacts included iron snips, an anvil, three iron hammerheads, a needle file, a wooden box, a lead backing sheet, a copper-alloy scabbard mount, an iron bell, and a blue glass bag-beaker. Later medieval ploughing will have removed any barrow that may have been raised over the burial. It has been suggested that this may have been the burial of an Anglo-Saxon smith.

27 *Silver cross set in the nasal piece of a helmet from Benty Grange (Derbs). The helmet was found during the excavation of a mound at Benty Grange by Thomas Bateman in 1848. The helmet has a boar on the crest.* Sheffield City Museum

As has already been said, these elaborate burials need not be un-Christian. Attention has been drawn elsewhere to the presence of crosses and cross-shaped decorations among the grave goods as possible indicators of the religious affiliations of the deceased. The use of crosses as decorative motifs on artefacts found in graves is inconclusive, and cannot be taken as evidence for Christian beliefs or even contact with Christianity. However, the presence of actual crosses, such as the cross-pendant from Winster Moor (Derbs) or the cross on the nasal of the helmet from Benty Grange (Derbs) (**27**) may reveal contact with Christian iconography, given the similarities with obviously Christian crosses on sculpture and in manuscripts. However, it is not entirely clear what the deceased or those who buried them invested in these symbols.

Burial in or near barrows was relatively common in some parts of the region in the seventh century, although not all burials were particularly lavish. For example, burials of the seventh or eighth century have been excavated at Garton Slack (Yorks) where there are over 30 barrows containing numerous prehistoric and Anglo-Saxon burials. At the Green Lane Crossing site there are two distinct groups of burials on either side of a barrow. There are over 30 burials to the west of the barrow containing a variety of artefacts, mostly iron knives, but also beads, necklaces, rings, ear-rings, and buckles. These burials are probably of seventh-century date. The burials to the east of the barrow are on a slightly different alignment, and contained no artefacts, although one of the burials was in a coffin that had hinges and clasps. Three miles to the north, at a site known as Garton Slack I, was another cemetery similar to the eastern half of the Green Lane cemetery, with a possible coffined-burial, and a few graves containing grave goods, including a purse with coins of the early eighth century, an iron knife and a bone comb. On present evidence it is difficult to place them any later than the early eighth century, but it is not impossible that burial both here and in similar locations continued much later. The cemetery at Thwing (Yorks) was also located near to a prehistoric landscape feature, in this case a series of Bronze Age enclosures, and it contained west-east aligned burials one of which contained an amber and glass bead and a knife and has been radiocarbon dated to AD 789-992. Finds, including a knife and keys, may have come from other graves at Thwing. A range of radiocarbon dates have been acquired and they suggest that the cemetery was in use into the later Anglo-Saxon period, as does associated settlement evidence of the eighth to tenth century. The radiocarbon dates so far published are AD 410-670, 434-643, 642-758, 650-860, 673-852, 724-961, 781-991 and 789-992 (cal).

By the seventh century the types and range of grave goods included in burials had changed from those found in the fifth and sixth centuries. At an earlier date, although there were many burials with no grave goods and some in which similar artefacts accompanied males and females, there was in many graves a sharp dichotomy between male burials, which typically included weapons, and female burials, which included jewellery assemblages. The occurrences of these typically 'masculine' and 'feminine' burial 'kits' were age-sensitive, and they were rarely found in the graves of the very young or the very old. By the seventh century, however, there was an increasing standardization of the 'feminine' burial kit, with less variation according to the age of the individual or the overall wealth of the grave. At the same time the masculine burial kit became limited to the very high status burials. There was also an increasing separation of the more wealthy and elaborate burials, which were often located in or near prehistoric landscape features, from the less elaborate burials in the row-grave cemeteries. The smaller number of elaborate burials may have been used within an increasingly stratified society to create and maintain a social elite which was employing highly visible and permanent above-ground markers — both barrows and churches — which were used to convey messages to more widely-flung audiences, drawing on a national, and in some ways, international repertoire of symbols of authority. These monuments, alongside the much smaller examples of weapon burials, may have been less markers of gender than markers of a regionally important social elite, signalling their exclusivity through where they were buried as much as how. Some of this signalling of elite status was achieved through what had hitherto been more widely used symbols of masculinity. It may even be that when women and children were buried near to the more elaborate male burials their status and significance was both determined by and signalled through their association with these symbols of elite masculinity.

By the early eighth century few burials contained any artefacts other than coffin fittings, but grave goods did not completely disappear from burials. Most of the items found in graves of the mid- to later Anglo-Saxon period are either jewellery or items that can be interpreted as the accoutrements of clothing, such as beads, small knives and dress-fasteners. For example, an adolescent burial from the late Anglo-Saxon cemetery beneath York Minster contained gold thread from a costume, and earrings and finger rings were found in other graves. One of the burials in the Ailcy Hill cemetery at Ripon (Yorks) contained a knife and a buckle, which may both have been present in the grave simply as the result of the burial of clothed bodies. The associated skeleton produced a radiocarbon date of AD 560-660. Items such as coins and combs were not, however, items of dress, and may have been deliberately placed in the grave. Our understanding of the significance of the presence of such small objects as coins and rings in graves is sometimes (especially in older and cursory excavation reports) hampered by the difficulty of determining whether they originally belonged to the grave or whether they are residual from earlier contexts or have been disturbed from later contexts. Nonetheless, the range of items found in graves of eighth- to eleventh-century date is greater than is often supposed, and is found in a wide range of cemeteries. A brief survey of such grave goods is instructive.

Two of the graves excavated beneath York Minster contained a coin, one of 841/2-848/9 and the other of 841-8, and at Repton (Derbs) in one burial there was a coin in the hand of the skeleton, which was of *c*.725 date. Four burials from the Ladykirk at Ripon contained decorated bone combs. At St Mary Bishophill Junior, York, an iron knife and schist whetstone accompanied one late Anglo-Saxon burial, and there was also a copper alloy buckle-plate at the waist and a coin in the hand of *c*.905-15 date. The skeleton in another burial was wearing a silver arm-ring. Excavations at St Mary Bishophill Senior discovered a tenth-century strap-end and interlaced silver wire, probably from a costume, which may have come from burials. Excavations of the church and cemetery built on the former Roman signal station at Scarborough revealed a coin of Cnut (1016-35) in one grave and a ninth-century jet cross on the breast of a skeleton. A ninth- or tenth-century bronze cross, possibly from a book cover, a ninth-century strap-end and a spear-head were also found during the excavations, and may have been associated with graves. An undated burial at Pontefract (Yorks) contained a pair of bronze tweezers. This burial belongs to the phase of burial pre-dating the Anglo-Saxon church of uncertain date, and another burial from this area has produced a radiocarbon date of AD 690 ±90 (*see* **11**). A burial at Barton-upon-Humber (Lincs), which is probably of tenth- or eleventh-century date, was accompanied by a pair of hazel rods or 'wands', which may have been a symbol of office, or have served to symbolize the Resurrection. At a later date, according to a burial sermon by the fifteenth-century priest John Mirk, a metewand, or meteyard, was regarded as a measuring stick that might be laid in the grave as part of the preparation for the Day of Judgement. In an inhumation burial at Swaby (Lincs) was a bone comb of possible Anglo-Saxon date. A buckle-plate was found in a triple grave from the church of St Andrew, York, and burials at St Helen-on-the-Walls have produced a pair of bronze tweezers, a belt mount and finger rings. A later Anglo-Saxon burial from Repton (in the phase post-dating the mass burial and mound) contained gold thread from a costume. In addition, although the evidence is hardly conclusive, it is striking that coins, knives and jewellery of mid- to late Anglo-Saxon date have been found in churchyards 'with considerable frequency', as Richard Morris (1983, 60-1) has observed. It appears to be the case, then, that burials of the eighth to eleventh centuries occasionally contain artefacts. This phenomenon has been more commonly observed in northern England, although future work may alter the emerging picture. This is relevant to our attempts to identify the Scandinavian influence on burial practices, because it has been traditional to argue that the deposition of grave goods had ceased by the early eighth century and resumed again following the Scandinavian settlements of the later ninth century. Given that artefacts do, however, occasionally occur in graves after the early eighth century, and the fact that many of the burials traditionally identified as 'Viking' contain little more than coins, a knife or jewellery, the supposed distinction between Scandinavian and indigenous burial practices is perhaps more blurred than has generally been recognized.

A trait of mid- to late Anglo-Saxon burials that may sometimes be missed during excavations concerns the placing of stones in the grave. At Kellington (Yorks) quartz pebbles were placed in later Anglo-Saxon graves, and at Whitby (Yorks) several of the graves of probable eighth- or ninth-century date have produced white quartz pebbles of varying sizes, a practice that has been observed in several other Anglo-Saxon cemeteries (Daniell 1997, 165). In recent excavations at Fillingham (Lincs) in one grave oval-shaped stones had been placed in the eye-socket of the individual, and stones had been placed in the mouth of two skeletons (**colour plate 7**). Given the absence of a consistent pattern it is difficult to ascribe meaning to the various items occasionally found in graves. Clothed burials and individual or local beliefs that are now beyond our ability to reconstruct, doubtless explain most examples. The public and communal funerary rituals were now being played out in the above-ground settings of funerary monuments.

Anglo-Saxon graves and grave furniture

The variety of types of graves and associated furniture (including wooden and stone coffins, and various forms of grave lining) is exposed most clearly by the excavations of the cemetery beneath York Minster. The cemetery dates to the ninth to eleventh century, and was built over following the construction of the later eleventh-century Norman cathedral. Most of the burials were laid out parallel with the Roman basilica within which they were contained (**28**). Both coffined and uncoffined burial occurred in this cemetery; there were also a few burials that contained charcoal and one burial that appeared to have made use of parts of a boat. In addition to the presence of purpose-made coffins, there were also four coffins that have been interpreted as reused domestic chests, and they had comparatively elaborate fittings in the form of locks and hinges. These four burials, which were for an adolescent, a young adult male, a middle-aged female and an elderly male, were located close together and it is possible that the similarity and proximity of their burials may indicate that the individuals concerned were in some way connected with each other in life. Two other burials were in wooden constructions that differed from conventional coffin burials and from the reused chests. In one, a child was placed in the grave on a single plank, which was not part of a coffin since there was no trace of any other

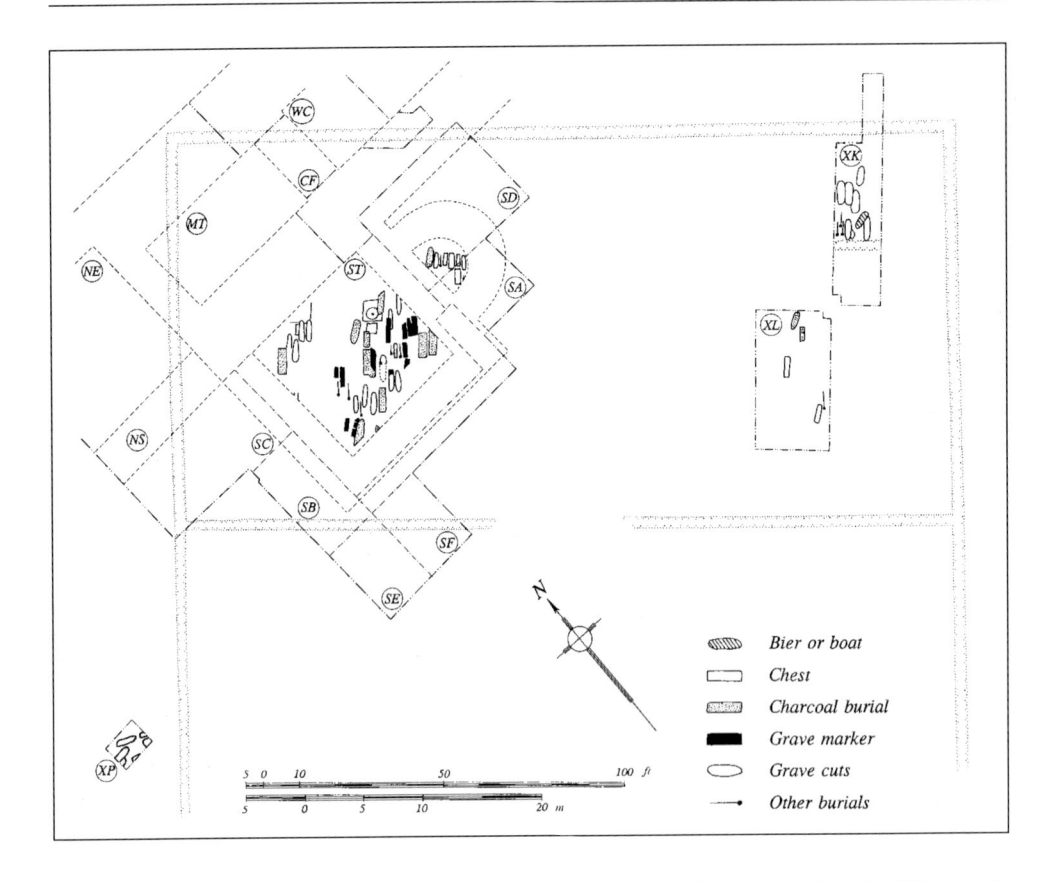

28 Excavations of the pre-Norman cemetery at York Minster. Royal Commission for Historical Monuments

wood in the grave. In the other, an adult was laid centrally between two rows of clenched nails, which has led to the suggestion that it was a clinker-built assembly, a construction technique in which boards were lapped and riveted together, and which is often associated with boats (**29**). The excavation of this grave revealed that whatever had been the original size of the clinker-built construction, it had been trimmed to a size no larger than that of a coffin. This burial has two other features of note. The skull of the deceased was surrounded by stones, and the grave was oriented east-west with the head to the east, unlike the other burials surrounding it which were oriented parallel to the basilica, south-west to north-east.

Seven burials excavated at York Minster are notable for the way in which the grave was prepared. Stones were placed in these graves to form a makeshift cist. Broken wall-facings were used to line the grave of an adult female. The use of the stones may have been a mark of status, but they may also have served some functional purpose, to support the grave, as the burial reused precisely the grave-cut of an earlier burial. Other burials had stones placed around the skull, which seems to have been a practice not untypical of later Anglo-Saxon burials.

29 Burial in parts of a boat from York Minster. This is a reconstruction of what the burial may initially have looked like, based on the location of the skeleton and nails found in the grave. After B. Kjølbye-Biddle in Philips 1995, Alex Norman

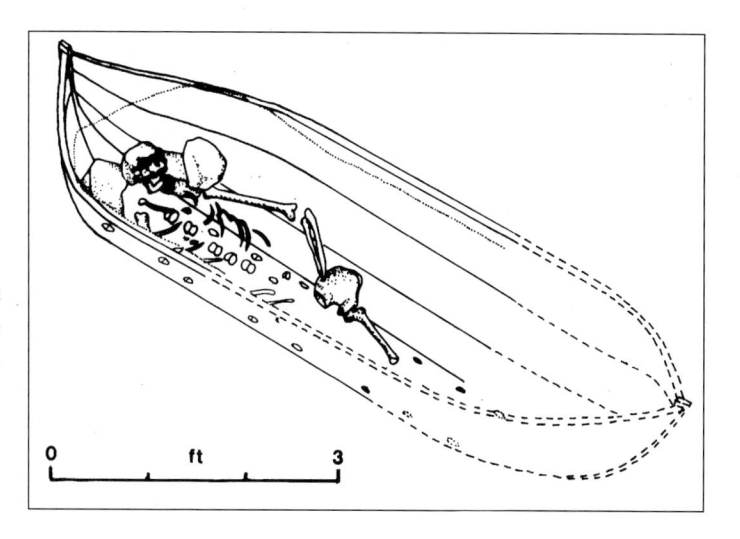

The twelve charcoal burials are enigmatic, and there are several possible interpretations of their significance. It is possible that the charcoal served a relatively functional purpose to soak up odours, or to mark the location of a burial. Indeed, charcoal is sometimes found on top of coffins in other cemeteries and it may, thus, have been intended to prevent later users of the cemetery from disturbing the burial. However, charcoal only appears once on top of a burial at York. The charcoal may conversely have had some symbolic association with the penitential ashes on which dying monks were sometimes placed, and may have symbolized penance for one's sins, humility, and the passion of Christ. Either way, the charcoal seems to signify that some additional effort had gone into the burial, suggesting that the deceased was someone of status, although only one burial containing charcoal among the later eleventh-century burials lay beneath a recumbent stone slab, which must have been another marker of status. The use of charcoal at York appears to have been a relatively short-lived tradition, which was used in the burials of both adult males and females. Charcoal burials have also been identified at St Mark's, Lincoln, Repton and St Helen-on-the-Walls, York. It appears to have been a tradition that was popular largely in the tenth and eleventh centuries, although the example from St Helen-on-the-Walls has produced a radiocarbon date of AD 1140±80 that suggests that the practice may sometime have occurred a little later. At Kellington bodies were placed on charred planks in the tenth and eleventh centuries. The significance of this is unknown, but it may have served a similar purpose to burial on a bed of charcoal elsewhere.

At Ripon the various burial grounds excavated within *c.*2-300m of St Peter's church display distinct characteristics, which suggest that they may have provided burial for distinctive parts of the local population (*see* **6**). Burial certainly took place within St Peter's church, although this may have been reserved for prominent members of the religious community or saints, such as Bishop Wilfrid who was buried on the south side of the altar, and St Ecgbert and St Wihtberht who are known to have rested there by at least the late ninth century. The crypt at Ripon, which was constructed in the later seventh century, may have been used for burial or the display of relics although there is no conclusive proof of this. There were at least four generations of burials at Ailcy Hill, to the east of St Peter's. The earliest complete burials excavated, which were aligned broadly west-east, had clearly disturbed earlier burials, which were apparently aligned north-south. The disarticulated bone from the north-south burials indicated that adult males and females and infants had been buried there. The earliest west-east burials were uncoffined and organized in neat rows. The next generation of burials disturbed these burials and was on a different alignment, west-north-west to east-south-east. Some of the burials in this phase were interred in chests with complex iron fittings including locks and hinges (**30**). Two of these burials have produced radiocarbon dates of 660-810 and 660-880 cal. AD. The west-east aligned burials apparently included only adult males and have yielded radiocarbon dates ranging between the later sixth and later ninth century. This has been explained as a sign of the adoption of the site for monastic burial, a claim possibly supported by the presence of chest-burials. Such forms of grave furniture have been associated elsewhere with monastic or episcopal burial grounds. The coffins from Ailcy Hill may have been reused domestic chests, as at York. The latest phase of burial activity excavated at Ailcy Hill is characterized by two unusual burials. One grave contained the remains of three individuals, and another contained the burial of a severely deformed individual, aged 14-15 years, who suffered from spinal tuberculosis and who had a pronounced distortion of the lower back. This period of use of the cemetery has been dated to the later Anglo-Saxon period from a radiocarbon date yielded by the deformed juvenile of 780-990 cal. AD. It may be that by the ninth or tenth century the cemetery had undergone another transformation and was being used to bury the socially excluded, including the deformed and, perhaps, felons, which is what the multiple burial may signify.

Thirty-six burials were excavated at the Ladykirk at Ripon (see above, p.22), and four of the burials within the chancel contained bone combs and two had comb cases, which have been dated on stylistic grounds to the later Anglo-Saxon period. These were probably the burials of priests, given both the location of the burials and the nature of the accompanying artefacts, which may have had some liturgical purpose. All of the other burials from this site were unaccompanied by artefacts. In addition, then, to there being different locations for burial in the vicinity of Ripon between at least the seventh and tenth centuries, there were also significant differences in the ways in which the dead were treated, presumably related to their role in local society or in the religious community.

At Repton there is similar evidence for a variety of burial rites. The tenth-century burials to the north of the crypt include both coffined burials and burials with stones set around the head, often called 'ear-muffs'. As we have seen, this practice was found at York Minster and it is also found at many other later Anglo-Saxon cemeteries, including Barton-upon-Humber, Fillingham (Lincs) (*see* **15** & **colour plate 7**), Kellington, Newark (Notts) and St Andrew, York where the cobbles cradling the skull may have served a fairly functional purpose since the individual concerned had been decapitated (**31**). A few burials around the crypt at Repton contained grave goods datable to the later ninth or early tenth century, although these may have been Scandinavian burials rather than being representative of indigenous practices (see below, p.110). To the west of the church was a two-celled sunken building which probably served as a mausoleum. It is likely to be of eighth- or ninth-century date, but it had apparently fallen into disrepair, although not

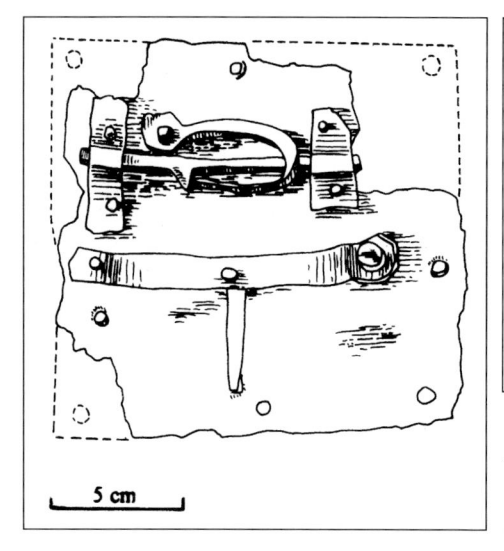

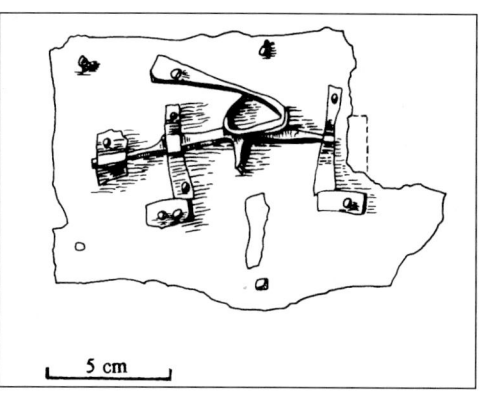

30 Locks from coffins excavated at Ripon (Yorks). After Hall and Whyman 1996, Alex Norman

necessarily out of use, by the later ninth century. It was used to inter the disarticulated remains of some 249 or more individuals. It has been thought to be a burial rite associated in some way with the activity of a Viking army that according to the Anglo-Saxon Chronicle over-wintered at Repton in 873-4. It has been suggested that the mass burial was that of a Viking warrior accompanied by grave goods and surrounded by the remains of his followers, collected from previous resting places. This conclusion is based in part on an antiquarian account of the contents of the mound, and in part on the presence of a number of artefacts among the bones, including an iron axe 'of early medieval type', a fragment of a two-edged sword, two large seaxes, a number of smaller seaxes and other knives, a chisel, a barrel-padlock key, fragments of precious metalwork, dress pins and coins of the 870s. Also significant is the absence of large numbers of bones, which is consistent with bodies having been exhumed and moved to a new site. A small number of bones were found stacked up by type in the corner of the mausoleum, and it may be that this was what the whole deposit once looked like, before being disturbed when it was opened up in the later seventeenth century. However, it is unlikely to be the murdered population of the monastery, or either Scandinavian or local battle dead, as there is insufficient wound trauma on the bones consistent with such a scenario.

The Chronicle entry provides a little information about events during the winter of the visit of the Viking army, which may help to explain the mass burial:

> In this year the army went from Lindsey to Repton and took up winter quarters there, and drove King Burgred across the sea, after he had held the kingdom twenty-two years. And they conquered all that land. And he went to Rome and settled there . . . And the same year they gave the kingdom of the Mercians to be held by Ceolwulf, a foolish king's thegn; and he swore oaths to them and gave hostages, that it should be ready for them on whatever day they wished to have it, and he would be ready, himself and all who would follow him, at the enemy's service

31 (left) Burial with cobbles set around the head from the church of St Andrew, York. The individual buried in this grave had been decapitated. York Archaeological Trust for Excavation and Research Ltd, York

It has been suggested that Burgred and Ceolwulf were members of rival Mercian royal families, with Ceolwulf being a descendant of the Mercian kings Cenwulf (796-821) and Ceolwulf I (821-3), and Burgred possibly being a descendant of Beornred, who had been a rival of Offa for the Mercian throne in 757. Whatever his origins, Ceolwulf II was certainly acceptable enough for Mercian bishops to witness his charters. Thus, there are grounds for suggesting that the Viking army may, in fact, have involved itself in internecine warfare. This places Repton in a different historical context from that in which it is normally considered. It is, moreover, apparent that the mass interment was not the result of a single act. Radiocarbon dates have been recovered from a sample of the bones that range from the eighth to tenth centuries, and it may be that the interment was the result of gradual accretion over a long period of time. Indeed, it is not unknown for bones to be exhumed and reburied in a single tomb in the Anglo-Saxon period. Bede records that the nuns of Barking Abbey (Essex) did this in their cemetery in the later seventh century owing to the restricted site on which the monastery was built. The fact that some of the bones were discovered stacked up according to type is an indication that the individuals whose remains were eventually deposited in the mausoleum had previously been buried elsewhere and were well decomposed before they were exhumed, since it would otherwise have been difficult to disarticulate them. Such a scenario is also supported by the absence of many small bones. Although the reasons for the cutting of a deep V-shaped ditch adjacent to the church are unclear, as is the date, it is possible that this act may account for the reburial of disturbed bones in the mausoleum.

The excavators, Martin Biddle and Birthe Kjølbye-Biddle, have suggested that the multiple burial at the south-west corner of the mound was a pagan 'sacrificial deposit'. While this is not impossible, such a burial is paralleled in other 'Christian' contexts, at Ripon, as we have seen, and also at the Gilbertine Priory site in York (see below, p.118). Whatever the real context for the creation of the mass burial, burial later continued around and against the slopes of the mound that covered it, indicating that it was not subsequently shunned for burial. I would not wish to deny the possibility that the bones under the mound have something to do with the Scandinavian raiders, but it seems likely that their involvement was only one factor that created this unusual discovery.

At Whitby recent excavations of the cemetery at Abbey Lands Farm, *c.*200m south of the medieval Abbey church, have revealed a series of west-east aligned burials arranged in rows, which probably date to the seventh or eighth century. As with the other cemeteries we have discussed, there was again a variety of burial rites. Many of the burials were in narrow graves, which suggest shrouded burial, for which confirmatory evidence survives in the shape of a single shroud pin. However, evidence for coffins has also been recovered. The coffins appear to have been simple wooden boxes, and where the wood has decayed it has left a stain in the ground around the skeleton, although in one case some fragments of the wood had actually survived. Metal strapping and other coffin furniture have been noted from two of the coffins. There are several unusual burials from the site. Two individuals appear to have been decapitated, with their heads subsequently being placed the wrong way round in the graves, with the jaws pointing away from the bodies. Several other individuals were buried face down, with their hands tied behind their backs and possibly their legs tied together at the knees. A cremation was also found, and it appears to have been placed in a small rectangular box, before being buried on the same west-east alignment as the inhumations. It is becoming increasingly apparent that cemeteries associated with churches from the seventh century included a variety of forms of burial.

Although the use of wooden coffins may indicate that a certain amount of investment had been made in a burial, it is inappropriate to use the presence or absence of coffins as an indication of the status of the people interred in any particular cemetery. Coffined burial was common in northern England and it was found in a variety of contexts. In describing one of the miracles performed by Bishop John of Beverley, Bede tells us that the servant of a thegn who was apparently close to death had already had a coffin prepared for him. In addition to the cemeteries we have already discussed, coffined burials of seventh- or eighth-century date have been excavated at Flixborough (Lincs), which was almost certainly the site of a religious community to judge from the finds from the site, and at Pontefract to the west of All Saints church, in the vicinity of another church of Anglo-Saxon date (*see* **11**). Burials of the tenth and eleventh century excavated adjacent to the contemporary church of St Mark's, Lincoln contained 'nail-like' iron finds, which may have been either nails for coffins (or possibly shroud pins). The cemetery at Thwing — which is not, however, near a known religious community — has also produced evidence for coffins of mid- to later Anglo-Saxon date. In contrast, the later Anglo-Saxon cemetery at Addingham (Yorks), which was located near to a site long associated with the archbishops of York and where there was probably a church of at least ninth-century origin, has produced no evidence for coffins. Nor have the broadly contemporary burials excavated near to the site of the monastery at Crayke (Yorks).

While the presence or absence of coffins does not offer any straightforward guide to the nature of a cemetery or to the identity of the people buried there, there may, nonetheless, be much to be learned from a study of coffins. The burial ground at Barton-upon-Humber which probably came into use in the ninth or tenth century has produced a variety of coffined burials (**32**). One of the coffins was an oak coffin of dug-out type. Another was comprised of loose boards placed in the grave, apparently without any form of jointing. One of the boards was a reused timber, to judge from the two holes drilled through one end, and these may have been the holes for a stool or a bench. The end timbers were probably also reused, given the evidence for beetle infestation which must have happened while the timber was above-ground. Another coffin at Barton appears to have been made from reused timbers, given that there are numerous peg holes and nails in the planks, which are not related to the construction of the coffin. It has been suggested that the timbers may have been reused from a bed. Five of the early coffins were joined with iron clenches and roves, and this implies a clinker-built construction. The size of the nails indicates that the timbers used for the coffins could have been no more than 15mm in thickness. This method of construction has encouraged speculation about the appearance of the coffins. Warwick and Kirsty Rodwell (1982, 292) have suggested that they may have been triangular in shape, or that they may have been rectangular with thin, concave sides. They have also suggested that these coffins may have been made of barkwood, possibly birch, which cannot be joined in conventional ways. Several other conventional coffins made of oak were excavated; some were held together by wooden dowels, although others also had nails.

By the tenth and eleventh centuries coffins appear to have been relatively common, although they were varied in form. At the church of St Andrew, York there is some evidence for wooden coffins in the form of nails, two of which still had timber attached. Another burial contained an iron strap hinge with a bifurcated scrolled terminal across the chest of the skeleton, which showed traces of mineralized textile, suggesting that the coffin had been covered with a pall. Remains of wooden coffins have been excavated at a site at Swinegate in York, which was probably the cemetery of St Benet's church until the twelfth century when the cemetery was built over. Of these coffins 40 were of plank construction, and most were held together by wooden pegs, with only one having nails. One was a dug-out tree trunk and there were two infant burials that had only a wooden lid covering the interment, one of which was distinguished by bearing a shallow inscription of the grid of the game 'Nine Men's Morris'.

Elaborate Anglo-Saxon stone coffins, or sarcophagi, have been found at a number of churches, and these may have been commissioned for saints, prominent ecclesiastics or lay lords. An impressive sarcophagus was discovered buried beneath the nave at St Alkmund's, Derby, and it has been dated on stylistic grounds to the ninth century (*see* **3**). The excavator suggested that it was made for St Alkmund, a member of the Northumbrian royal family who was murdered in the early ninth century during a factional dispute. We know that St Alkmund rested in Derby (then called 'Northworthy') by the later ninth century, and it may be that the sarcophagus was made for him. However, we also know that Ealdorman Æthelwulf of Berkshire, who was killed while fighting the Danes at Reading (Berks) in 871, was taken from Reading 'into the province of the Mercians to the place called Northworthy, but in the Danish tongue Derby'. Accordingly, Martin Biddle (1986, 8) has remarked that the sarcophagus could equally as well have been a fitting resting place for a ninth-century ealdorman, i.e. for Æthelwulf. The sarcophagus was so elaborate that it was probably intended to be seen rather than to be buried.

32 Coffin from Barton-on-Humber (Lincs). A coffin of tenth- or eleventh-century date in the process of excavation. Mike Parker Pearson

A slab discovered at Wirksworth (Derbs) seems originally to have been part of a shrine, although when it was discovered in 1821 it had been reused upside down over a coffin two feet beneath the floor of the church (*see* **4**). Art historians have variously dated the slab to the seventh, eighth or ninth centuries. It depicts the death of the Virgin, the descent into Hell, Ascension and the apocalyptic representation of the Lamb on the Cross. Its iconography, then, represents death, judgment and resurrection. The panel is divided into parallel upper and lower registers, dominated by images of Christ and the Virgin respectively. Roberta Gilchrist (1994, 31-2) has recently commented that the iconography of the Wirksworth slab may suggest that the church had once been a house for religious men and women, given that there are both male and female associations on the slab which would be an appropriate opposition for such a 'double house'. Six sculptural fragments found at South Kyme (Lincs) appear to have once been part of a shrine, which might indicate that it was the site of some now lost cult (*see* **5**). A panel at Hovingham (Yorks) may also once have formed part of an elaborate shrine (**colour plate 1**). The iconography of the panel emphasizes the role of Mary in various scenes from Christ's life, and Jane Hawkes (1993, 260-1) has suggested that the shrine may have been made for a female saint.

Other than the examples mentioned above, Anglo-Saxon stone coffins are rare in the region, but have recently been found at Kirkdale (Yorks). Admittedly, close dating of stone coffins, unless decorated, is difficult, however the famous sundial at Kirkdale was apparently carved onto a reused portion of a stone coffin in the middle of the eleventh century. That example of reuse, and another excavated example of a stone coffin, reveal that stone coffins were a feature of Anglo-Saxon burial practices at Kirkdale. In some cemeteries, as we have seen at York, stone linings of graves are found, and at St Mark's, Lincoln one of the earliest burials, probably of the late tenth or early eleventh century, was placed in a grave lined with limestone rubble. Such grave linings may have been cheaper, less prestigious alternatives to a stone coffin. At Newark recent excavations at the castle have uncovered a late Anglo-Saxon cemetery containing at least 70 burials and probably many more. All of the burials are aligned west-east and contain no grave goods, and radiocarbon dates suggest that the burials belong to the tenth or eleventh century. A few of the burials had 'ear-muffs' and several were outlined by stones. At Fillingham a cemetery has been excavated which is of probable later Anglo-Saxon date. The burials were placed in shallow graves straight onto the bedrock, and were lined with stones and several had stones placed around the head (*see* **15, colour plate 7**).

Generally between the seventh and the eleventh century people were interred in individual graves, which were aligned more or less west-east. However, exceptions to this are found. It is clear, for example, that the basic alignment for burials in a cemetery might change during successive phases of use, as we have seen at Ailcy Hill, Ripon and at Whitby. The excavations at York Minster reveal that grave alignment might be dictated by the layout of buildings surrounding a cemetery (*see* **28**). There are also examples of multiple burials, such as the charnel house at Repton (if that is how we may interpret it) and the multiple burial beside it, and the triple burial at Ailcy Hill, Ripon. At the site of the Gilbertine Priory of St Andrew, York, the first tenth- and eleventh-century phases of the cemetery associated with an earlier church (probably the church of St Andrew mentioned in Domesday Book) includes four double burials (**33**). In one burial the arms of one skeleton were wrapped around the other, and another grave contained three individuals — two adult males with a female placed diagonally across their chest. Multiple burials and careless arrangements of the body in the grave, alongside evidence for decapitation and hands and legs tied, have recently been identified as being characteristic of execution cemeteries, containing the burials of felons who were excluded from burial in consecrated ground, something which appears to have occurred from at least the tenth century. At Walkington Wold (Yorks) a number of unusual burials have been excavated which were cut into one of two Bronze Age barrows. Ten of the 12 skeletons excavated had been decapitated, and one had its hands tied. As seems to be common of such burial sites most of the skeletons (11 out of 12) have been sexed as male. Although there are grounds then for suggesting that some of the multiple burials from the cemeteries thus far discussed were the burials of felons of some sort, this interpretation seems unlikely within a churchyard setting, especially at St Andrew's where the triple burial may have been within the church. There is also the problem at Whitby that the unusual burials, including decapitations and bodies with hands and legs tied, occur in an otherwise orderly cemetery associated with a major religious house. This evidence may throw into question the notion that victims of execution were invariably excluded from churchyard burial.

The fate of the Anglo-Saxon dead

There was little guarantee that the deceased would rest undisturbed in their grave for long. Although in some excavated Anglo-Saxon cemeteries there was little evidence of inter-cutting of graves, indicating that care was taken to mark the precise location of burials, in many other instances graves were disturbed by later burials. At Pontefract, in one grave the bones of the first occupant were moved to one side to accommodate a second burial (*see* **23**), showing that while burials were sometimes disturbed by later burials, the bones of the original occupant of the grave may be carefully stacked up around the later burial. There is also clear evidence that bodies might be moved from their original resting-place. As we have seen at Repton, many of the individuals whose remains eventually ended up in the mausoleum had been previously buried elsewhere. Another striking example of the movement of bodies comes from Addingham. This cemetery has a number of unusual internal chronological and spatial characteristics (*see* **9**). There is little evidence of inter-cutting of graves, which suggests a relatively short chronology for this burial area; there are several empty graves, and a number that contain the remains of more than one individual. The empty graves (which contain traces of human bone) are in the western part of the burial ground, whereas those with both primary and secondary interments are to the south and east, where the graves are set closest together. Max Adams (1996) has suggested that at some point after the disarticulation of the body individuals were exhumed and reburied in graves to the east, with the bones of either the original occupant or the newcomer being placed in a pile at one end of the grave, something which appears to have happened more than ten times in

33 Double burial from the church of St Andrew, York. This burial contained two adult males. York Archaeological Trust for Excavation and Research Ltd, York

a sample of fifty or so graves. This possibly occurred because there was some focal point to the east and burial close to this was regarded as desirable, and if it was not possible initially it was undertaken later. The removal of bodies from graves is not unknown in the Anglo-Saxon period, and it certainly happened at Raunds (Northants) where the reuse of stone coffins may have been the reason. This was not the case at Addingham, and, assuming that it was not simply the result of encroachment of some other activity onto the western part of the cemetery, it may be that an element of social competitiveness was being played out through the removal of bodies towards some focal point.

A number of churches in the region were clearly built over earlier burial grounds, as we have seen. This does not necessarily mean that the preceding cemetery was not associated with a church, but it does indicate that some Anglo-Saxon church-builders had no qualms about building on cemeteries and disturbing graves. The late eleventh-century Norman cathedral at York was built over the late Anglo-Saxon cemetery, although much of the area of the cemetery was covered with cobbles, as part of a 'landscaping' exercise by the Norman builders. Churches were also built over burials at Repton, Ripon (Ladykirk), Pontefract (see **11**, **12**), Kellington, Barton-upon-Humber, Barrow-upon-Humber (see chapter 2), and successive phases of rebuilding at a number of excavated churches in York and at St Mark's Lincoln disturbed earlier burials. As we have previously seen (above pp.40-1), Anglo-Saxon burials were also sometimes disturbed by the construction of castles (as at Newark, York and Pontefract) and other domestic buildings (as at Swinegate in York, Pontefract and at Addingham where the manorial buildings to the west eventually encroached onto the cemetery).

Death and the display and exchange of artefacts

The grave was not only the place where artefacts were displayed during the funerary procedures. It is notable that in Anglo-Saxon wills the heriot payments made to a lord, often the king, on the death of his man, consist of items similar to those that had been found in graves at a much earlier date. They include weapons, jewellery and horse-fittings, in addition to money. For example, Wulfric Spott, a major landholder in the north Midlands, left a will c.1004, in which he granted to his lord 'two hundred mancuses of gold, and two silver-hilted swords and four horses, two saddled and two unsaddled, and the weapons which are due with them'. Now such items were to be rendered to a person's lord rather than placed in the ground. It is also, perhaps, significant that the heriot payment consisted of items associated with fighting. This is also true of ecclesiastical wills. For example, c.953 Bishop Theodred of London left the king his heriot of 200 marks of red gold, two silver cups, four horses, two swords, four shields and four spears along with a number of estates. Whoever a person was, and whatever life experiences they may have had, there remained a symbolic, if not always real, association between lordship and fighting equipment, which were very much masculine symbols of power. Although wills survive only from a much later date than the period when the types of artefacts they describe as heriot payments were deposited in graves, the wills may nonetheless offer some clues about the disappearance of grave goods. It may be that one factor was that weapons, in particular, came increasingly to be used at the moment of death as payments to a lord or the king.

Artefacts also continued to be used in association with death in the context of hoarding and in what may have been ritual deposition in rivers. Hoarding during the Anglo-Saxon period is usually interpreted as the burial, for safety, of treasures, which for some reason were not recovered at a later date. This certainly may have been true in many cases, but it is not entirely persuasive and other explanations are possible. As Guy Halsall (2000) has recently asked of hoards, did all of their owners die before they could retrieve them, and without telling anyone else where they had put them? Or were they all so forgetful that they simply could not remember where they buried their treasures?! In cases where hoards were deposited in churchyards (such as at Goldsborough, Yorks) or in mounds (such as Lilla Howe, Yorks), it does not seem very plausible that the treasures were placed there in order to hide them, given that both churches and mounds are highly visible in the landscape and are locations known to contain wealth. It may be that this hoarding served some ritual purpose, although it is, admittedly, difficult to know what this purpose may have been. Ritual deposition in rivers may also explain the large numbers of finds, particularly of swords, that are found in rivers, which have previously tended to be attributed to chance loss. The river Witham east of Lincoln has, for example, produced a seventh-century shield boss, an eighth-century silver hanging bowl, a silver gilt ornament of three linked pins, a Viking Age axe, stirrups, knives, spearheads and swords. At Skerne (Yorks) the skeletons of animals (including horses, cattle, sheep and dogs, none of which showed signs of butchery for consumption), four knives, a spoon-bit, an adze and a sword in a wooden scabbard of willow poplar with fleece lining were found associated with the oak piles of a jetty or bridge abutment. Across the country it has been estimated that at least four times as many Viking Age swords have been found in rivers than in burials or churchyards (where they may once have been in a burial). Swords were large items not easily lost, one would assume, and they were expensive and treasured items. As Halsall (2000) has said, 'it defies all credibility to suppose that the pre-Conquest English habitually dropped and lost them by accident whilst crossing streams and rivers, or whilst wandering into bogs'. The possibility of ritual deposition has to be allowed. Although it may be difficult to square the notion of ritual deposition of artefacts with traditional notions of what constituted acceptable Christian burial, the available evidence may necessitate us reassessing our views of what was acceptable in a Christian context. Indeed, law-codes and ecclesiastical commentaries of the later Anglo-Saxon period make it clear that 'superstitious' practices continued to be known, and condemned, long after English society had become Christian.

Viking burials

A number of burials in the region have commonly been cited as examples of 'Viking' burial. These include the cremation cemetery at Heath Wood, Ingleby (Derbs), the inhumations with grave goods and the mass burial at Repton, the barrow burials at Cambois, Bedlington and at Camphill near Bedale (Yorks), and the burials accompanied by swords from Kildale and Wensley (Yorks). It is worth reconsidering the premises on which the argument that these are Viking burials rests. It has been traditional to identify the settlers on the basis of the appearance of supposedly alien burial rites in the later ninth and earlier tenth centuries in parts of northern and eastern England. Yet, as we have seen, burial practices in those regions were not uniform in the ninth century, and it is important to note that burial practice was not uniform in contemporary Scandinavia either, where cremation, inhumation with and without grave goods, ship burial, and burial under cairns and mounds were all practised, often in the same region or even the same cemetery. Thus, the identification of burial by or of Scandinavians might not necessarily be straightforward.

There is certainly a handful of burials from the region that it would be perverse to try to explain as anything other than Scandinavian. The cremations may, indeed, be those of Scandinavians — although we might note that cremations of probable eighth-century date have also apparently been found among inhumations at both Whitby and Thwing, but admittedly not on the same scale as at Heath Wood, Ingleby. The cemetery at Heath Wood comprised 59 barrows, of which around a third have been excavated. Some, and perhaps all, of the barrows covered the site of a funeral pyre, upon which the burned bones of men and women have been found (**colour plate 6**). Sacrificial offerings of cattle, sheep, dog and possibly pig have also been found. A number of metal items, some of Scandinavian type, have been found inside the barrows including two broken swords (possibly the result of ritual 'killing' of the swords), iron buckles, wire embroidery, a copper alloy strap-end, iron spade, and a ring-headed pin. This burial rite is virtually unknown in the ninth or tenth century in England. The only comparable examples (e.g. Hesket in the Forest (Cumbria), Claughton Hall and, possibly, Inskip (Lancashire)) are single burials, not cemeteries, and there is some doubt about the identification of the latter two as Viking Age cremations, as opposed to Viking Age inhumations in a place previously used for cremation.

Of the rest of the burials generally interpreted as those of Scandinavians, they appear to represent a short-lived revival of elaborate burial display. These include six inhumation burials from Repton. The burial of an adult male (grave 511) contained a necklace with two beads and a silver Thor's hammer, a copper alloy buckle, an iron sword, two iron knives, an iron key, the tusk of a wild boar and the bone of a jackdaw. The burial of another adult male contained an iron knife. Two others may have contained weapons, and there was another burial with an iron knife, and a female burial with a gold finger ring and five silver pennies of the mid 870s. Theweapon burials are unusual in the wider context of ninth-century burial practices in northern England, and these have been interpreted, not implausibly, as the burials of Scandinavian settlers.

However, the other burials are not exceptional, and in the context of the evidence cited above for the occasional occurrence of artefacts in graves in the ninth century we should perhaps not be as certain as we have previously been that burials with a few artefacts are those of Scandinavians. We should also remember that late ninth-century English society may have known ritual deposition of artefacts in association with other funerary rituals. Moreover, the artefacts placed in both burials and other deposits were commonly of indigenous rather than Scandinavian origin. One wonders how big a step it would have been for indigenous people to place artefacts in graves in the context of contact with incoming groups who may sometimes have used such a burial rite. More to the point, people place artefacts in graves for a reason, as part of a dialogue with other groups, and given the location of most of the burials with artefacts from a generation either side of 900 near to churches or barrows with which indigenous society was familiar, it is likely that the burials had resonance for the indigenous communities even if they themselves did not bury their dead in this manner. Repton grave 511 contained a coffin, and a post-hole at the eastern end of the grave, which suggests that the grave had been marked above ground in some way. One wonders whether this grave combined Scandinavian funerary custom (burial with grave goods) with English practices (adjacent to a church, coffined burial, and above-ground marker). Wooden coffins are not unknown in ninth-century Scandinavia, but are not common and are widely regarded as a foreign import. It is a possibility that grave 511, located near to the church, is telling us something important about the processes of assimilation of the Scandinavian settlers to indigenous funerary practices and society.

Burials and social display

Although grave goods had largely disappeared from burials by the eighth century, this does not mean that burial had ceased to be a medium for social display. The location of burials, in or near mounds or churches, and the use of above-ground markers increasingly became the means by which the elite signalled their wealth and status (see also next chapter). The elaborate burials that date to a generation either side of 900 witnessed a brief return to elaborate funerary display in the grave, which, while clearly influenced by the Scandinavian settlements, primarily reflects not innate ethnic differences but a society undergoing major transitions in political authority, lordship and ecclesiastical organization. Social crisis and competition for power were often manifest in elaborate burial displays in the early Middle Ages.

One notable feature of these burials is that they are overwhelmingly of males, and the associated artefacts consist almost solely of items that carry clear masculine symbolism — weapons, or items with agricultural, hunting or trading connotations. It is also striking that a number of examples of stone sculpture of the earlier tenth century include warrior images or scenes from heroic culture (**34,52,53,54,55,57**). It appears that for a brief moment of intense social stress it was to the male and the masculine that communities looked to ameliorate that disruption, to renegotiate local power structures, to make claims to land and to return the community to its status quo.

Some recent studies have hinted that even after the decline of the use of grave goods gender continued to be an important factor determining the ways in which individuals were buried. Analyses of Anglo-Saxon churchyards regularly comment on the different treatment accorded men, women and children in the grave, indicating explicitly or implicitly that this may have something to reveal about contemporary gender roles or perceptions and that gender was still relevant to funerary arrangements. There is certainly some evidence for seemingly contemporary zones in cemeteries, characterized by different types of grave or demographic profile, at Hartlepool (Cleveland), Winchester

Graves

(Hamps), Raunds (Northants), Jarrow (Northumb) and Withorn (Scotland). There are also notable clusters of male burials at some sites — such as Ripon, Hereford, and Burrow Hill (Suffolk) — but we have to be careful when drawing conclusions about gender roles and relations on the basis of this evidence as it may relate to the use of some burials grounds, or parts thereof, for members of associated male religious communities. A similar pattern at Southampton may be accounted for by the use of the site by a disproportionately male population of seasonally migrant craft workers and traders. There is no evidence to suggest that after the seventh century men and women were routinely treated in different ways in the funerary context. This may not simply be because we are no longer able to see so easily such distinctions with the disappearance of grave goods — as we have seen there remained many other ways of distinguishing or elaborating graves. Rather than gender, it appears to be factors relating to wealth, social status, family and occupation that become more important in determining burial practices. This may account for the clustering of burials around particular features in churchyards, such as funerary monuments, or access routes through the churchyard. Whatever claims to power or influence were being staked through such burial strategies they are a long way off from the dichotomous gendered burial displays of the fifth and sixth centuries. In churchyards while it might be more likely to be through male burials that statements were made about family status it was not exclusively so.

34 Warrior on Anglo-Saxon sculpture at Norbury (Derbs). This sculpture is of tenth-century date. Jim Williams

The later Middle Ages

Burials of the twelfth to fifteenth century continue to show variation, although few burials are found outside churchyards by this time, and most are aligned west-east. Diversity continues to characterize coffins, the form of the grave, the position of the body in the grave and, occasionally, the placing of artefacts in graves.

Grave goods

Artefacts other than coffins are rarely found in graves of the later Middle Ages, but the exceptions often provide useful information about attitudes to death and to the deceased. At the Gilbertine Priory of St Andrew, York, half a seal matrix was found in deposits associated with disturbed burials in the north chapel, and it may have been a grave deposit. The seal depicted a gloved hand holding game animals and it had been deliberately broken, an action consistent with cancellation. In another grave two perforated plates of copper alloy were found around the damaged knee of an adult male, and they presumably were intended to perform some curative role. The copper alloy stains on one of the excavated skeletons suggests that some items made of copper alloy were placed in the grave. Other finds from disturbed soil in the vicinity of burials, such as a knife with an ivory handle and a copper alloy dagger chape, may conceivably have come from graves. One burial to the south of the nave contained a lead chalice and paten, and another contained a paten, indicating that the deceased were priests. Chalices have also been found in graves at the Cathedral and St Mark's in Lincoln, Flawford (Notts), Wharram Percy (Yorks), St Leonard's hospital in Chesterfield (Derbs) (**36**), and York Minster. At Monk Bretton Priory (Yorks) a burial containing a chalice and paten was beneath a grave slab that depicted a chalice. On the whole chalices and patens seem to be found in graves of thirteenth-century or later date. However at St Leonard's, Chesterfield a lead paten (the presumed chalice was too badly disintegrated to analyze) was found in a stone-lined grave, and the skeleton has produced a radiocarbon date centred on the late eleventh to early twelfth century (**35**).

A papal bull — a lead seal attached to a papal document — was found in the hand of a skeleton excavated at All Saints, Peasholme Green, York. Papal bulls have also been found in disturbed contexts in churchyards at Beverley and York, and they may conceivably have come from graves. In the later medieval cemetery at St Helen-on-the-Walls, York, one grave contained a lead object that may have been a pilgrim's badge. Another grave contained a necklet of twisted wire, and the skeleton from this burial has produced a radiocarbon date of AD 1170 ± 80.

Long wooden rods have been found in 10 graves at the Augustinian friary in Hull, and a number of interpretations of their significance have been offered, including the suggestion that they were symbols of pilgrimage or of some form of office-holding, and even that they were used for self-flagellation (**37**)! The grave of an adult female contained a leather girdle (a belt looped round the waist with a long strap dangling to the ankles), which was a fashionable courtly garment of the fourteenth century. There is good evidence from several sites that some individuals were buried clothed. In some cases this may have been a reflection of the lack of care that was taken over preparation for their burial. In other cases, such as the burials of ecclesiastics, this was clearly an indication of their status. There was a later medieval written and artistic tradition that ecclesiastics were expected to be properly attired to meet Christ, and this may explain why they were buried in their robes. The coffin of Archbishop Walter de Gray (1216-55), which was opened during restoration work at York Minster in 1968, contained a silver-gilt chalice and paten, a gold ring set with a sapphire, an emerald and a ruby, a pastoral staff of walrus ivory set

35 Burial of priest from St Leonard's Chesterfield (Derbs). This burial contained a lead paten and the powdered remains of what may have been a chalice. The burial also had large shaped stones set around the head, and has been radiocarbon dated to the end of the eleventh or early twelfth century. In this photograph the stone lining of the grave can be seen, and it consisted of at least four courses of stones. The grave was covered by large flat stones. The only surviving skeletal remains were the legs and one arm curved around the paten. The head end had been destroyed by the construction of a modern drain. Alison Walster, ARCUS

with stones, and textile fragments, including the remains of a cushion of silk and gold thread placed under his head, two bands of silk and gold thread near his head, and the leather soles of his shoes. The almost complete destruction of his grave-clothes suggests that he was buried in linen rather than the embroidered silk vestments found in the graves of other medieval archbishops (Ramm 1971, 127-9). The coffin of Archbishop Godfrey de Ludham of York (1258-65) was also opened in 1968 and discovered to have been lead-lined, which, along with embalming, created the right conditions for the survival of both body tissue and fabric. The coffin contained a painted wooden pastoral staff, a gold ring set with a sapphire, a silver-gilt chalice and paten, and remains of a cushion, mitre, stole, woollen pallium with appliqué Maltese crosses, and leather shoes. Priestly vestments were found in graves excavated in the Chapter House at Lincoln Cathedral, and one grave contained remains of a silk chasuble and a coarse sack-like wrapping made from cow hair. The skeleton in one grave had remains of a textile cross woven with threads of gold placed on the forehead, and two twigs placed in the shape of a cross were found on the chest of another skeleton.

Graves and coffins

Many of the excavated cemeteries from the region of later medieval date contained a variety of types of coffin and grave lining. Various types of wooden and stone coffin have been found. On the whole it is difficult to say whether the more elaborate coffins, including those that were decorated or those wooden coffins with fittings of some complexity, were made for the social elite, but in some instances they certainly were. Archbishop Walter de Gray was buried in a stone coffin beneath a Purbeck marble effigy surmounted by a canopy that rests on nine Purbeck marble columns. The coffin was painted with a highly colourful life-size depiction of the archbishop, who was shown holding a cross staff and vested with the full pontificals. Painted coffins may not have been uncommon for the elite. In a later source, Adam of Domerham's *History of Glastonbury* describes the visit of Edward I and Queen Eleanor to Glastonbury in 1277 to witness the translation of what were believed to be the remains of King Arthur and Queen Guinevere. The bodies were said to have been placed in painted coffins, which were presumably made either in the twelfth century (when the two bodies had first been exhumed) or the late thirteenth, in honour of the translation. Whoever was buried in those coffins it was thought appropriate that someone of royal status should have a painted coffin.

36 Lead paten from Chesterfield (Derbs). Priests would often have two chalices and patens, one set made of silver for use during church services, and another set for their burial. The latter set would normally be made of a low-grade metal such as pewter or lead. Alison Walster, ARCUS

Wooden coffins (as opposed to the metal fittings of wooden coffins) rarely survive, but the waterlogged conditions at the Augustinian priory site at Hull resulted in the survival of 39 later medieval coffins, from a total of over 240 excavated burials (**38**). Of these coffins, three were decorated and 38 were made of Baltic oak which presumably has something to reveal about later medieval trading connections in Hull, and also about the acquisition of raw materials by those involved in the funerary industry (see below, p.178).

Stone coffins are found more often in the later Middle Ages than they are in the Anglo-Saxon centuries. Many of the burials at the Gilbertine priory of St Andrew, York, for example, were contained in stone coffins. Four of the six burials of the thirteenth or early fourteenth century in the north chapel were in stone coffins. The other two were, however, in wooden coffins, one of which had iron fittings. Given the location and the form of the coffins these six burials may have been those of high status members of the laity, since they include two adult females and they may have been patrons of the Priory. Other indications of the status of these individuals is provided by the secular imagery from the seal matrix which was found in association with these burials (see above, p.113), and a fragment of stone which may have been part of a canopy for a shrine or tomb recess. In the east cloister alley a further ten inhumations were excavated, of which three were placed in stone coffins which appear to have had wooden covers (**39**), and two were placed in graves lined with roof tiles — a form of grave lining also found at Clementhorpe nunnery in York (**40**). Other burials around the cloister at St Andrew's were in wooden coffins. Again, this may have been a favoured area of burial for important members of the lay community. One adult burial in the area of the chapter house was marked by an upright, uninscribed stone slab (**41**), two infant graves were lined with roughly hewn stones, and one adult male burial at the east end of the presbytery was placed in a grave lined with lime. An inscribed Roman sarcophagus was reused for a burial in the nave in the thirteenth century, presumably for someone of importance.

It is, as at an earlier date, simplistic to identify the more prestigious later medieval burials simply on the basis of the form of the burial. At the Gilbertine priory of St Andrew, York, for example, there are 25 burials which do not appear to have been provided with coffins, but while this may indicate poorer burials, their location in the crossing of the church would conversely seem to imply that they were the burials of more prestigious individuals. Another group of five graves — one of which was empty, another

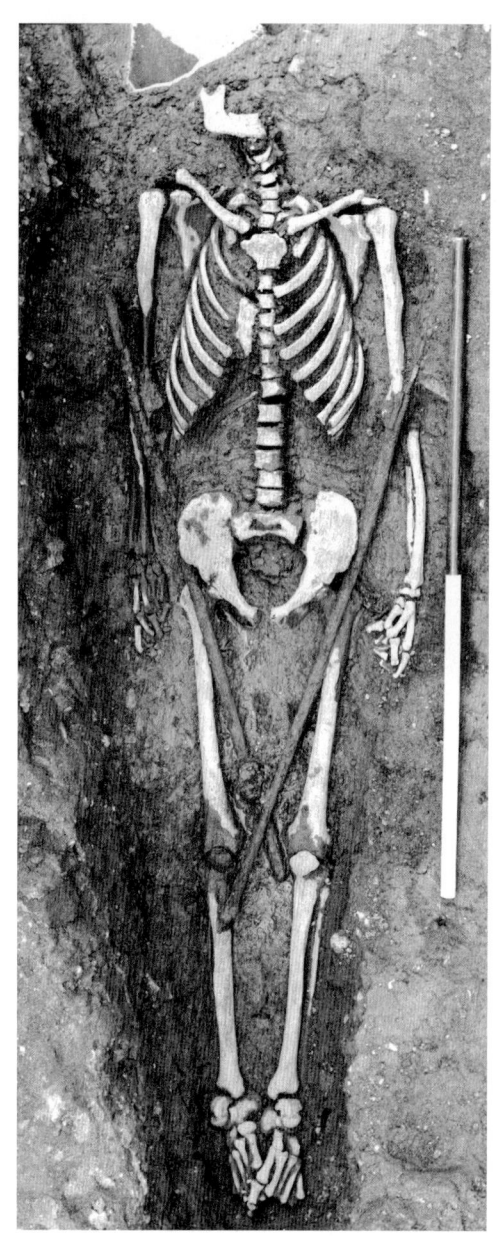

37 Burial from the Augustinian friary at Hull (Yorks). In this burial of an adult male two wooden rods were discovered crossed on top of the body Humber Field Archaeology

of which was lined with lime, and the others of which had no coffins — were located in the presbytery, and it may be that despite their relative material poverty these were the graves of important individuals, perhaps grouped together under an altar. Little is known about the use of Gilbertine priories for burial by members of the laity, but it is likely to have been an option as members of the later medieval ruling classes favoured burial in religious communities. That this was the case at the priory of St Andrew is indicated by the presence of female burials, as women cannot have been members of the priory. The evidence of two wills, by Alice de Fiskergate and Marion Redmane, reveals that they left land and money in return for burial at the priory. The growing influence of lay patrons has recently been emphasized by a study of the window glass from the priory. The thirteenth-century window glass, which made little use of colour and eschewed figural representations, was replaced in the fourteenth century with more colourful glass, incorporating figural and heraldic designs, as a result of the influence of the aesthetic preferences of a wealthy secular patron. Financial considerations make it unlikely that the poorer laity were normally buried at the priory, although servants and members of the lay workforce may have been.

At the Augustinian friary site in Hull, the one burial containing a coffin made of English oak was found in a prominent position within the friary, in the choir, and may have been the burial of a member of the friary community. Whatever the case, it is striking that the indigenous material was used for a burial in a prestigious location, whereas all other surviving coffins located elsewhere in the church (in the nave, north transept and cloister) used imported timbers. Thus, the use of imported timbers need not necessarily indicate burials of the highest status.

38 Burial from the Augustinian friary at Hull (Yorks). An adult female in a coffin which has produced dendrochronology dates of AD 1338-50. A 26-week foetus was buried in a smaller coffin placed inside that of the adult, presumably its mother. Humber Field Archaeology

It is unusual to find burials with stones set around the skull after the eleventh century. Rare later examples are found at St Mary's, Stow (Lincs) where the practice continued into the thirteenth century, and the hospital of St Leonard in Chesterfield, which may be late eleventh-, or early twelfth-century in date. At the priory of St Andrew, York, a decapitated individual buried some time in the later Middle Ages (the context was difficult to determine) had cobbles placed around the skull. The cobbles may have served a functional purpose.

Most excavated graves of later medieval date are oriented west-east. Although in more recent centuries it is not uncommon to find priestly burials oriented east-west, so that, it is said, the priest would rise up at the Resurrection to face his flock, this does not appear to have been a medieval tradition. Priestly burials of later medieval date, which have been identified from the presence of chalices and patens, normally face the same way as other burials. The only east-west oriented burial at St Andrew's, York was in the cloister garth, and the body had been decapitated and cobbles had been placed around the skull. Given the location of this burial it is difficult to see the reverse orientation as having sinister significance, although at other sites such an orientation may have done. This has been suggested at, for example, the cemetery of St Margaret's, Combusto, Norwich 'where those who have been hanged are buried', and where many burials were oriented east-west, north-south or south-north.

39 *Burials in stone coffins at the Gilbertine priory of St Andrew, York. These burials were excavated in the south-east corner of the east cloister alley.* York Archaeological Trust for Excavation and Research Ltd, York

Generally bodies were placed in individual graves, but there are occasional examples of double burials, such as the four double burials in the nave of the priory of St Andrew, York, in the early fourteenth century (*see* **33**). There were also double burials at St Helen-on-the-Walls, York (**42**). These may represent family groups, and this is suggested by the not infrequent request in wills for burial with or near a family member. There is some evidence that tombs or graves might be reopened in order to add other burials. In his will of 1448, William Styward asked to be buried under a marble stone where his mother lay in the church of St Helen-on-the-Walls. In such instances, grave slabs would have served not only to commemorate the deceased but also to identify the precise location of their burial.

The fate of the deceased

The later Middle Ages witnessed the not infrequent disruption of cemeteries, and the building of churches and other buildings over cemeteries. The Gilbertine priory of St Andrew, York was constructed over the cemetery of an earlier church towards the end of the twelfth century, and in the late thirteenth and early fourteenth century major modifications to the priory both sealed and, in some cases, cut burials. The stone coffins in the north chapel were disturbed during this phase of rebuilding. A cobbled surface to the south of the nave sealed a number of burials but was then cut by other burials which were then sealed by a new cobbled surface. It has been suggested that there may have been some sort of dispute over this surface, which appears to have formed a path leading to the nave, which would explain why it successively sealed and was then cut by burials (Kemp and Graves 1996, 149).

The rebuilding and extension of churches had implications for the bodies that had been buried in the churchyard, often resulting in them being disturbed (see above, p.43). There is some evidence that little care was taken to avoid disturbing earlier burials. This is indicated by the level of inter-cutting of burials and also by instances of articulated limbs found overlying other interments, as has been found at St Helen-on-the-Walls, suggesting disregard for earlier burials. On the other hand, at St Mark's, Lincoln the foundation dug for the tower in the twelfth century encountered a burial in a

*40 Grave lined with tiles from the Gilbertine priory of St Andrew, York. This burial was excavated in the south-east corner of the east cloister alley, near to the burials in stone coffins (see **39**). York Archaeological Trust for Excavation and Research Ltd, York*

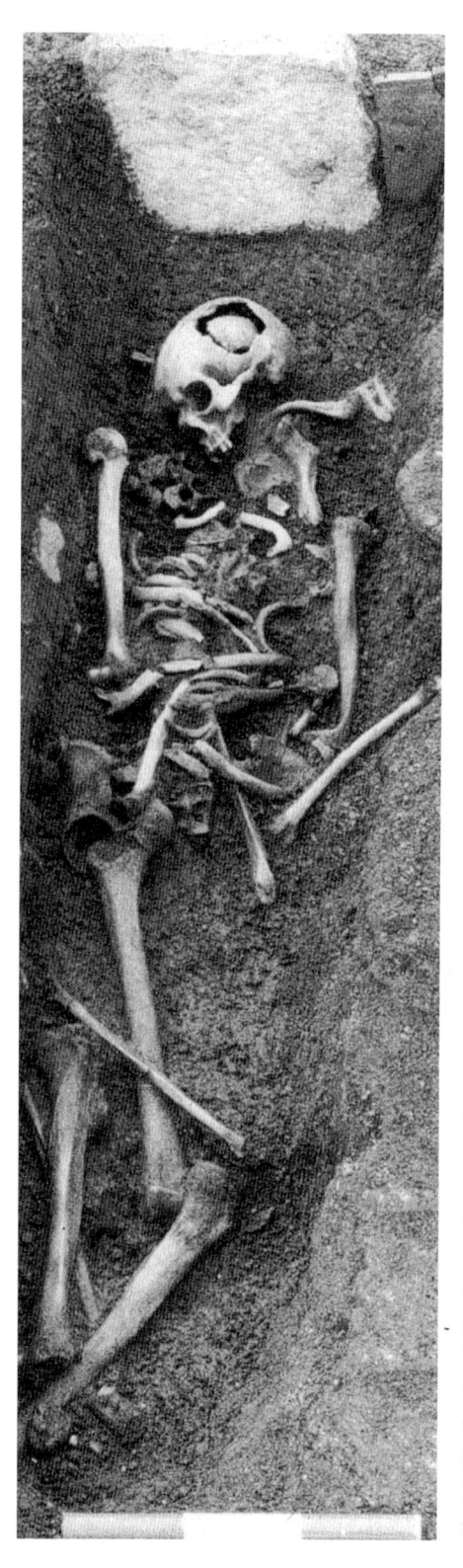

41 (left) Burial marked with a stone marker at the Gilbertine priory of St Andrew, York. This burial was excavated in the area of the former chapter house. There was also a tile placed upright next to the stone marker. York Archaeological Trust for Excavation and Research Ltd, York

stone cist, but the builders appear to have taken care not to disturb this burial during their work, even though it was partly surrounded by new masonry.

In an unusual example of the post-mortem movement of bodies, in the later twelfth century, William son of Ernis granted the church of Long Sutton (Lincs) to the priory of Castle Acre (Norfolk) along with a site on which he intended a new church to be built, and he instructed that the bodies buried in the existing church should be taken to the new church. Charnel pits have been identified in a number of cemeteries, and are referred to in documents, and this was where bones disturbed by subsequent burials or building work were often placed. At St Mark's, Lincoln the south porch constructed in the mid-sixteenth century had a small sealed charnel house beneath it. The porch was constructed largely from grave monuments and architectural features from another church or churches, and it may be that the charnel was also brought from another church, as there is no evidence of a major graveyard clearance or disturbance in the sixteenth century at St Mark's. It has been suggested that the function of the new south porch may have been to preserve on holy ground the remains of individuals who had had to be moved from their original resting place. Following the Act of Union of Parishes in 1549, eleven churches in Lincoln were declared redundant, and the fabric of most was sold on as building materials. A further nine churches were demolished at other points in the sixteenth century. On logistical grounds it is probable that the building material for the porch at St Mark's, and hence also the bones, came from one of the other churches in the Wigford district, possibly the church of St Edward King and Martyr, since its parish was brought within the parish of St Mark's by the Act of Union of Parishes.

Death and the display of artefacts

While few objects are found in graves of the later Middle Ages, the transfer and even destruction of artefacts was still widely associated with burial. As at an earlier date, death was clearly a moment when property and movable wealth were handed over to heirs and other beneficiaries through the provisions made in wills, and through customary practice within the family and the community (see chapter 3). There is also some documentary evidence that the disposal or breaking of items associated with the deceased was a practice that occurred in the later Middle Ages. Examples include the breaking of seals associated with both lay and ecclesiastical lords. This appears to have been a practice that occurred in the church or at the site of the burial, and this may begin to explain such finds as the broken seal matrix from the priory of St Andrew, York (see also Daniell 1997, 151-2). There is also some evidence that noble households sometimes cast items into the grave of their lords.

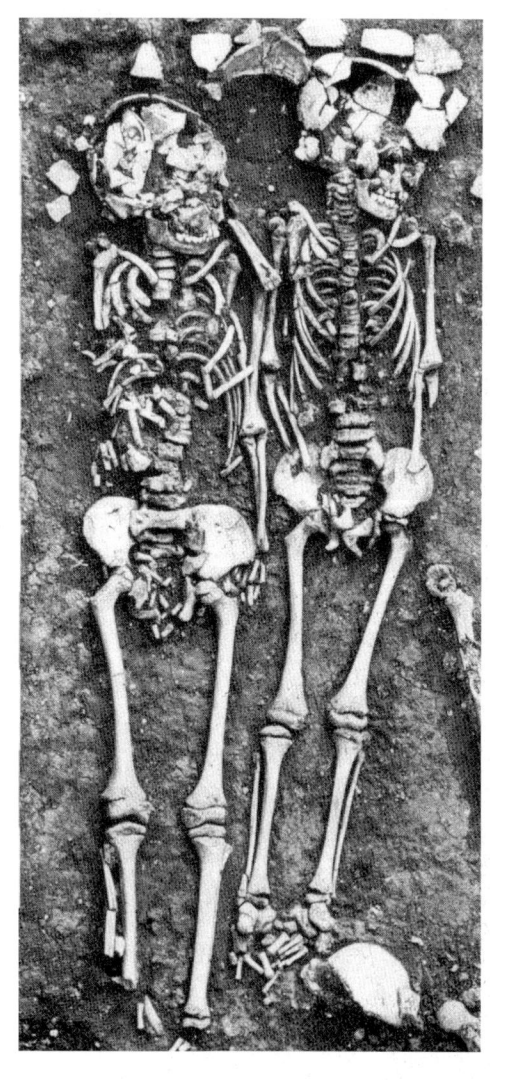

42 Double burial from St Helen-on-the-Walls, York. This grave contained two juveniles, both probably under 10 years of age. York Archaeological Trust for Excavation and Research Ltd, York

Noble households were usually closely involved in making arrangements for the funeral of the lord, and the funeral often marked the moment at which the household of a lord was formally broken up. Sometimes this was marked by the casting off of the symbols of office into the grave of the lord.

It has recently been suggested (Parker Pearson and Field 2001) that the ritual deposition of artefacts in rivers may have continued into the later Middle Ages in some regions. It is certainly notable that the river Witham near Lincoln has also yielded medieval artefacts in addition to the Anglo-Saxon artefacts, which are comparatively better known. Later medieval finds include swords, axes, a crossbow-bolt, an iron helmet, knives, chainmail and six iron candlesticks. While it is not impossible that these are simply 'chance losses', the possibility that votive deposition in rivers continued and perhaps had some sort of funerary significance is not entirely implausible. There are plenty of examples from the later Middle Ages of individuals and communities involved in religious or spiritual practices that did not conform to the expectations of the Church, and which might be condemned (see pp.89, 178). It is perhaps significant in this context that the river Witham through Lincolnshire was lined with later medieval religious houses. There were at least ten abbeys and priories, four hospitals and eight monastic granges. Was it the case that through the Middle Ages this river retained from an earlier time a 'strong spiritual sense of place' (Parker Pearson and Field 2001), which was reflected in both the location of religious properties and continuing votive deposition?

Death was also a moment at which various payments had to be made, both to lords and to the Church. Mortuary payments were commonly made in the form of clothing or animals, as we have seen. A group of ghost stories preserved at Byland Abbey (Yorks) *c*.1400 (see below, p.167) include a story of a man who met a group of people 'passing along the King's highway. And some rode sitting on horses and sheep and oxen, and some on other animals; and all the animals were those that had been given to the church when they died.' The ghosts in this story are riding the animals that they had given as mortuaries to the local church. Thus, long after grave goods had ceased to be common, death remained a moment at which goods, including animals, clothing and other personal artefacts, had to be exchanged.

Jewish burials

Excavation at the Jewish cemetery at Jewbury, York has provided important insights into the burial practices of the medieval Jewish community, and has revealed significant contrasts with non-Jewish burial practices (on the foundation of the cemetery see above, p.51). There was much less evidence of the disturbance of burials at Jewbury than is normally the case in medieval cemeteries. Given the relative density of burials in many parts of the cemetery this indicates that much care had been taken to avoid disturbance. It has been argued that Jewish custom may have had a much greater concern with avoiding the disturbance of burials (Lilley 1994, 307). Just 12% of burials at Jewbury were intercut, and only in 1.7% of instances were the bones of the earlier skeleton disturbed. By comparison, over 35% of the later medieval burials at the priory of St Andrew, York were intercut, and over 60% of the burials of St Benet's, York were intercut. One of the intercut burials at Jewbury contained the disarticulated remains of an adult male and a child, and the latter appears to have been disturbed when the adult was buried. One explanation for this may be that it was an attempt to create a family plot.

Most of the burials were contained within wooden coffins made from oak and Scots pine, and were joined with iron nails. Many of the coffins were held together by iron nails, and twenty had iron fittings, including corner brackets and brackets placed around the sides, which are comparatively rare (only one other example has been found in York, at the priory of St Andrew) (**43**). The coffins with fittings were clustered together and this, along with the rarity of this form of coffin, may indicate that the people buried in such coffins were a distinct group. Given that the fittings may also have served to strengthen the coffins, it has been postulated that they were the coffins of Jews in Lincoln who had to be transported to Jewbury for burial, a practice that continued until they acquired their own cemetery some time before 1290 when the Jews were expelled from England. There is some evidence for a few shrouded burials, in the form of antler 'toggles' positioned above the head, which were possible shroud fasteners. The tightly constricted bones of some skeletons may also indicate shrouded burial (although the same effect could conceivably have been achieved in a narrow coffin).

The burials were all aligned roughly southwest-northeast, and may have been arranged in this way in alignment with the boundaries of the property, which the Jewish community had acquired for the cemetery, and perhaps also so that they faced the entrance to the cemetery. Comparison with other excavated Jewish cemeteries suggests that there was not a standard alignment for Jewish burials. The normal burial position at Jewbury was with fully extended arms and legs, which is in contrast with other later medieval cemeteries where a high proportion of bodies were laid out with the arms resting on the body. Six burials at Jewbury, which lay outside the main cemetery area, were characterized by unusual burial positions. One had its arms folded across the body at 90, a second had the left arm on the right pelvis and the right arm flexed over the chest, a third had the left arm flexed at 90 over the chest and a fourth had the arms folded over the lower chest. Two of the burials had unusual alignments, one was east-west and the other had the head to the north end of a grave with a normal alignment. It has been suggested (Lilley 1994, 358) that these burials may have been those of the socially excluded — apostates, suicides, people of ill repute or baptized Jews perhaps. Certainly, they appear to be the graves of individuals who had deliberately not been given a burial that was normal for the cemetery. Most graves at the site were in individual grave cuts, but a few grave cuts contained more than

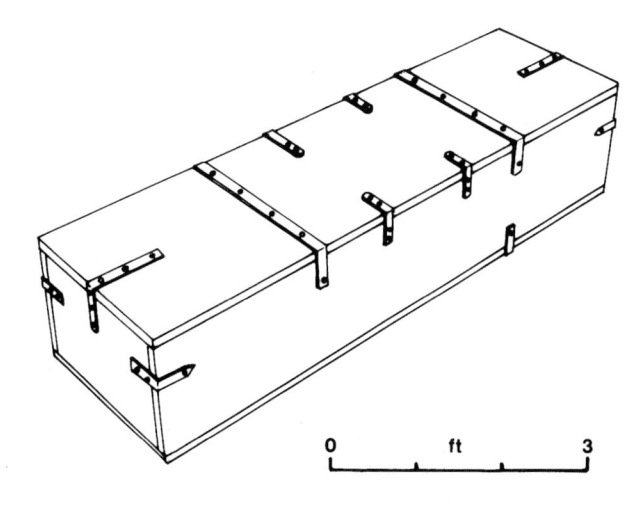

43 Reconstruction of a coffin from the cemetery at Jewbury, York. After Lilley 1994, Alex Norman

one burial, which may have been the graves for family groups or it may represent occasions when several individuals had to be buried at the same time.

Conclusion

Even with the decline in the use of grave goods after the seventh century it is clear that burial practices were anything but uniform. The form and alignment of graves and the positioning of bodies could vary enormously both within and between cemeteries. From time to time artefacts were still placed in graves, and it is clear that death remained a time when everyday artefacts, clothing and animals had to be handed over in the form of mortuaries, heriots, symbols of office and perhaps even votive deposition if that is how we may interpret the evidence from the river Witham. Yet despite this variation it is not easy to relate the form of a grave in any straightforward manner to the status or wealth of the individual buried there. The location of a grave may have more to reveal, as it is clear that wealth and status were determining factors in the burial of some individuals within churches or in certain favoured places in the churchyard.

5 Remembering the dead: memorials, commemoration and care of the soul

This chapter examines the various means by which the dead were remembered and commemorated in the Middle Ages, and the ways in which they sought to ensure the safe passage of their soul to Heaven. Commemoration may take many forms, and serve several purposes. For the wealthy various types of monument were available. In the Anglo-Saxon centuries stone crosses, grave slabs, grave markers and name stones are extremely common in many parts of northern England, and many of these were clearly intended both to mark a grave and to serve a commemorative role. Shrines and sarcophagi that were probably designed to be displayed rather than buried are also occasionally found. In the later Middle Ages the dead were commemorated by various types of grave slabs, effigies, brasses and tombs, and also by the prayers offered in the chantry chapels they established or in the guilds of which they were members. Commemoration was also afforded by the patronage the wealthy were able to give to churches through the window glass, fonts, architectural fabric and church plate that bore the names and the insignia of their patrons, and which were often used to invoke prayers for them. Indeed, forms of commemoration served not only as a reminder of the importance of a person, and by association their family, in the living world, but they also played an important role in ensuring the safe passage of the soul of the deceased, being a reminder of the need, or even a request, for prayers. Much lay investment was made in ensuring post-mortem prayers and services, most notably in the later Middle Ages through the endowment of chantry chapels.

For the rest of society forms of commemoration were undoubtedly just as important as for the wealthy, although they were less elaborate and expensive. Excavation has revealed that many Anglo-Saxon and medieval graves were marked with wooden markers, which may have served some sort of commemorative purpose — at the very least they must have been intended to identify the location of someone's grave, and to help prevent later disturbance. The dead of the poorer sectors of society might also be remembered in a sense by burial in or near prominent locations or features in the landscape, or near the commemorative monuments of the wealthy. In the later Middle Ages, for some of the poorer members of society membership of a religious guild was a possibility, and would ensure a decent funeral and sufficient post-mortem prayers, although they had to be able to pay their subscriptions. Some guilds also provided funerals for the poor of their community. On the whole, however, if we are to discuss further the poorer members of society we need to ask different questions of our evidence. We cannot discuss funerary monuments as they do not survive, and may scarcely have existed, for the poor. Instead, we need to think about the more general provisions of the Church for the poor, the experiences of the poor during attendance at church, so-called 'popular' notions about the dead, and the role that the poor played in the commemorative arrangements for the wealthy.

Commemoration in the Anglo-Saxon period: seventh, eighth and ninth centuries

By the eighth century elaborate assemblages of artefacts in graves were virtually unknown, which was in sharp contrast with the burial practices of previous centuries. Whatever the precise reasons for this transformation in burial practices (see above pp.17, 92-3), it is clear that it was not related to a cessation in the use of funerary display to express aspects of social status. As we have seen, the treatment of the dead in the grave did not become uniform, and differences are discernible in grave furniture, the dressing of the body and the placing of artefacts in the grave. However, increasingly it was to be above ground that display was focused rather than in the grave. Grave markers and grave slabs are not uncommon in northern England in the eighth and ninth centuries, and burial also commonly occurred in or near monuments of various types — including churches, mausolea and barrows. Reliquaries containing the remains of several individuals and furnished with inscriptions also served to commemorate the dead. Finally, for some of the most prominent members of society commemoration was achieved through written text. Thus, there was a variety of means by which the wealthy could be commemorated, although, as we shall see, this commemoration was often not long lasting.

Grave markers

To some extent most of the deceased members of society were commemorated in the short term if only passively and if by no other means than by their burial in a communal cemetery, which continued to be a focal point for burial. However, some were commemorated actively and for longer, or in more individual ways, through the provision of above-ground markers which served both to commemorate the dead and to make statements about them, their role in society and their families and peers that were also relevant to the living. A number of elaborate, and sometimes inscribed, stone grave slabs and crosses of eighth- or ninth-century date survive from northern England (see **1, 20, 21, 44**), and while crosses did not necessarily normally serve a funerary or commemorative purpose, inscriptions on a few suggest that some, at least, did. Those at Thornhill carry Old English and runic inscriptions recording for whom the monument was erected (see **20,21**). A cross shaft from Hackness (Yorks) is carved with both runic and Latin inscriptions to an Abbess Oedilburga (see above, p.32) (**45**). There are other examples of stone grave markers and crosses inscribed with personal names from elsewhere in northern England (e.g. Urswick, Carlisle and Bewcastle (Cumbria), Monkwearmouth and Jarrow (Co. Durham)). This adds considerable weight to the argument that stone crosses may have been employed to commemorate individuals, effectively serving as sculptural *liber vitae*. However, this form of commemoration in stone bearing inscriptions was far from common and only the very wealthy members of the lay or, more commonly one suspects, ecclesiastical elite were commemorated in this way.

At York, in the cemetery excavated beneath the Minster, a number of small, upright incised stone grave markers, or stelae, were found which are unparalleled in England. They date to the seventh to ninth century. They include the name of the deceased, and one inscription reveals that at least some were erected above the graves of the individuals commemorated: '+ Here [beneath this?] turf [or tomb?] rest the [remains?] of Wulfhere' (*see* **2**). The quality of the carving on some of the fragments is very varied, which suggests that two different hands were at work. This may indicate that the markers were reused and new carvings added. None of these markers was found *in situ* above a grave, and many had been reused as building material or in a couple of cases as parts of a composite stone coffin. The lack of weathering of the stelae has encouraged speculation that they were originally displayed within a building. This was presumably a church or chapel. Although the Anglo-Saxon location of St Peter's

44 Anglo-Saxon sculpture from Bakewell (Derbs). These sculptures have been stacked up in the porch of the church. Jim Williams

has not been firmly established, it was presumably in the vicinity. The emphasis on literacy on the stelae is paralleled on contemporary monuments at other religious communities such as Hartlepool (Cleveland), Monkwearmouth and Jarrow, and it is in contrast to the majority of monuments from the region, which do not bear inscriptions. It may indicate that they were made for an ecclesiastical, or at least a literate, elite.

At Whitby (Yorks) several simple stone crosses, some inscribed with individual names, have been excavated, and, as at York, the lack of weathering suggests that they were set up inside the church. It has been suggested that they were skeuomorphs of wooden crosses, and that they may have been intended to commemorate the wooden cross set up by King Oswald (633-42) before he engaged his pagan enemies in battle, and at which many miracles later occurred (Cramp 1993, 69). On the other hand, the similarity of the Whitby crosses to the cross carved on the base of St Cuthbert's wooden coffin, and the close relationship between Abbess Ælflaed of Whitby (d.714) and St Cuthbert (d.687), may suggest that the monuments at Whitby and Lindisfarne were linked in some way (Karkov

1999, 135). Stone grave covers and markers were doubtless relatively rare at this early date. More common may have been wooden markers. Evidence for the marking of graves in wood in the eighth or ninth centuries has been identified at Thwing (Yorks). Such markers may not have been the sole preserve of the wealthy. Many burials excavated from cemeteries of seventh- to ninth-century date reveal a lack of inter-cutting of graves, and this suggests that many burials were marked in some way above ground.

It may not only have been monuments inscribed with words and names that served commemorative functions. An unusual early carving of a mounted warrior — armed with a small round shield, sword and seax and wearing armoured shirt, long hose and heavily pleated skirt — on an eighth-century cross shaft from Repton (Derbs) may have served a commemorative purpose (**46**). The scene with the warrior derives from late Roman depictions of an emperor, and it has been suggested, on the basis of the form of the sculpture and its likely date, that the warrior was King Æthelbald of Mercia, who was murdered in 757 and buried at Repton (Biddle and Kjølbye-Biddle 1985).

Although some stone crosses served commemorative purposes, we have to remember two important points about such monuments. The first is that crosses need not necessarily have been erected at or near a burial, not least because in the Anglo-Saxon centuries it was not uncommon for a prominent person to be commemorated in more than one place, especially those with saintly pretensions. Secondly, it is far from likely that all crosses were used to commemorate individuals. Many more may have served simply liturgical functions (**47**). Nonetheless, this does not preclude them from having later become foci for burial. This was certainly the case when the burial

45 Anglo-Saxon sculpture from Hackness (Yorks). This cross-shaft is of late seventh- to early ninth-century date, and carries inscriptions in Latin and runes. After CASSS volume III, copyright University of Durham, Tom Middlemass

46 (above) Anglo-Saxon sculpture from Repton (Derbs). This sculpture is of eighth-century date and was found during recent excavations. The excavators think it may represent King Æthelbald of Mercia who was murdered in 757 and buried at Repton. Copyright Repton Excavations, photograph by Malcolm Crowther

47 (right) Anglo-Saxon sculpture from Bradbourne (Derbs). The cross had been broken up at some point in its history, but was reconstructed in the early part of the twentieth century. Phil Sidebottom

places were decided for St Cuthbert on Lindisfarne and for Abbot Sigewine at the monastery in the north of England described in the early ninth-century poem *De Abbatibus*. St Cuthbert requested burial 'near my oratory towards the south on the eastern side of the holy cross which I have erected there', and the body of Abbot Sigewine was placed 'for blessed quietude by the figure of the tall cross, which he himself had set up'.

Relics

As we have seen (above, pp.20-1), the coffins in which some individuals were entombed were so elaborate that it is likely that they were intended to be positioned above-ground. Examples include the sarcophagus from Derby (*see* **3**) and the panels and fragments that had probably once formed sarcophagi at Wirksworth (Derbs) (*see* **4**), Hovingham (Yorks) (**colour plate 1**) and South Kyme (Lincs) (*see* **5**). The individuals accorded such treatment are likely to have been both socially powerful and also probably saintly. Evidence for reliquaries, in the form of lead plaques inscribed with personal names, has also been found during excavations at both Kirkdale (Yorks) (**48**) and Flixborough (Lincs) (**colour plate 3**). The form of the inscriptions and of the personal names indicates that these plaques date to the eighth or ninth century, and they had presumably once been attached to boxes or chests. Indeed, the inscription from Kirkdale includes the word *ban-c[yst]*, which means 'bone-chest' or 'coffin'. Both of the lead plaques were excavated in contexts that suggest that they had been deliberately discarded at some point. The lead plaque from Kirkdale had been partially melted down when discovered beneath a layer which included eleventh-century pottery, and that from Flixborough was discovered in a rubbish pit. There was clearly no guarantee that those considered important enough to have their remains stored in a reliquary would continue to be commemorated or venerated. Indeed, there is another example of the recycling of funerary artefacts from Kirkdale in the form of its eleventh-century sundial, which it has recently been suggested was carved on a reused part of a stone sarcophagus (above, p.28).

Burial location

Commemoration was also achieved in a sense by where a person was buried. In the seventh century there was an increasing concern with monumentality in burial practices for the aristocracy. Burial in or near barrows, prehistoric monuments and churches became increasingly common during the seventh century. There is no reason to regard these as competing pagan (barrows, prehistoric monuments) and Christian (churches) practices, as there was nothing un-Christian about elaborate elite display. Burial in striking settings in or near above-ground markers may have served not only to commemorate the important status of the deceased but also may have been intended to stake claims to land on behalf of the families of the deceased. Such elite burials were also commonly accompanied by other burials, and although it is difficult to know who else was buried there — members of the family or kin-group, members of the household, other followers, members of the local community — they were presumably people who sought to gain some prestige for themselves and their remaining family through burial near to the monuments of the elite.

Although it is difficult for us to read at this remove, it may also be that where in a burial ground a person was buried had much to reveal about the life they had led, the forms of commemoration that they would receive and their likely fate in the afterlife. Indeed, contemporary continental sources indicate that where a person was buried in a churchyard might reflect the sort of life that they had led. Sinners, while not necessarily excluded from churchyard burial, were sometimes buried away from the favoured places, and less care was often taken over their burial. For example, according to Gregory of Tours (d.594),

Palladius, count of Javols, committed suicide, and although his body was accepted for burial at the monastery of Cournon (France) he was buried in ground away from the rest of the Christian community because of the stigma attached to his death. The burial location of such individuals may also have served to indicate, indeed to determine, the fate that awaited them in the afterlife (Effros 1997). Although it would ultimately be divine judgement that determined the fate of the soul, an appropriate burial and the prayers of living Christians were also important to easing the passage of the soul. For the Church to prejudice this must have both alarmed people and served to underline the sacral authority of the Church in this world and the next. There is no reason to doubt that continental examples provide an appropriate parallel for Anglo-Saxon England, and, indeed, the late seventh-century penitential attributed to Archbishop Theodore of Canterbury (d.690) indicates that the treatment of the deceased might vary according to their social status. For example, only monks and members of the ecclesiastical hierarchy would receive masses on the day of their interment, lay Christians would receive masses three days later, while the families of penitents would first have to fast and give oblations for seven or thirty days. The penitential also states that anyone who commissioned improper forms of commemoration, especially for heretics or penitents, would be obliged to perform penance for a year. Those who committed suicide were permitted masses if they had been suffering from insanity, but other suicides were only permitted to have alms and prayers. The clergy were increasingly becoming spiritual intermediaries between the living community and God, determining appropriate post-mortem commemoration, and access to salvation.

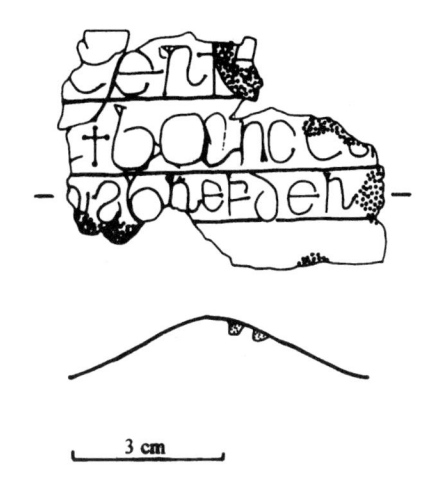

48 *Inscribed lead plaque from Kirkdale (Yorks).* After Watts and Rahtz 1997, Alex Norman

Written commemoration

Those who were elevated to sainthood often had *Lives* written about them. From our region there are *Lives* of Bishop Wilfrid written by his contemporary, the monk Stephen, of Guthlac (d.714) written by the monk Felix between *c.*730 and 749, and an anonymous *Life* and both prose and poetic *Lives* written by Bede about St Cuthbert. These *Lives* served to commemorate the saint and also, indirectly, other members of their religious communities and their lay and ecclesiastical contemporaries. The *Life of St Gregory* written about Pope Gregory the Great (d.604) by a member of the community of Whitby in the late seventh or early eighth century contains much information commemorating the achievements of various members of the Northumbrian royal family, especially relating to matters of religious observance. Such works clearly had some popularity as, for example, the *Life* of St Guthlac was drawn on in two poems of late eighth- or early ninth-century date and it was translated into vernacular prose towards the end of the ninth century. In addition, information concerning the special, particularly pious, qualities of some individuals was often recorded in narrative works, such as Bede's *Ecclesiastical History*.

Political issues clearly affected whether or how a prominent individual was commemorated in writing. Particularly instructive is the different treatment meted out in writing to the abbesses Hild (d.680) and Ælflaed of Whitby. Although Bede describes Hild's death, which was the good death required for someone to achieve sanctity, he does not record her dying words, nor does he say how or where she was buried. By contrast Bede has much more to say about Ælflaed, both in his *Ecclesiastical History* and in his prose *Life of St Cuthbert*, and in doing so he indicates that she was a religious woman who maintained an interest in the politics of her church and of Northumbrian society, as well as in the lives and careers of her family. Much is also said about Ælflaed in the anonymous *Life of St Gregory* written at Whitby. For example, when the bones of King Edwin (d.633) were discovered and taken to Whitby, only the names of the current abbess, Ælflaed, and her mother, Eanflaed, were recorded in a passage noting the fame of the monastery at Whitby — Hild is absent. There is some evidence to suggest that Ælflaed played a major role in the early eighth century in preserving the memory of members of her family and abbey, and also in determining who was excluded from the record. The names of Ælflaed and her mother Eanflaed (d.704) are recorded in the Lindisfarne *Liber Vitae*, but not that of Hild. Several members of Ælflaed's family are commemorated in stone at places associated with her. One of the commemorative stones from Whitby is inscribed with the letters +AHHAE+ which may commemorate Acha, who was the sister of Ælflaed's grandfather, King Edwin, and the inscription on a cross from Hackness (**45**), a daughter house of Whitby, may either commemorate Edwin's queen, Æthelburh, or, more probably, a later Abbess Æthelburh who accompanied Ælflaed to the death-bed of King Adlfrith of Northumria in 705. Whatever the identifications, it is striking that the written and the sculptural record relating to Whitby and Hackness commemorate a number of abbesses and hallowed queens, some of whom were certainly related, but apparently excluding Hild. It appears that Ælflaed had been successful in promoting the commemoration of her own family members above those of others, including Hild. The commemoration and the manipulation of the dead was an important means by which family power and authority could be established and maintained (Karkov 1999).

In sum, in the seventh, eighth and ninth centuries commemoration of the dead was achieved by a variety of means, including location, above-ground monuments, and, for the wealthy and the powerful, through both words and images. Who was commemorated, how long they were remembered, and whether and for how long prayers were offered for their souls was, of course, determined by the living community.

Commemoration in the tenth and eleventh century

Stone sculpture became increasingly common in northern England in the tenth and eleventh centuries and is found in at least three times as many places as in the eighth and

Remembering the dead: memorials, commemoration and care of the soul

49 Sculpture in situ above a grave at St Mark's, Lincoln. After CASSS volume III, copyright City of Lincoln Archaeology Unit

ninth centuries. This later sculpture is also much more explicitly funerary in nature. There are many more grave slabs and covers. Moreover, the iconography of the crosses, which includes many more images of secular figures than at an earlier date, suggests that more of them may have served to mark graves and/or to commemorate particular individuals. The commemoration of the laity became increasingly common in the tenth and eleventh centuries. Prior to this monuments were largely reserved for saints, abbots and kings.

Stone monuments

A number of sculptures of the later Anglo-Saxon period have been excavated *in situ* above a grave. Excavations at St Mark's, Lincoln revealed the grave of an adult male, which was marked by a stone marker with interlace decoration, placed over the chest (**49**). The burial was part of a row of burials that had grave markers, although only one survived, the others being identified from the presence of stake holes. In the cemetery excavated beneath York Minster the stone sculptures found there were in a context sealed by the footings of the Norman cathedral. The excavations confirmed that the sculpture was, indeed, of Anglo-Saxon date, a fact that previously had only been inferred on stylistic grounds. They also confirmed that the sculpture served a funerary purpose (**50, 51, 52**). Many of the excavated burials had decorated grave slabs above them, and some had end-stones, some of which

50 Excavation of later Anglo-Saxon cemetery at York Minster. Grave slabs with end-stones.. Royal Commission for Historical Monuments

had clearly been cut down and reused from previous contexts. Thus, some monuments are stylistically rather earlier than the archaeological context in which they were found. Another grave slab was a Roman inscribed stone to which an Anglo-Saxon inscription had been added — 'Pray for the soul of Costavn'. This indicates that the community using the burial ground in the later Anglo-Saxon centuries was prepared to reuse earlier monuments, which is particularly striking because at the same time they were also innovating in the production and display of stone sculpture. There are a few grave-markers that incorporate Scandinavian iconography — such as Sigurd (**52**) and Wayland the Smith — revealing that the Scandinavian influence had been absorbed into the commemorative repertoire of this cemetery. It is difficult to say who was burying their dead in this cemetery — the indigenous populations or the Scandinavian newcomers. Yet, whichever group used the cemetery, and it may have been both, a variety of strategies were clearly employed to commemorate the dead. Either the Scandinavians were prepared to reuse earlier monuments, or the indigenous population was prepared to adopt new Scandinavian motifs, or perhaps both communities were prepared, at the very least, to bury their dead in the same place. It may have been social status rather than ethnic allegiance that determined who was buried in the York Minster cemetery and what sort of monument was used for their grave. The excavations at York also revealed two infants (one 3-5 years, the other 10-12 years) with stone grave markers, suggesting that status could be inherited in later Anglo-Saxon York, and not simply acquired through one's actions.

Remembering the dead: memorials, commemoration and care of the soul

51 *Sculpture and burials from York Minster.* Royal Commission for Historical Monuments

52 *Sculpture and burials from York Minster. This panel depicts the heroic figure of Sigurd, plunging his sword into a dragon.* Royal Commission for Historical Monuments

53 (left) Cross-shaft from Nunburnholme (Yorks). A carving of the heroic figure Sigurd and another figure, probably monstrous, was added to this sculpture, partly obliterating the image of a priest above. The feet of the priest are still visible below the two lower figures. After CASSS volume III, copyright University of Durham, Tom Middlemass

The York excavations were also important in confirming that the monuments would have been painted. A few small fragments retained traces of pigments, and they reveal that the relief carving was enhanced with different colours from the backgrounds. Other York sculptures from St Mary, Castlegate and the Clifford Street excavations, and sculptures from Middleton, Otley and Burnsall (Yorks) also retained traces of pigment. The funerary monuments of the Anglo-Saxon period were, it is clear, highly colourful artefacts. They may also have been set with precious stones and metal, to judge from the incidences of sockets set into sculptures.

It was once thought that some aspects of later Anglo-Saxon stone sculpture were 'pagan', particularly scenes which carried images derived from Norse mythology and those images which depicted activities which one would not normally associate with the Church (for example, hunting or the brandishing of weapons). However, this view has recently been revised. The body of stone sculpture from northern England is now widely regarded as belonging to a Christian milieu. It has been argued by Richard Bailey (1997, 77-94) that both scenes derived from Norse mythology and other secular scenes could be interpreted as Christian teaching and art 'being presented in Scandinavian terms', in which parallels were drawn between Christian themes and Scandinavian mythology and pagan beliefs. There are, for example, possible parallels drawn on a cross-shaft at Nunburnholme (Yorks) between depictions of the Scandinavian legend of Sigurd (who killed a dragon and after tasting its blood learns of the treacherous plans of his stepfather, Reginn) and eucharistic images. Both involve enlightenment through consumption, of the dragon's blood and the Host respectively (**53**). Parallels may also have been intended between images of St John with

54 (right) Cross-shaft from Leeds (Yorks). Note the image of Wayland the flying Smith from Norse mythology in the bottom panel of the cross-shaft, which is accompanied by images of evangelists and ecclesiastics, birds and figures with wing-like cloaks. Is a link being made between Wayland and winged angels and evangelists? After a reconstruction of the cross-shaft by Peter Brears, Alex Norman

his eagle and Wayland the flying smith on a cross-shaft at Leeds (Yorks) (**54**). Other images may have had resonance for both Christian and pagan viewers. For example, the snakes on a cross-shaft at Masham (Yorks) may have been understood as either the serpent at the end of the world from Scandinavian mythology, or the dragons and leviathans of Isaiah, Job, the Psalms and Revelation, or both. The figure with two birds perched on his shoulder at Kirklevington (Yorks) may have been understood either as Odin and his attendant ravens, or as a Christian symbol of resurrection, if not as an individual, recently deceased, warrior (**55**). Such images may have been deliberately ambiguous, and intended to have multiple meanings. The Anglo-Saxon Church had long proved itself adept at absorbing the aristocratic ethos of society, and there is, in fact, little about the tenth-century stone sculpture of the region that can be regarded as unacceptable within a Christian milieu. It has recently been suggested by David Stocker (2000) that the tenth-century sculpture often drew on images of saints in its depictions of secular rulers, thus demonstrating the interrelatedness of lordship and the Church in the tenth century.

The sculpture was also a very visible manifestation of lordship, and of a period of contact and acculturation between the settlers and the local populations, drawing on both Scandinavian and indigenous motifs. Most of the sculptures were apparently displayed in or near churches. The grave slabs were clearly funerary monuments, and the stone crosses may also have served as memorials to individuals. The figures depicted on some of the sculptures were perhaps intended to be, not (or not only) gods or heroic figures, but real and identifiable warriors (*see* **34, 55, 57**). The proliferation of stone monuments in the tenth century was seemingly under secular influence as the local elite employed them both to signify their status and their political allegiances, and to memorialize themselves or their peers. The increasing secular influence on sculpture is suggested by the iconography that both becomes increasingly diverse and displays many more 'secular' images, and by the range of churches with which it is associated, both major religious communities and other fairly ordinary 'parish' churches. Regional patterns in the ornamentation, form and iconography of the sculpture have been identified, and, in addition to this reflecting the locations of schools of sculptural production, it may also reflect regional polities, in which lords signalled their allegiances and status through the commissioning and display of

55 (left) Cross-shaft from Kirklevington (Yorks). Is the figure on the cross-shaft Odin with his attendant ravens? Or a Christian image, perhaps of St John the Evangelist? Alex Norman

particular forms of sculpture. For example, there was a transformation in the form and ornamentation of the monuments of northern Lincolnshire in the tenth century away from styles typical of the North towards styles of ornamentation much more reminiscent of southern styles. David Stocker has linked this with both the capture of Lincolnshire by King Edmund and attempts to reunite the province of Lindsey with southern England and the diocese of Canterbury (the most significant development of which was the re-establishment of a bishop of Lindsey). He has described the later tenth-century monuments of northern Lincolnshire as 'the colonial monuments of the southern church'. The elite of northern Lincolnshire appear to have been memorializing themselves in distinctive regional fashions through which they reflected their cultural and political allegiances. As they sought to consolidate their authority they used the Church, and their patronage seemingly extended beyond the major churches of the region to a new group of local or manorial churches. In the Peak District of Derbyshire and southern Yorkshire, sculpture is noted for its lack of Scandinavian influence. It may be that the elites of those regions were using sculpture to assert their regional identity and perhaps also to signify their allegiance to the southern rulers. Indeed, there is documentary evidence to show that lords were being encouraged to buy land from 'the heathen' by Edward the Elder, the West Saxon king who was eventually to begin the conquest of areas of Scandinavian settlement.

Tenth-century sculpture in Yorkshire and Lincolnshire is different from the sculpture that preceded it, not only in terms of ornamentation, but also in terms of location and function, since much more is clearly funerary than had previously been the case. At most churches there is sculpture from only a small number of monuments, and Paul Everson and David Stocker (1999, 76-9) have suggested that many of these sculptures were the founding monuments in a new generation of parochial graveyard. However, there are a number of churches with many more sculptures. On the available evidence the distinguishing factor does not appear to be that these were the mother churches of the region, but rather that these churches were located in trading places (usually riverine or coastal), such as St Mark's and St Mary-le-Wigford (in what has been dubbed the 'strand' of Lincoln), Marton-on-Trent, Bicker (on the fen edge) (Lincs), St Mary Bishophill Senior (in what has been identified as a beach market-place on the banks of the Ouse in York), Yarm, Kirklevington, and Lythe (Yorks). These graveyards with exceptional

56 Sculpture from Levisham (Yorks). This beast has been much debated. Some believe that it echoes Scandinavian style, but others have argued that it owes much to indigenous carving styles. It is not implausible that contemporaries would have viewed it differently according to their previous experiences of animal ornamentation. Alex Norman

numbers of monuments may, then, belong to unusual settlements with distinctive elite populations, with a sizable number of newcomers (in the form of merchants) whose social competitiveness was played out, amongst other ways, through funerary display.

As has already been observed (above, p.111), there may be a connection between the warrior imagery and scenes from heroic culture displayed on some of the stone crosses and the probably slightly earlier funerary displays of weapons and other symbols of elite male lordship. For a short time, in a turbulent situation, in the later ninth and early tenth century masculine and military imagery was once again employed in the processes of social negotiation through burial display, both in the grave and above ground. Warrior and heroic imagery is found on sculpture at, for example, Middleton (**57**), Skipwith, Weston, York Minster (Yorks) (*see* **52**), Norbury (*see* **34**) and Brailsford (Derbs). It is impossible to say who commissioned this sculpture. However, it might be appropriate to draw parallels with the historically attested role of aristocratic women in preserving dynastic memory and commemoration in other early medieval societies. Stone sculpture was not common in the Scandinavian homelands and the styles and motifs found on tenth-century sculpture in northern England are really only paralleled in Scandinavia on jewellery, weapons, fabrics, wood and bone-working. Women are thought to have played a part in the transmission of cultural and artistic traditions through the domestic environment.

A form of monument peculiar to the tenth century is the so-called 'hogback' monument, of which over 100 examples survive (**58**). Although there may be similarities to be drawn between hogbacks and pre-Viking shrines of seventh- to ninth-century date, the very act of burying numerous members of the secular elite under such stone monuments was an innovation. The hogbacks also carry iconography, which amalgamates pagan and Christian themes, and David Stocker (2000) has suggested that they may have been used to commemorate the conversion process. The hogbacks were clearly intended to resemble houses — they often have roofs, they appear like bow-sided halls, and one even has a door. Many have beasts holding on to the gable ends of the roofs, often with them in their mouths, and they appear to be muzzled bears. Stocker's interpretation of these monuments suggests that the house was intended to represent the lord and/or his family, and the bear was a symbol of conversion from paganism to Christianity. Although the bear had some negative symbolic qualities (e.g. sloth and lust), it was also thought to give its cubs life by holding them between its paws and licking them, thus making it a suitable symbol of conversion.

'Viking' burials

The problems of identifying the burials of the Scandinavian settlers in the later ninth and tenth centuries have already been discussed (above p.33-4). The most clearly Scandinavian burial site in the region is that at Heath Wood, Ingleby (Derbs), and this provides an example of the use of barrows to mark the status of, and presumably commemorate, the deceased. There are 59 barrows, of which around a third have been excavated (**colour plate 6**). Many, and perhaps all, of the barrows covered the site of a funeral pyre, upon which burned human bones remained, alongside metal items and cremated animals. The barrows are mostly clustered into four distinct groups, which recent earthwork survey suggests is a real phenomenon rather than the product of differential survival. These may have been associated with distinct family or kinship groups. Not all of the barrows certainly contained human remains, and it has been suggested that these were 'cenotaph mounds' put up to commemorate individuals buried elsewhere. However, the most recent fieldwork revealed a cremation off-centre in the mound, and this has led to speculation

57 Cross-shaft with from Middleton (Yorks). After CASSS volume III, copyright University of Durham, Tom Middlemass

58 Fragment of a hogback monument from Dewsbury (Yorks). Jim Williams

that earlier excavations may have missed evidence for cremations because they excavated through the centre of the mound. The visibility of the mounds, which showed up black against the surrounding red-coloured soils, and the investment in the cremation cemetery at Heath Wood, which included the possible use of ship strakes as funerary biers in addition to the raising of mounds and the creation of ditches, may be indicative of 'instability and insecurity of some sort . . . a statement of religious, political and military affiliation in unfamiliar and inhospitable surroundings' (Richards *et al* 1995, 66). This combination of ship symbolism, cremation, mound burial and sacrifice is, perhaps, the most overt statement of 'Scandinavianness', of 'otherness', found in northern England. Here, for once, we probably can see the Scandinavian settlers behaving in a self-consciously 'Scandinavian' manner.

The leaders of the Scandinavian settlers showed themselves to be adept at adopting the indigenous styles and insignia of lordship, including, it is suggested, burial and forms of commemoration. There is no doubt that the Church and the material culture associated with it were important elements in the consolidation of power over parts of the region in the tenth century, and this may begin to explain why the newcomers so easily adopted churchyard burial and the indigenous practice of raising stone monuments, irrespective of their personal religious beliefs, and it may also begin to explain the relative dearth of burials accompanied by grave goods. The Church offered a more visible, permanent marker of status and means of commemoration in the form of above-ground markers, both churches and stone monuments, and this may have been where investment was placed. Stone monuments in a churchyard provided a very visible, public statement, which permitted an individual, a family or community to convey a distinctive political and cultural message through their form and decoration. However the Scandinavian settlers chose to bury their dead, it is clear that commemoration with stone monuments was quickly adopted. It is their influence on the production of stone sculpture that was the most distinctive element of Scandinavian forms of commemoration, and this influence was clearly wedded to indigenous forms of commemoration. Stone sculpture was scarcely known in Scandinavia in the ninth century, with the exception of the island of Gotland which had a collection of carved stone monuments, but which are very different in form from the monuments found in England. The people who commissioned stone monuments in England in the tenth century, and those who made them, were drawing on a combination of traditions. Yet, while lords of this period were clearly drawing on forms and expressions of lordship familiar to them in either Scandinavia or England, they were also modifying lordship and its insignia at the same time. Thus the stone sculpture of the tenth century did not simply mirror the interests and insignia of lords, but rather it was used to create new lordly ideals and images.

The Norman Conquest

As we have seen (above pp.39-42), the Norman Conquest created a number of changes to the funerary landscape of England, in particular concerning where the elite were buried, as many of the newly-arrived elite faced a choice about burial in either England or Normandy. This, in turn, had an impact on where the dead were commemorated, and on associations between lordly families and given churches. The later eleventh century and early twelfth century saw the rebuilding of many parish churches, and the foundation of many religious houses by new Norman lords. Many subsequently chose to be buried in these churches. In many ways, these new church foundations were, in themselves, monuments to their founders and patrons. In some instances new Norman lords tried to enhance their associations with newly encountered, or newly-founded, churches. For example, Robert de Lacy founded a Cluniac priory outside his castle at Pontefract (Yorks) in 1090, and there is evidence to suggest that he moved his parents from their original resting-places to be buried on either side of the altar of St Benedict under marble slabs, thus increasing his familial associations with this foundation. On the other hand the political instabilities of the later eleventh and early twelfth century often discouraged such close associations with a given house. Earl Waltheof, the last English earl of Northampton, was executed at Winchester (Hamps) in 1076 following his revolt against William the Conqueror and buried at Crowland Abbey (Lincs). His widow Judith, a niece of William the Conqueror, was not buried at his side, perhaps for understandable reasons, and is traditionally thought to have been buried at a nunnery in Elstow (Northants). Later Waltheof's heir, Maud, was buried at Scone in Scotland having married David I of Scotland, after her first husband, Simon I de St Liz, died on crusade and was buried abroad. There was, thus, no continuity in the burial practices and locations of commemoration of the members of this particular earldom, apparently due to a combination of political intrigue and dynastic factors. Similar factors, although they are much harder to trace, may have lain behind the strange burial strategies of the counts of Brittany and lords of Richmond (Yorks). Both Alan I and Alan II were buried in Bury St Edmunds (Suffolk), while the next count, Stephen, was buried in York and his son Alan III was buried at Bégard (France). Although the religious houses at both Bury St Edmunds and Bégard were patronized by the earls it is not immediately apparent why successive earls were buried in such diverse locations. Other reasons which may lie behind such inconsistencies in aristocratic burial traditions include the apparently increasing

59 Grave cover from Dewsbury (Yorks). The cross-shaft carved in high relief on this stone is surrounded by two dragons. There was originally an inscription on the stone, but 'hic iacet . . .' ('here lies . . .') is the only part now legible. Jim Williams

preference for the newly founded religious orders, such as the Cistercians and Augustinians, directing patronage, and desire for burial, away from the older Benedictine houses. Gilbert de Ghant refounded the Benedictine house at Bardney (Lincs) and both he and his son Walter (d.1139) were buried there, but Walter's son, Gilbert II, chose to be buried at his Augustinian foundation in Bridlington (Yorks) where he had been baptized and brought up. Whatever lay behind the various aristocratic strategies, one thing is clear: if the Normans wished to commemorate their *Normanitas* through their funerary practices it is striking that so few of them chose to be buried in Normandy (Golding 1986).

The Norman Conquest also had a direct impact on commemoration of the deceased in some places as cemeteries were obliterated in the wake of castle-building campaigns, as happened at Newark, Pontefract and York (above pp.40-1), and even in the face of ecclesiastical building campaigns, as can be seen from the excavations at the Norman Cathedral at York. On the whole, however, it is difficult to link transformations of cemeteries directly to the Norman Conquest. In any case, as we have seen, transformations in the organization of cemeteries could hardly be claimed to be a Norman innovation, nor did it cease to occur after the early years of Norman rule. Finally, elaborately decorated monumental stone sculpture, both grave covers and crosses, appears to have gone out of fashion after the eleventh century. Few examples of stone grave markers can be dated to the twelfth century, although the tradition did not completely die out and notable exceptions may be found — such as the elaborate grave covers at Conisbrough and Dewsbury (Yorks) (**59**), and the crosses at Keddington, Revesby, Minting, Lincoln (the Cathedral, St Mark's and St Botolph's), Digby, Aunsby, Londonthorpe and Castle Bytham (Lincs). This continuing tradition in some regions may have been especially significant in the face of a new ruling elite, and we should not forget that these were expensive items, which took time to make. However, it was not to be long before standing crosses had ceased to be commissioned and grave slabs became increasingly plain, commonly decorated only with a cross. Moreover, many pieces of sculpture were incorporated into the fabric of churches built or rebuilt in the eleventh and twelfth centuries, suggesting that their function and resonance had ceased to be relevant. For example, at Glentworth (Lincs) a tenth-century grave-marker was reused in the north jamb of the west window of the tower, and appears to have been an original feature of the late eleventh-century church tower. The Repton rider stone (*see* **46**) was discovered near to the church in a pit (possibly used for scaffolding during building work), which was probably dug in the eleventh century, since it cut later Anglo-Saxon burials, but was itself cut by an eleventh-century charcoal burial. It is, however, possible that the very fact that some Anglo-Saxon monuments continued to be visible in the fabric of churches indicates that they were respected as special, even holy, monuments. Examples include sculptures reused in the fabric of churches at Great Hale, Hougham, St Mary-le-Wigford, Lincoln (Lincs), and Kirkdale. On the other hand, many more pieces were lost to view in these building campaigns, and it is doubtless inappropriate to seek single explanations for the fate of stone sculpture production and display, or simple interpretations of what this may have to reveal about attitudes to the dead of an earlier era and political regime.

The later Middle Ages

For all of the laity the need to assist the soul was everywhere made apparent in churches, but there were many more ways of providing forms of commemoration and aids to the soul for the wealthier members of society. The funerary monuments, chantry chapels and guilds of those members of the laity who could afford them impinged on everyone else because of their very visibility and because of the space they took up in parish churches. Indeed, the religious experiences of parishioners could be greatly affected by the monuments to the wealthy as they blocked access to parts of the church and obscured their view of the altar and the Host, which gave rise to many complaints.

Funerary monuments
Later medieval churches were full of monuments to the deceased, so much so that it is possible to speak of a veritable invasion of churches by the secular. Some churches, in effect, became the mausolea of leading families. This development did not go without comment, or criticism. The fourteenth-century preacher from the Gilbertine priory at Sempringham (Lincs), Robert Mannyng, commented in his penitential manual for the laity that lords wanted to have 'Proude stones lyggyne an hye on here grave', which would lead to damnation in death. In William Langland's *Piers Plowman* of the later fourteenth century, the poet criticizes the ostentatious display in friaries, particularly commenting on the stained-glass windows in which donors were depicted. However, the target of his criticism is less the secular ostentation than the means by which money had been obtained to pay for it (Martindale 1992, 167). On the whole, however, it is striking that there is little contemporary comment on, or condemnation of, this development in patronage, and it may be because it was of too great a benefit to the Church to be condemned. Indeed, ecclesiastics seem to have actively encouraged it, and many monasteries had on display an effigy of their founder and of subsequent patrons. The only exception to this appears to

60 Grave covers in the porch at Bakewell (Derbs). This collection shows the range of crosses to be found on medieval grave covers and some of the types of other symbols that accompanied the crosses. Jim Williams

have been cathedrals, which seem to have been dominated by monuments to bishops and members of the cathedral clergy. It is not clear whether this was because cathedral communities sought to retain their churches as their own preserve, or whether it was because the competition was too great for secular lords, who were better placed to make an impact with their monuments in other settings. Not only was a secular influence largely absent from the funerary monuments and chantry chapels of York Minster, but it was also conspicuous by its relative absence in the decorative work of the Minster. Had his plans been realized, however, the intended chantry foundation for Richard II in York Minster would have had a major impact on the church, as it was envisaged as involving 100 priests and six new altars. Perhaps only royalty could really compete in the cathedral environment.

Monuments were not always erected at the place where a person was buried. Moreover, some individuals were commemorated by more than one monument set up in different places. Perhaps the most famous example of that from our region concerns Queen Eleanor of Castile, the wife of Edward I, who died in 1290 at Harby (Notts). Crosses were set up at the places where her body rested on its way to London, including Lincoln, Grantham and Stamford (Lincs). Her body was buried at Westminster and her heart in the Dominican friary in London, while her viscera were buried at Lincoln Cathedral, where a gilded bronze effigy to her was placed. It is now lost but it may have

61 Grave covers in the porch at Bakewell (Derbs). Jim Williams

been similar to that still in Westminster Abbey to judge from a seventeenth-century drawing of the Lincoln monument.

Grave slabs

As we have already seen (above p.143), the elaborate grave covers of the Anglo-Saxon period gave way in the twelfth century to plainer flat or coped grave slabs, usually decorated with a cross. It is clear that a great deal of choice was available to patrons and that even at the same church a wide variety of types of cross and occasionally other motifs may be found on grave slabs. Many of the 300 slabs discovered at Bakewell (Derbs) when the south transept was rebuilt in 1841 are now stacked up in the porch of the church (**60 & 61**), and they bear testimony to the variation in types of monument to be found at a single church. Crosses are sometimes accompanied on grave slabs by other items. These include, most commonly, swords (presumably symbols of masculinity and the right, not to mention wealth, to bear arms), and shears (possibly a symbol of the feminine identity of the person for whom the slab was made, being a relatively common domestic item). Chalices, patens and books were symbols of priestly or monastic status. Indeed, excavations at Monk Bretton Priory (Yorks) revealed that a grave slab depicting a chalice was placed over a burial containing a chalice. Other symbols found less commonly on grave slabs include knives, keys (possibly, as some have argued, a symbol of office-holding used for stewards or mayors, but more likely another feminine symbol), and shields (sometimes bearing coats of arms). Bows and arrows are found on slabs at Baslow (Derbs)

(**62**) and Melsonby (Yorks), and a hunting horn on a belt or balderic is found on slabs at Baslow, Bakewell, Hope and Darley (Derbs), and both of these emblems may have signified that they were the monuments of forresters. Grave slabs at Baslow and Sprotborough (Yorks) include both a sword and priestly symbols (chalice, book, paten), but it is not clear what this signified. It may have indicated both the aristocratic and priestly status of the deceased, if it does not simply reflect the reuse of a monument and the addition of new symbols.

Grave slabs might be set up over burials both inside and outside churches, although few now survive *in situ*. Coped slabs, such as those at Ackworth, Darrington and Methley (Yorks), were clearly designed to lie in the churchyard, and, indeed, these three monuments all have small drilled holes, which were presumably intended to allow water to drain off (**63**). Flat stones may have been located either inside the church or in the churchyard. Grave slabs were not only important elements of the commemorative repertoire of the wealthier sectors of later medieval society, but they also served practical functions, such as identifying the precise location of burials, which enabled, amongst other things, the reopening of graves to receive subsequent burials. For example, in his will of 1448 rector William Styward requested burial in the choir of the church of St Helen-on-the-Walls, York, 'under a marble slab beneath which lies my mother's body'. The terms of this will also remind us that grave slabs were not simply made of stone. Slabs made of marble and alabaster are also known: for example, the alabaster slab at Norbury (Derbs) (**64**) probably made for Elizabeth, wife of Ralph Fitzherbert, who are both commemorated by one of the alabaster tombs in the church (**69**). Wills sometimes provide evidence for the commissioning of particular types of monument. In 1376, Sir Marmaduke Constable requested burial in the church at Flamborough (Yorks) and asked for three 'marble' (the word may also have signified alabaster) slabs to be made and placed over the graves of his father, his mother and himself. Sir Thomas Ughtred requested in his will of 1398 a marble slab and two brasses to be placed over the tomb of his parents in Catton (Yorks), although he wished himself to be buried in the church of the Dominicans at York.

As was the fate of earlier monuments, later medieval grave slabs were not immune to recycling. Many, such as those at Bakewell, were to be built into the fabric of churches, and lost to sight, until uncovered at a later date during renovation work, for example.

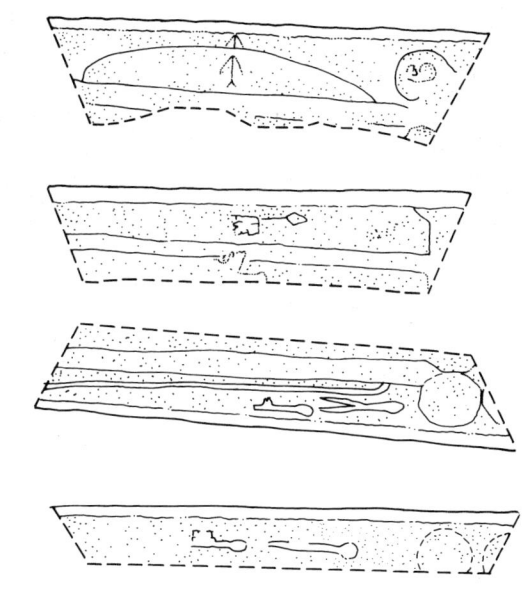

62 *Grave slabs reused as window lintels from Baslow (Derbs). The slabs have been cut down to serve their new purpose.* Jo Mincher

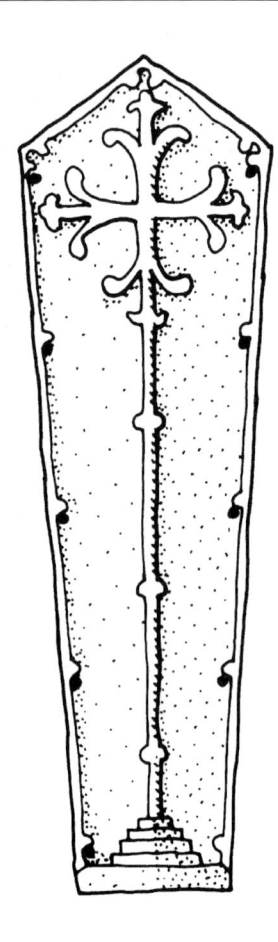

Remembering the dead: memorials, commemoration and care of the soul

63 (above left) Grave cover from Darrington (Yorks). This slightly coped stone has a series of small drilled holes along the edges, which were presumably intended to drain off water collecting behind the moulding. Jo Mincher

64 (above right) Alabaster slab commemorating Elizabeth Fitzherbert at Norbury (Derbs). Jim Williams

Others were incorporated into the fabric of churches so as to remain still visible. For example, slabs were used intact as window lintels at Bradbourne (Derbs), Wath-upon-Dearne (Yorks) and Baslow, where five were reused for the windows of the clerestory built in the fifteenth century (**62**).

Monumental brasses

English brass manufacture began in the thirteenth century. The production of figure brasses developed into an industry in London in the 1280s and 1290s largely in response to ecclesiastical demand, with the earliest being made for bishops and abbots. Figural brasses existed alongside cross-brasses, which were clearly influenced by the long-

65 Monument to Nicholas Fitzherbert at Norbury (Derbs). Jim Williams

standing tradition of carved relief cross-slabs in stone. Other forms of brass included those that were simply inscriptions made up of brass letters set in stone or Purbeck marble, such as those made for Dean William de Lessington (d.1272) and Archdeacon Simon de Barton (d.1280) at Lincoln Cathedral.

Brasses began as an ecclesiastical art form and monument, but by the earlier fourteenth century had been adopted by lay lords. They offered commemoration both through the images depicted and through words. There was a repetition of style and imagery in many brasses, including the posture of the figures, the clothing they wear, the display of heraldic devices, the invocation to pray for the souls of the departed, and so on, yet there was still room for some variation and personalization of brasses. In particular, smaller brasses do not maintain the stylistic consistency of larger brasses, and they demonstrate much greater evidence for stylistic and iconographic experimentation (**66, 67**).

Brasses were not uncommonly reused. The brass of Sir Anthony Fitzherbert at Norbury (Derbs) (d.1538) has on the reverse the figure of a woman, who may be Matilda de Verdun (d.1316). This brass had probably come from the dissolved abbey of Croxden (Staffs). A Flemish brass at Topcliffe (Yorks), which depicts Thomas de Topcliffe and his wife (1391), has also been reused, because on the reverse there is a depiction of part of a kogge, or trading ship, used by Hansa merchants. A small brass at Hampsthwaite (Yorks), depicting a civilian of *c*.1350-60 was reused in 1570, when someone scratched an inscription on the figure. The Hampsthwaite brass is a rare survival of a brass to a civilian figure that is shown wearing a tight-fitting jacket, a cape with a hood, a belt with a pouch and dagger attached, and tight-fitting hose.

There are a number of carved slabs with crosses or busts from the region into which brass letters have been set. The lettering appears to have been an afterthought rather than an integral part of the design. For example, at Stow (Lincs) an Ancaster slab with the bust of a woman has an epitaph in brass letters which reads *'Alle men that bere lif/Prai for Emme was Fuk wife'*. Such creations are not necessarily the work of brass manufacturers and could have been created by masons from letters they had purchased. The lettering on a slab at Thornton-le-Moor (Lincs) is made up of a mixture of styles of letters, which may have been plundered from other tombs. Brass was also occasionally used to make effigies, such as that apparently made for Bishop Robert Grosseteste at Lincoln.

66 Brass from Sprotborough (Yorks). This late fifteenth-century brass commemorates William Fitzwilliam and his wife. There is a lion at his feet, and a dog at the feet of his wife. Jim Williams

Brasses may be dated and provenanced by a variety of means: the inscription (both its content and form), by the styles of the engraving, and by the style of the dress and armour depicted. We have to remember, however, that brasses might be commissioned long before the death of the person or people they were to commemorate, or have been made long afterwards, so the date of manufacture and the date of the death recorded in the inscription may not be the same. Workshops in London led the way in producing high quality brasses for an expanding market, although the importance of regional workshops, in places such as York, Lincoln, and to a lesser extent, Boston and Stamford (Lincs), is increasingly being recognized. Brasses also came into England from the continent, Germany and Flanders in particular. Brasses were commonly set into slabs, often of Purbeck marble, or mounted on tombs, thus the setting of the brass was an important component of its impact. One of the earliest brasses from the region was made in York for Archbishop William Greenfield (d.1315), and it was associated with an elaborate tomb.

67 *Brass from Tideswell (Derbs). This brass commemorates Robert Lytton (d.1483) and his wife Joan (d.1458). Not only was the brass made at least 25 years after the death of Joan, but the style of dress suggests that it may have been made some time after the death of Robert. Lytton was Under-Treasurer of England in the reign of Henry VI.* Jim Williams

The brass is badly worn, but there are signs that the archbishop was depicted beneath a canopy, as was common on contemporary brasses being produced in London, although the engraving of the clothing was much more 'fiddly' and refined than on London brasses, which has encouraged speculation that the York engravers were used to working either on a smaller scale or in a different material, such as glass (Binski 1987, 78).

There are similarities between brasses and effigial sculpture. The subject matter is commonly the same, and lords are usually depicted in their military finery, and ecclesiastics in their robes of office and accompanied by ecclesiastical equipment. Brasses provided an opportunity for lords to display their heraldic devices, and were part of the way in which wealthy families could dominate their local churches. However, it is important to note that few lords only patronized their local churches, and for many the local church may not even have been the main focus of their devotion or commemoration. Brasses were not even necessarily placed where the deceased was buried. An instructive example comes from Cowthorpe (Yorks) where there is an elaborate, although partly lost, brass to Brian Rouclyff, a lawyer who became Baron of the Exchequer in 1458, and his wife, Joan (**68**). The brass shows their coats of arms, those of the Rouclyffs and the Hammertons, impaling various other family arms, and shows the couple holding a model of a church, which was presumably intended to represent the church of Cowthorpe. A now lost part of the inscription, which was recorded in 1845, apparently described Brian Rouclyff as the founder of the church (he was responsible for rebuilding it in the 1450s). There is also a small memorial at the bottom of the brass, in the form of a bier covered by a pall, to John Burgh, who was the maternal uncle of Brian Rouclyff, for whom his nephew requested special prayers in his will. Nonetheless, in spite of this brass being commissioned, Brian Rouclyff requested in his will that he be buried in the church of the Friars Minor, York, and he also asked for a monument to him to be set up in London.

The evidence of wills occasionally illuminates the processes by which brasses were commissioned. It seems to have been not uncommon for women to be commemorated in brass only once their husband had died. Occasionally it can be shown that men who had been married more than once, following the death of their first wives, asked for both their wives to be depicted on their brasses. For example, Thomas Stathum of Morley (Derbs) stipulated in his will of 1469 that he wanted to be buried in the south side of the chancel of the church at Morley, and he asked for a marble slab to be placed above him in which were set three brass images, of himself and his two wives. His second wife, Elizabeth, was still alive at the time that the will was written. Sir John de Quintin of Brandesburton (Yorks) also asked for a brass depicting himself and his two wives in his will of 1397. However, only his first wife Lora appears on the brass. His surviving wife, Agnes, who was probably left to carry out the task of commissioning the brass, clearly had other

68 *Brass from Cowthorpe (Yorks). This fifteenth-century brass was made for Brian Rouclyff, a lawyer who became Baron of the Exchequer in 1458, and his wife, Joan. After Stephenson 1898*

ideas and she asked in her own will of 1404 to be buried next to her second husband, John de Wassand, at Sigglesthorne (Yorks) instead, which doubtless explains her absence from the Brandesburton brass. The will of John Langton of Leeds, whose brass is unfortunately partly lost, asked for the arms of himself and his wife, and also those of their sons and their wives, their daughters and their husbands and the arms of other ancestors to be displayed on the monument.

English brasses appear to have declined in popularity in the 1350s and 1360s and Flemish brasses made major inroads into the English market, especially in the eastern half of England where Flemish merchants did most of their trade. While the Black Death may have been a factor, the fact that brass manufacture was becoming increasingly diverse in the 1330s and 1340s may have led to a perceived decline in the quality of English brasses and encouraged those who wished to purchase brasses to look to the continental market.

Tombs and effigies

By the thirteenth century it had become common for the wealthy to be commemorated with an effigy, which displayed not just who they were but which also indicated their social and economic status. Tombs and effigies were certainly commemorative but they were also symbols of wealth, of both the deceased and of their heirs who would usually have been responsible for overseeing the completion and erection of the monument. These monuments were commonly focal points for competitive display between leading families, and monuments were an important means by which wealthy families expressed their dominance within a locality, and reinforced their associations with a particular place. These monuments were commonly painted, although paint rarely survives today, and this enhanced the impact of these monuments.

It was not uncommon for the monuments to the members of a particular family to dominate a particular church. For example, in the later thirteenth century William de Ros, the patron of Kirkham Priory (Yorks), was buried in the priory church before the altar, and his son Robert (d.1285) was interred in a marble tomb in the south part of the church. The marble tomb of William de Ros (d.1316) was on the north side of the altar and the stone monument to his son William (d.1343) at the south. The gatehouse at Kirkham was also adorned with de Ros heraldry, emphasizing the association of this family with the monastery. Wills reveal that monuments to the Lords Darcy and to members of the de Fauconberg, Brus and Latimer families were erected at Gisborough Priory (Cleveland), although they have largely been lost following the subsequent destruction of the church. At Norbury there are numerous monuments to members of the Fitzherbert lords of the manor, including alabaster tombs (**65, 69**) and slabs (**64**), brasses, a stone effigy (**70**) and window glass incorporating coats of arms and images of members of the Fitzherbert family (**colour plates 21, 22**). The church at Thornhill contained several monuments to members of the Saville family, and it also possesses window glass with inscriptions that record the generosity of the Savilles, who clearly expected prayers in return (**71**).

Knightly effigies were statements of worldly successes as much as they were reflections of spiritual concerns. There was a degree of experimentation in the earliest effigies, but by the later thirteenth century the cross-legged knight holding his sword was becoming something of the norm. A short-lived form of monument of the early fourteenth century

Remembering the dead: memorials, commemoration and care of the soul

69 Monument to Ralph and Elizabeth Fitzherbert at Norbury (Derbs). The Yorkist collar of suns and roses is just visible. The monument includes the only surviving depiction of the Yorkist collar with a boar pendant. Jim Williams

saw effigies of knights depicted as if poised for action. Often they are shown drawing their sword as if about to leap into action. Later, however, this gave way to the depiction of knights in what Colin Platt (1981, 45) has called 'martial repose', and eventually to a more peaceful repose. Hands held together in prayer became increasingly common. The knights on effigies from the region are many and varied. Contrasting examples of monuments are found at the churches of Norbury (Derbs). The monument of Sir Henry Fitzherbert at Norbury shows him ready for action, in the process of drawing his sword. He also has the typical cross-legged pose of the thirteenth century and early fourteenth century (**70**). In contrast the other Fitzherbert monuments at Norbury show the knight armed but in prayer (**65, 69**). There are clear contrasts between the monuments from Sprotborough (Yorks) where the knight is shown fully armed with sword and shield but in prayer, and those at Tideswell (**72**) or Harewood (*see* **75**), for example, where a rather more peaceful position is struck.

Effigies, tombs and brasses generally depicted the deceased as a young person. This was probably intended to present the person at the age of 33, which was the age at which Christ died and which many theologians argued would be the age that everyone would attain at the Resurrection.

The depiction of women on tombs and effigies was influenced both by images of the Virgin, and by contemporary literary notions of the ideal of feminine beauty. Literary

154

conventions dictated that women should have a long neck, high forehead, small lips, small, high breasts, narrow waist and long arms and fingers. These conventions were adopted in the funerary monuments of women, and paint may have been used to achieve the other ideals of blonde hair, black eyebrows and white skin (Coss 1998, 74). Effigies of women appeared later than those of men, and few can be dated to before 1280. They tend to be depicted in a more serene pose than knightly effigies (**73, 74**). The joint effigy, tomb or brass was an important means by which links between leading families could be displayed, and they were an opportunity to display various coats of arms. Effigies of women often bear the coats of arms of their husband or father on their gown.

Effigies provided an opportunity for a display of the heraldic arms of the deceased. Indeed, it may not be coincidence that the knightly effigy seems to have emerged as a form of funerary monument at about the same time that the earliest listings of arms are found, that is, in the early thirteenth century. The importance of displays of arms in the construction and signalling of lordship is brought home in a famous dispute from the 1380s between Sir Richard Le Scrope of Bolton Castle (Yorks) and Sir Robert Grosvenor over who had the right to use a particular heraldic device. Both parties called witnesses who listed where they had seen the two families display their heraldic symbols. Tombs were mentioned alongside window glass, wall paintings, manuscripts, charters, seals, wall-hangings, vestments and inn signs. Scrope eventually won because he was able to demonstrate that his ancestors had fought under their arms, but the case reveals that the display of arms was important to registering ownership of them and that heraldic devices were public acclamations of status and identity. That this status was particularly masculine in character is revealed by the public, hereditary and military connotations of heraldic devices. The importance of the visibility

70 Effigy of Sir Henry Fitzherbert at Norbury (Derbs). Jim Williams

Remembering the dead: memorials, commemoration and care of the soul

71 *Windowglass from Thornhill (Yorks). This drawing was made in the nineteenth century. The window shows the dead rising from their graves.* Alex Norman

72 *Tomb from Tideswell (Derbs). It is not known for whom this tomb was made. No inscriptions or coats of arms survive to narrow down the range of possibilities. The knight does, however, wear the collar of esses (see p.157).* Jim Williams

of heraldic proclamations of status is emphasized by one of the witnesses called Sir Robert Laton, who declared that in his youth his father had instructed him to write down all the arms of princes, dukes, earls, knights and barons and learn them by heart. Clearly, learning heraldic devices was an important part of knightly training. Whether, however, members of wider society could always be relied upon to recognize these symbols is another matter.

Effigies could also be used to show the political allegiances of the deceased through their wearing of insignia, of which the most famous are the Lancastrian and Yorkist livery collars. The appearance of collars on monuments does not prove that the person so depicted had actually been awarded the collar as a badge of office, as it may simply have been depicted as a sign of long service to one of these royal houses. The Lancastrian collar of esses (it is not certain what they stood for) appears to have originated among the retinue of John of Gaunt, duke of Lancaster, in the later fourteenth century and was worn by his followers, or at least it was at times when it was politically expedient to do so. These collars are not uncommon on monuments in the region. Two of the alabaster Redmayne tombs at Harewood show the recumbent figures wearing the collar of esses, alternating with garter ribbons in one instance and with roses in the other (**75**). Women also wear them on their effigies, which may indicate that they did so in life. For example a monument in the church at Methley (Yorks) of Cecily Fleming shows her wearing the collar of esses. The corresponding Yorkist collar consisted of suns and roses, and is found on, for example, the tomb of Sir Ralph Fitzherbert at Norbury, where it is shown with a boar pendant. There is some evidence that monuments made without collars had them added later, such as on a brass at Gunby (Lincs).

Tombs and effigies often carried inscriptions. Commonly these record the name, date of death and personal details of the deceased, but sometimes they ask the reader to

73 *Effigy from Sprotborough (Yorks). Note the angels holding the pillow on which the woman's head rests. This is a fourteenth-century monument.* Jim Williams

Remembering the dead: memorials, commemoration and care of the soul

74 Effigies from Tideswell (Derbs). These two females effigies are of different dates to judge from the style of carving and clothing, and were later placed together. Jim Williams

75 Collar on effigy at Harewood (Yorks). This early fifteenth-century effigy is of Richard Redmayne. He wears the Lancastrian collar of esses, interspersed with ribbons. Author

pray for the soul of the deceased, or they alert the reader to the fact that the same fate awaits them. For example, the tomb of John Barton at Holme (Notts), who died in 1491, carries the inscription 'Pity me, you at least my friends, for the hand of the Lord has touched me' (**77**). This inscription is in stark contrast to the proud statement about his wealth that is written on the east window that he paid for (see below p.165), and also contrasts with the inscription that formerly existed on a window in his manor house which read 'I thank God and ever shall/'tis the sheepe hath payed for all'. This reflects not only his wealth but also that he had benefited greatly from the population decline over the previous century which had made specializing in sheep rearing much easier and more profitable than arable.

Tomb chests normally had figures carved on the sides of the monument, and they were biblical figures, saints and clergy or else members of the family of the deceased. The latter are often described as 'weepers', yet they are normally depicted not in expressions of grief but in graceful poses, serving as a reminder of who the person had been through the depiction of other people in their social world. Weepers also often included saints and angels, who, presumably, were expected to offer assistance to the soul of the deceased. Angels were also sometimes used to hold up heraldic shields. Good examples of the use of a variety of types of weepers survive at Harewood, where there are six fifteenth-century and early sixteenth-century alabaster tombs with effigies of couples, the sides of which feature angels and saints. The Fitzherbert monuments at Norbury also feature numerous relatives (**65, 69**) (the tomb of Sir Nicholas Fitzherbert appears to depict both of his wives (**76**)), saints and angels. The tomb for Bishop Henry Burghersh of Lincoln (d.1340) depicts among the weepers Edward III and his sons. In contrast, an unusual monument from Fenny Bentley (Derbs) depicts the couple, Thomas Beresford (d.1473) and his wife Agnes Hassall (d.1467), commemorated in shrouds, and the sides of the monument are filled with shrouded depictions of their sixteen sons and five daughters. Yet in spite of the anonymity of the individuals depicted, it is clear for whom the monument was made from the

76 *The wives of Nicholas Fitzherbert at Norbury (Derbs).* On the end panel of the tomb of Nicholas. Jim Williams

77 Tomb of John Barton at Holme (Notts). The living images of John Barton and his wife lie above, while below is a cadaver with the inscription 'Pity me, you at least my friends, for the hand of the Lord has touched me'. Jim Williams

inscriptions on the side of the tomb that name Thomas and Agnes, and also their third son Hugh, who is the only one of the children named. The fact that the children are all depicted in shrouds, and the style of the armour depicted around the cornices of the tomb belongs to the sixteenth century, suggests that the tomb was made many decades after the death of Thomas and Agnes, perhaps by the heir of Hugh, the only son named. This monument is a reminder of the fallacy of dating a monument by its inscription, as it was clearly made much later than the date of the death of the individuals depicted.

An important class of monument that survives but rarely is the wooden tomb. Wood should not necessarily be regarded as an inferior medium for commemorating the dead. Wood was easily painted and the bright colours applied were both striking and capable of conveying messages about the status and identity of the deceased. The most impressive example from our region is the wooden tomb of Sir Roger Rockley (d. 1534) at Worsborough (Yorks), which depicts Sir Roger in life above a cadaver below (**colour plate 24**). Such monuments, and similar monuments in stone (such as that to John Barton at Holme), serve both as reminders of the fate that awaited the viewer of the monument, and also offered hope of resurrection to an eternal life.

Alabaster was a material that became increasingly popular in the fourteenth and fifteenth century, and the quarrying and carving of it were activities located largely in the Midlands (see below pp.180-1). Fine examples of alabaster tombs survive at Harewood and Norbury, as we have seen, and at Aston-on-Trent (Derbs), where traces of paint on the tomb remind us that alabaster tombs might be painted. A unique relief in alabaster survives at Bakewell. It depicts the arms of the Foljambe family, and was made *c*.1375. It probably shows Sir Godfrey Foljambe and his wife (**78**).

Church fabric and fittings

The patronage of churches by the wealthy also served as a form of commemoration. On some occasions it was clearly intended that there should be some spiritual return for the patronage of a church. For example, in the mid-twelfth century Alexander son of Osbert, and his son Nigel, granted 920 acres of land to Sempringham Priory (Lincs) 'that we may be brothers and sharers in their prayers, and may have a burial place in their church, and as full service as one of their number'. Other patrons arranged to have either their heraldic symbols or inscriptions naming themselves added to the items they had paid for. For example, a fifteenth-century window from All Saints, North Street in York carries depictions of St Christopher, John the Baptist and St Anne, and the words 'Pray for the souls of Nicholas Blackburn senior once mayor of the city of York and Margaret his wife' (**79**). It was a medieval belief that the sight of St Christopher every morning would offer protection against premature death, and as such this window, in addition to commemorating Nicholas and Margaret Blackburn, would also have been a welcome image for other parishioners. Robert Goldyng of Hull requested in his will of 1453 that he should be buried in the Charterhouse just outside the town, and he left money for a new window, which was to depict the Virgin, John the Baptist, and St Thomas Becket, and at the feet of the Virgin was to be an image of the donor genuflecting. Gilbert, Earl of Angus gave to Kyme Priory (Lincs) vestments of blue velvet bearing his arms in 1377. Even where such obvious statements of patronage were not made, the patron who provided items for a church might be long remembered. For example, at Kirkham Priory the baptismal font was discussed by several witnesses to a court case of 1496-7, and while they could not agree on how long it had been there — estimates ranged from 20 to 40 years — there was consensus on who had donated the font, a parishioner called John Delaryne.

78 Alabaster monument to Sir Godfrey Foljambe and his wife at Bakewell (Derbs). Jim Williams

79 Window depicting St Christopher from All Saints, North Street in York. Royal Commission for Historic Monuments

Parishioners who could afford it often left in their wills items of equipment, new fittings or money for additions or repairs to the fabric of churches, and such donations clearly also became the subject of competitive largesse. In his will of 1451 Sir Thomas Cumberworth of Somerby (Lincs) left vestments to Lincoln Cathedral and St Katherine's, Lincoln, which were specifically said to bear his arms. He also left vestments and equipment to Thornton Abbey (Lincs), the Carthusian house at Hull, to the parish church at Somerby and to poor churches in the area; he left relics to the churches at Somerby and Stain in Withern (Lincs); and he arranged for lead to be purchased for the roof of the chancel at Somerby and the nave at Stain (Essex). Sir Geoffrey Luttrell of Irnham (Lincs) left money in his will of 1345 to 'the use of the fabric of the church of Irnham', and for the fabric of Lincoln Cathedral, and he also made donations to Sempringham Priory, the Dominicans and Franciscans of Stamford, the Cistercians of Vaudey Abbey (Lincs), and Hampole Priory (Yorks). He also left money to images in a number of churches — the image of the Annunciation of the Blessed Virgin Mary in St Paul's Cathedral, the image of St Mary in Canterbury Cathedral, and that of the blessed Mary in St Mary's Abbey, York. The will is specific about where the images were depicted — the south wall at St Paul's, the vault underneath the choir at Canterbury and beyond the north door at York

— which may indicate that Geoffrey had been on pilgrimage to these places to visit the devotional sites, and so we should not view such bequests cynically, they may well have been real and relevant elements of the spiritual and devotional life of the will-maker. The wealthier inhabitants of Hull in the fifteenth century left bequests for the fabric of the church including lead for the roof, money to hire masons, donations for windows and for paving the church. Others left money for a new antiphoner, for the construction of the reredos, for the painting of new images above the altars, for vestments and a cupboard to keep them in, and others left lengths of cloth. In 1372 John Wyga gave money for the building of a new aisle in the church at North Kelsey (Lincs), and in 1440 John Whytebrede left money in his will to enlarge the parish church of Gosberton (Lincs). Such contributions to churches, which were doubtless very welcome, would probably have ensured that the donor was long remembered. To ensure this, some patrons asked to have their name entered in the bede-roll, a list of persons who were to be remembered in prayer on the anniversary of their death.

The fact that donors such as Sir Thomas Cumberworth specifically asked that their coats of arms be displayed on vestments meant that even the illiterate, who may not have been able to read inscriptions recording who had purchased items for the church, would be able to identify the patron. At York, in the church of St Denys, the donor of a window called Robert (possibly Robert de Skelton, a Chamberlain of York in the mid-fourteenth century) is depicted in the window, which requests prayers for the souls of himself and his wife, actually presenting the window to the church. It has been suggested that one of the reasons why medieval window glass sometimes survived the Reformation and the destruction of religious imagery that often accompanied it was because, for example, saints were believed locally to depict patrons of the church in the guise of the saint. This has been argued for the figures of St George and St James at Barton-on-Humber (Lincs), who were thought to be Henry and William Beaumont, and the figure of St George at Long Sutton (Lincs) was thought locally to be John of Gaunt (Hebgin-Barnes 1995). Whether or not these interpretations were misguided, it suggests that images displayed in churches might easily come to be associated with their patrons, even if they ostensibly appear to depict saints.

Contemporaries did not always approve of these secular displays within churches. For example, the late fourteenth-century poem *Pierce the Ploughman's Crede* describes a Dominican friary as follows:

> Wyde wyndowes y-wrought y-written full thikke,
> Schynen with schapen scheldes to schewen aboute, [shaped]
> With merkes of marchauntes y-medled bytwene, [merchants' marks placed]
> Mo than twenty and two twyes y-noumbred
> Ther is non heraud that hath half swich a rolle, [herald]
> Right as a rageman hath reckned hem newe. [counted]
> Tombes opon tabernacles tyld opon lifte, [raised]
> Housed in hirnes harde set abouten, [corners]
> Of armede alabaustre clad for the nones, [for the nonce]
> Made upon marbel in many maner wyse,

> Knyghtes in her conisantes clad for the nones, [cognisances]
> All it semed seyntes y-sacred upon erther;
> And lovely ladies y-wrought leyen by her sydes
> In many gay garmentes that weren gold-beten.

We have to place this patronage of churches in context. While endowments were often undoubtedly made to secure intercessory prayers and burial in a favoured location, there were other potential benefits. For example, it seems certain that one reason why donations were made to religious houses in some regions was because the work they often subsequently undertook on reclaiming heath, marsh and fen and on maintaining roads and bridges (for which some houses such as Holland Bridge (Lincs) were especially founded) would bring benefits to the neighbouring properties of a patron. Patronage of churches was also a means for the wealthy to establish their position in local society. Indeed, it may have been more the socially aspirant, such as merchants and lords new to an area or recently elevated in status, who were more concerned to display their wealth and social prominence in local churches. We should not overlook the fact that many of the very wealthiest lords had their own private chapels within their residences and that they may rarely have ventured into the local church and may have been little concerned with displays of wealth there. Indeed, wealthier lords did not simply limit their largesse to their own parish churches, as we have seen from the wills of Sir Thomas Cumberworth and Sir Geoffrey Luttrell. Money for commemoration and for prayers for their souls was often widely spread.

The impact of the Black Death on artistic production is a matter for much debate. In addition to affecting the commissioning and production of individual monuments, it also took its toll on building projects. Many churches undergoing building campaigns on the eve of the Black Death did not see them finished for many generations. It is difficult but to conclude that the Black Death played a part in this, either because of the death of patrons or craft workers, or because the priorities of patrons changed, and funding was directed away from grand, communal building schemes (of the nave and aisles) to more personalized initiatives (chantries, chapels, porches, donations of fixtures and fittings). For example, the major building campaign at the church at Patrington (Yorks) was almost complete by 1349, but for half a century afterwards the steeple went without its spire, and its chancel in English Decorated style was finally finished off with an east window in fifteenth-century Perpendicular style. At Ashbourne (Derbs) the rebuilding of the church in the early fourteenth century was not completed, and the north aisle, which was obviously intended, did not match the south aisle. Other churches were reduced in size. The church at Wharram Percy (Yorks) had lost both of its aisles by 1550, and the windows from the aisles were reset in the blocked up archways. On the other hand there is evidence that many churches experienced building campaigns in the fourteenth and fifteenth centuries, such as at Tideswell (Derbs) and Thirsk (Yorks). The effects of the Black Death on ecclesiastical fortunes during the fourteenth and fifteenth century were not uncommonly ameliorated by the wealth of individual patrons, such as the merchant and former mayor Thomas Nelson who paid for the re-glazing of the east window at Holy Trinity, Micklegate in York, and the clothier John Barton at Holme who rebuilt the parish church, seeing to it that his contribution was recorded in the east window: 'Pray for the soul of John Barton of Holme, merchant of the Staple of Calais, builder of this church, who died 1491, and for Isabella his wife' (see the contrast with his tomb, above p.159). The wealthy founders of chantries also enhanced the fortunes of churches. This may, indeed, have been a factor in the continuing building programme at Thirsk, following the foundation of a chantry by the cleric and royal official Robert of Thirsk in 1415.

It is arguable that the lay parishioners were able by one means or another to maintain their churches far better than the clergy themselves. This, at least, seems to be the conclusion to be drawn from an early sixteenth-century account of the state of church fabric in Lincolnshire which indicates that the defects of naves and towers, for which the parishioners were responsible, were far less serious than those of chancels, for which the rector (in the guise of either the clergy or their patrons) were responsible, and monastic patrons appear to have been the most negligent when it came to repairing churches. A striking account of the ways in which ecclesiastical patrons might neglect church fabric comes from Scredington (Lincs) in 1336. The parishioners complained that 'it rains upon the high altar in such a manner that when it is raining and there is also a wind the chaplain cannot celebrate at the altar, or sits in the desks or even in his place for matins'.

The Black Death had a major impact on later medieval society (see below pp.181-4), but this impact has been a subject of much debate and remains controversial. Its impact on artistic production is no less problematic. Many scholars believe that from the middle of the fourteenth century artistic developments directly reflected the socio-economic changes and the quality of the piety that the Black Death brought about. Such a conclusion has been made about all forms of artistic endeavour, from church-building and architecture, to the production of brasses, tombs and effigies, to glazing, manuscript illustration and, even, the increasingly widespread use of the vernacular in manuscripts. It is certainly true that some artistic styles appear to have come to an abrupt end as a result of the death of master craftsmen or the disappearance of specialist workshops (see below, pp.183-4), but it is difficult to make a case that there was a wholesale transformation of artistic production in general, or of funerary monuments in particular, in the immediate wake of the Black Death. Another important impact on the arts was the increasing penetration of foreign art and craftsmen into England, particularly as the fifteenth century progressed, which was doubtless facilitated by the shortage of indigenous craftsmen and artists. The different schools of artistic endeavour were, however, affected differently. Flemish brasses appear to have become relatively common, especially in eastern England (see above, p.153), in the later fourteenth century, but it was not until the fifteenth century that foreign styles and craftsmen had come to dominate the production of sculpture, glazing and manuscript illumination. Only architecture appears to have retained its vigour under indigenous influence. The Black Death certainly had a major effect on the cultural world of later medieval England, but it was not uniform and affected different fields of artistic production in different ways.

Guilds and chantries

As we have seen (above pp.80-81), guilds and chantries were founded in many different contexts and for a variety of expressed reasons. The nature and number of the prayers, masses and other aids to the soul they offered varied greatly, as did, in consequence, the forms of commemoration that they provided. The wealthy and the executors of their wills often expected to be able to exert control over their chantry chapels long after they had died, indicating that they believed they would be remembered and their soul prayed for in perpetuity. The executors of Adam de Banke (d.1411) of York required the chaplains of his chantry in All Saints, North Street to be resident constantly and to refrain from celebrating masses elsewhere, and they also stipulated in detail what were to be the duties of the chaplain, especially on the anniversary of the death of the founder. These arrangements make it clear that chantries impinged on the activities of the other clergy in the church and on the religious experiences of other parishioners, as they stated that the chaplain was to wear 'a surplice, to sing the canonical hours and parochial masses on every Sunday and festival with other chaplains, clerks and ministers of that church'.

Prayers, masses and repentance of sins

Strictly speaking, the souls of all the faithful benefited from masses and it was not essential for individuals to be personally named in order to gain salvation. Nonetheless, the fact that those who were wealthy enough to write wills sought to ensure that they were specifically named and prayed for, especially in their own chantry foundations, suggests that individualistic concerns were relevant, and it may have led to concern among the less wealthy who could not afford the care for their soul that the wealthy could ensure. One means of acquiring the necessary post-mortem prayers for the poorer members of society was through membership of a guild. In many ways guilds were effectively collective chantries, and were able to offer prayers for many more individuals than chantries, providing that the membership subscriptions could be met. It is difficult to measure contemporary attitudes to the benefits that being able to pay for large numbers of masses were expected to bring. Clearly, the wealthy must have thought that they would be effective, as donations for prayers are commonly the biggest financial outlay made in wills. There is also the implication that payments for prayers and commemoration will ensure that the social hierarchy will be maintained in the next life, to the advantage of the wealthy and influential in this world. Nonetheless, there are some contemporary comments that suggest that it was not as simple as that. In his *Handlyng Synne*, Robert Mannyng tells a tale of a wealthy evil man who bribed church wardens to be allowed burial in a tomb in the chancel, but his body was later ripped out by devils and thrown outside the churchyard. In another of Mannyng's tales, a lord is rebuked by a peasant for allowing his beasts to defecate on graves in the parish churchyard. The lord replies that there was no need to show respect as they were only the bones of 'churls' (peasants). The peasant, however, reminds him that 'Erles, cherles, al at ones/Shal none knowe youre fro oure bones'. Mannyng says that this was a popular local adage, and if so it may suggest that it was popularly thought that in the next life all would be equal, and therefore that extra buying-power in this life, whether for monuments or prayers, was not necessarily the decisive factor that would determine one's fate.

The importance of being appropriately prayed for after death is emphasized by the details contained in a collection of ghost stories from Yorkshire, which were written *c*.1400, and preserved in a manuscript in the possession of Byland Abbey (Yorks).

Although preserved in a monastic context they may provide some insights into the beliefs of wider society. In one story a ghost appears to a tailor and tells him that for certain things he had done he had been excommunicated and he asked the tailor to go to a priest and ask him to absolve him, and to arrange for the correct number of masses to be said for him. The ghost also says that he has appeared to the man because that day he had not heard mass. The tailor then went to York where he acquired an absolution for the man whose ghost he had met and was instructed to bury the absolution in the man's grave. The tailor subsequently went to all the orders of the friars in York and acquired the necessary masses. The tailor then met the ghost again who told him that he had been tormented by devils until his absolution had been buried in his grave. In another ghost story a canon of Newburgh Priory (Yorks) appeared to a man and said that he had been excommunicated for hiding silver spoons, and asked him to retrieve the spoons, take them to the prior and seek absolution for him. Another ghost, who had been a servant, asked the person to whom he appeared to ask for his master's pardon and absolution. A child who had not been baptized appeared to his father wriggling in a stocking, saying that he had been buried without receiving a name. He was duly baptized and was then able to walk instead of wriggling. These stories provided a warning that the dead might sometimes be tormented by things that had happened in their lives, and by issues that had been left unresolved. They also suggest that the living would have to help out the dead in order that they may rest in peace. The intended audience for these ghost stories appears to have been the wider community rather than the family, since it is to people living in the vicinity rather than to family members that the ghosts generally appear.

While there may, then, have been popular concern with being appropriately prayed for and with the torment that the soul might experience if the living did not intercede on its behalf, the extent to which this meant that the laity in general adhered to the teachings of the Church or fully understood its messages must be open to doubt. It is difficult to measure the depth and qualities of later medieval spirituality. There is much documentary evidence at our disposal, but the picture that emerges is contradictory. Some contemporary commentators suggest that the laity were not very religious, rarely attended church and paid little attention when they did, others indicate that worship was an important aspect of the lives of the laity and that they made great efforts to learn their parts of the services.

Guilds and chantry chapels as monuments to the dead

In addition to providing for prayers and masses to be said for the souls of the deceased, guilds and chantry chapels provided tangible reminders of the deceased. In doing so they also transformed the appearance of churches, resulting either in building campaigns or in alterations to the spatial organization of churches. The Burgh and Thonnock chantries at Gainsborough (Lincs) resulted in the building of an additional chapel, chantries at Beckingham and East Kirkby (Lincs) led to the rebuilding of aisles in the parish church, and that of John of Harrington at Harrington (Lincs) was located in an 'oratory built at my cost on the south side of the parish church'. Ralph Lord Cromwell, Lord Treasurer of England, founded a chantry at Tattershall (Lincs) in the early fifteenth century in collegiate form, including seven chaplains, six secular clerks and six choristers, and in doing so rebuilt the church alongside his castle. He also built an almshouse as part of the chantry complex. Accounts of the college reveal that he installed windows depicting the history of the Holy Cross, the Magnificat, St Clare, the Seven Corporal Acts of Mercy and the Seven Sacraments. Guilds also had an impact on the fabric of churches. The guild of St John the Baptist at Gosberton was responsible for a new window in the south aisle, at Hogsthorpe the guild of St Mary built the porch, and north windows in the parish churches of Owersby and Kirkby cum Osgodby (Lincs) were provided by guilds. The members of two guilds in Kirton Lindsey (Lincs) made annual contributions for the upkeep of the church of 2d each, and at Hagworthingham (Lincs) the church benefited from rents from the guildhall and from occasional collections from dancing and festivities held there. The guild of St Peter and St Paul at Boston (Lincs) added a new aisle to the church of St Botolph in which their altar was placed.

Some churches had numerous chantries or guilds, resulting in much of the space within those churches being given over to meet the spiritual needs of select groups within the parish. Twenty-two parish churches in York (just over half) are known to have contained one or more perpetual chantries at some point during the later Middle Ages, and St Saviour's had as many as eight. The parish church at Newark (Notts) had at least thirteen chantries, which was an exceptional number. The fabric of many churches continues to carry the marks of where chantry or guild chapels had once been, in the form of piscinas or wall-brackets for holding altar candles. York Minster has little surviving evidence for the location of chantry chapels, in the form of piscinas, wall-brackets or screens, but records of sixty or so altars, many of which served chantry chapels, has enabled a partial reconstruction of where some of the altars were positioned in the later fourteenth century following the rebuilding of the choir begun after 1360.

The creation of guilds and chantries also had an impact on the wider landscape. A few resulted in completely new buildings. The battle at Towton (Yorks) in 1461 between rival Yorkist and Lancastrian factions where thousands died (see above, p.49) was followed by the foundation of a chantry chapel. Edward IV requested indulgences of seven years for those who came to pray for the souls of the dead, patronage continued under Richard III, and in 1486 the chantry chapel was said to have been a 'splendid chapel expensively and imposingly erected from new foundations'. Chantry chapels erected on battlefields were clearly political statements and were utilized to serve the interests of both the victor and vanquished over successive periods. Some chantries were founded with the additional role of increasing divine worship by providing a chapel for a community that had previously not had one. A number of outlying hamlets and fen edge settlements in Lincolnshire acquired chapels founded as chantries, such as Kinnard's Ferry and Amcotts in the parish of Owston, with that at Amcotts being founded in the mid-fifteenth century specifically to save the inhabitants from the winter floods as they made their way to the parish church. Chantries had an impact on urban topography following the building of houses to accommodate chantry priests. For example, at West Tanfield (Yorks) a house was built adjacent to the churchyard for chantry priests in the later fourteenth century, and at about the same time a house was built in Newark by Dame Alice Fleming to provide for chantry priests in the church in return for which they had to say a daily prayer for the founder. At York a number of patrons purchased urban properties and even established new properties on the street fronts of churchyards to provide rents to support chantries, effecting another transformation in the urban landscape as a direct consequence of the need for prayers and masses for the wealthy.

Saints

As we saw in the previous chapter, would-be saints had to prepare appropriately for their death as the first stage of demonstrating their sanctity. Once death had occurred then it was necessary for post-mortem demonstrations of sanctity, in the form of miracles and translations. Before his burial in Lincoln Cathedral, Bishop Hugh cured a blind woman, and collections of post-mortem miracles allegedly performed by Richard Rolle survive. St John of Beverley apparently miraculously foretold the imminent collapse of the tower, c.1213, when a great light was seen shining from his tomb. The translation of a saint from their original resting place to another nearer to God was an important indication of their power, and a means by which the cults of long-dead saints could be given new emphasis. This *translatio* normally involved the movement of the saint to a holier position closer to God, which usually meant either translation nearer to the altar, or into a higher (that is, either taller or else in a higher position in the church) shrine. The remains of St Hugh of Lincoln were translated in 1280 in the presence of King Edward I and Queen Eleanor, the archbishop of Canterbury and 230 knights. St John of Beverley was translated in 1037 by Archbishop Ælfric of York, from his tomb at the east end of the nave to a position near to the high altar. There was a whole series of rituals associated with a translation, and the body of the saint was commonly said to have been found to be incorrupt and sweet-smelling and to emit light. Although there could be a physiological basis for such a bodily state, such as the effects of embalming or of placing the body in a sealed coffin, the main point about this description was that the saint's corpse represented his soul, and it revealed that the saint was enjoying the 'sweetness and light of heaven'. The saint had overcome the rot, decay and stench that were the bodily decay of ordinary people (Finucane 1981, 60).

Charitable bequests

One means to ensure the safe passage of the soul was through charitable works. The stimulus to undertake such acts were the words of Christ in Matthew 25: 35-6:

> For I was hungry and you gave me food, I was thirsty and you gave me drink, I was a stranger and you welcomed me, I was naked and you clothed me, I was sick and you visted me, I was in prison and you came to me.

To these acts there was later added the requirement to bury the dead, which was enjoined in the apocryphal Book of Tobit (chs 2, 11). These were the Seven Corporal Acts of Mercy. These acts informed the majority of charitable bequests made in wills in the later medieval period. A window in the church of All Saints, North Street in York depicts a wealthy man performing the six works that derived directly from the words of

Christ. A fifteenth-century wallpainting in the church of SS Peter and Paul at Pickering (Yorks) depicts the Seven Acts of Mercy (**colour plate 23**). Doubtless such images served to remind parishioners of the importance of these undertakings. Further encouragement to undertake charitable works was provided by images of saints who were associated with charity. A window in the church of St Martin, Coney Street in York depicts the appearance of Christ to St Martin in a dream to tell him that he was the poor person that he had clothed. Many other churches have depictions of St Anne, commonly teaching the Virgin to read, who was a model of pious and charitable living: for example, in windows at All Saints, North Street in York and Norbury (**colour plate 22**), on an alabaster tomb at Burton Agnes (Yorks) and on a wallpainting at Corby Glen (Lincs). Several York churches also had images or lights dedicated to St Sitha of Lucca, who was the patroness of housewives and servants, and particularly noted for her charitable provisions to the poor. The performance of charitable acts is not always easy to document. Wills sometimes record charitable works that are to be carried out after the testator's death, but we should not overlook the fact that many other charitable acts may have gone unrecorded, precisely because they had been carried out long before a will was drawn up.

Many wills simply made a general provision for the poor. The will of Sir Thomas Cumberworth, for example, left money to the poor and clothing for those who were to attend commemorative services. Other wills indicate more specifically what the money they left was to be used for. Margaret Bramshowe (d.1471) left her household utensils to poor newly-weds and Joan Johnson (d.1474) left turfs and wood fuel for 'the poor of Christ'. However, in other wills it seems clear that the Seven Acts of Mercy greatly informed bequests to the needy in later medieval wills, and it is also apparent that acts of charity were generally not indiscriminate but were targetted towards particular groups (Cullum and Goldberg 1993). The feeding of the poor was provided for in the will of Robert Sutton of Lincoln in 1451/2 which indicated that ten quarters of wheat and malt were to be divided 'for my soul' among the poor. Richard Parke of York (d.1461) left money for a dole of bread to the poor outside his house every Friday for a year, thus leaving no doubt about who had provided it. Thomas Bracebridge of York (d.1437) left money for a thousand farthing loaves to be distributed to the poor. Some left money for a wake or *convivium* for poor neighbours, such as Isabella Barry (d.1391) who left 20s for a wake for her poor neighbours, and Alice Pund (d.1390) who left 40s for the same. Perhaps more realistic of the ways in which such charity was provided was the instruction in the will of John de Preston of York to give the poor the leftovers from his wake to add to the 2s for bread he also left. Clothing was commonly left in wills. In York, for example, John de Gysburn bequeathed cloth to make tunics for the poor in 1390, and in 1387 Elena Milys requested that her clothes be given to the poor, saving only the garment that was to be used for her mortuary. Richard Croull (d.1460) left five shirts, ten pairs of shoes and seven pairs of hose signifying, respectively, the Five Wounds of Christ, the Ten Commandments and the Seven Acts of Mercy.

The requirement to visit the sick and to receive strangers appears to have been commonly met through bequests to hospitals and maisonsdieu. For example, in 1391 Elizabeth de Eston, a baker in York, left 4s to the four leper houses in the city and 7s to each of the maisonsdieu. The latter were often founded during a person's lifetime, and they permitted their founder to exercise charity throughout their lifetime. It is, as has already been noted, important to remember that wills only provide a partial insight into the piety of later medieval people, and actions during their lifetime were just as important in assisting their soul, although apt to be overlooked in wills. Money for repairs to roads or bridges may also have been influenced by the requirement to receive strangers. Bequests to prisoners were less common, although prisoners could be regarded as deserving of charity given that there were biblical precedents reminding medieval people that even the saintly, such as SS Peter, Paul, Catherine and John the Baptist, experienced periods of imprisonment. Many churches carried images of such saints. For example, St Catherine is depicted on the wall painting at Pickering, as is St John the Baptist, who was a common sight in the wall paintings and windowglass of the region. Joan Gregg of Hull left money in 1438 for a variety of charitable purposes, including ten pounds to be used by her executors to redeem prisoners, and one pound was left to the prisoners in York jails. In 1429 John Osay of Hull left ten pounds for prisoners, which along with other money for the blind, poor and lame, was 'for my soul and the souls of all my benefactors'. Nonetheless, there appears, if wills may be relied upon, to have been less concern to provide for prisoners than for other needy individuals. Finally, the requirement to bury the dead is rarely specified as a charitable bequest in wills. A rare exception comes from the will of James Lounesdale (d.1495) who left money for those who did not have the means to be buried. One reason for this may have been that in ensuring provisions were made for their own burial testators may have believed that they had fulfilled this requirement, and many left items for their funeral that could be reused for other funerals.

In many wills a bequest to the needy was accompanied by the requirement for the recipients to pray for the soul of the deceased, and it was not uncommon for the benefactor to indicate some way in which their munificence would be recognized. On the whole, however, it is difficult to conclude that the only reason for bequests to the poor and needy was for their intercessory powers on behalf of the souls of testators. The fact that wills commonly specify precisely which groups are to benefit from the bequest suggests that the real needs of the poor were taken into account when wills were drawn up. The doctrine of Purgatory was central to the faith of the laity and the performance of charitable acts was regarded as an essential component in ensuring the safe passage of the soul through Purgatory.

Texts

The wealthy also had the option of being commemorated in text, in particular in the devotional and fictional works that they commissioned, and in some cases wrote. Sir Geoffrey Luttrell, a Lincolnshire knight, commissioned an illuminated manuscript in the 1330s or early 1340s — known to us now as the Luttrell Psalter — which, among many other images, depicts him on horseback, preparing to go off to war (**colour plate 18**). Yet, interestingly this image was commissioned long after Geoffrey had ceased to be an active participant in war, effectively rendering it a memento of his younger, fighting days, rather than a picture of the reality of the time when it was made. This image in the psalter, as much as the military effigies we have already discussed, emphasizes the importance of certain kinds of military trappings to men of status, irrespective of the reality of their situation. Another reason why the image of Sir Geoffrey on horseback is only partly a 'real' representation is related to changes in warfare in the earlier fourteenth century. Fighting on horseback had long been the preserve of the knightly classes, distinguishing them from the lowly foot-soldiers, but in the early fourteenth century fighting on horseback had been shown to be extremely ineffective, especially in the wars against the Scots. Michael Camille (1998) has recently argued that the interplay between image and reality was important in medieval depictions of knights. A contemporary chronicler described the great army that Edward I led into Galloway in 1300, of which Sir Geoffrey had been a member, in the following terms:

> The king with his retinue set out immediately against the Scots. They were not in coats and surcoats but were well armed and mounted, on costly great horses, so that they would not be taken by surprise. There were many rich trappings of embroidered silks and satins, many fine pennons on lances. The neighing of the horses could be heard from far away, and everywhere the mountains and the valleys were filled with sumpter horses and carts bearing the provisions and equipment for the tents and pavilions.

This image of preparation for war was belied by reality, and many military historians have attributed the disastrous defeats of the English at the hands of the Scots to the very paraphernalia described here, and shown in manuscript illuminations. Knights on horseback easily became mired in the mud, and if they fell off their horses they were left like 'helpless and turned-over tortoises', as Camille has put it. Indeed, it is notable that there was a proclamation in 1327 that made it law that even the great magnates had to fight on foot if necessary, and at the battle of Halidon Hill 13 July 1333 the English dismounted and fought on foot 'contrary to the habits of their fathers', and won a resounding victory against the Scots after decades of defeat. After that, few medieval battles did not involve the knightly class dismounting. Yet however inappropriate the image of Geoffrey in practical terms, it retained its symbolic power. This was also in spite of the proclamations of moralisers of the day, such as Peter, archdeacon of Bath, who had much to say about these displays, describing how knights 'embroider their saddles and blazon their shields with scenes of battle and tourney, delighting in a certain imagination of those wars which, in very deed, they dare not mingle in or behold'. Knightly status, in England at least, was very uncertain, because it was not hereditary, even if in practice many families retained the status because of their landed assets. Moreover, knighthood had begun centuries before as a relatively subservient role, but one that had over time come to be more closely associated with the aristocratic classes. What marked out knights from those further down the social ladder was the right to bear a coat of arms, and the fact that they fought on horseback. It is no wonder that whatever the practicalities of warfare in his day that someone like Sir Geoffrey Luttrell would want to be seen in his psalter on horseback in all his heraldic finery.

We should not underestimate the importance of ideals in medieval societies, and it is simplistic and artificial to separate 'image' from 'reality', as the two were powerfully interwoven. The dominant forms of masculinity, sometimes dubbed 'hegemonic masculinity', are specifically dependent on creating and maintaining the social ascendancy of a particular form of masculine identity, that involves not simply force or violence but extends into the organization of private life and of cultural norms. The winning of hegemony for men of the later medieval aristocratic and knightly classes to some extent entailed the creation of models of masculinity which were partly, if not largely, fantasy figures, bearing little relationship to the experiences of most men. Indeed, their authority rested not solely on what they were or did, but on what sustained their power and what large numbers of other men supported and aspired to. Few men were King Arthur, Charlemagne, or Guy of Warwick (a legendary hero of English Romance literature), but many aspired to be like them, or to be associated with them, and participated in sustaining the contemporary resonance of both historical and fictional characters. Of course, the relationship between cultural models of masculinity and the actual experiences of men were rarely straightforward, and there is much to debate about how far, for example, chivalric ideals were consistent with the 'realities' of the period. There was also something of a tension between the need for service and commitment to one's lord on the one hand, and the individual achievements of the knight errant valorized in much of the literary output of the later Middle Ages on the other.

The psalter is in fact the major reason why we remember Sir Geoffrey Luttrell, although this was doubtless not the intention. Other manuscripts from the period that were both devotional works and also commemorated the importance of the family who commissioned them include the Grey-Fitz Payn Book of Hours, which was probably made in the first decade of the fourteenth century for Sir Richard de Grey of Codnor Castle (Derbs) as a wedding present for his bride, Joan Fitz Payn. The manuscript is illuminated with the heraldic arms of the families, and one folio depicts Joan wearing a heraldic mantle being blessed by Christ (**colour plate 16**).

Conclusions

Previous studies of commemoration of the dead in the medieval period have tended to concentrate on monuments, but it is clear that in order to provide a more comprehensive picture of commemoration we need to draw on other types of evidence. The dead might be remembered in a variety of ways. Although it is difficult to see at this remove how the poorer members of society commemorated their dead, we can see the messages they would have been confronted with on a regular basis about the fate of the dead in the afterlife and what they could do in this life to ensure that their soul did not go to Hell. We can also see the part that the poor played in the commemoration of the wealthy dead, and there was clearly felt to be a reciprocal relationship between the poor and the wealthy in this respect.

6 The living and the dead

In previous chapters the role of the living in providing for the dead has been discussed. The living were, of course, ultimately responsible for burying the dead and for preparing their body, coffin and grave for the interment. They were also responsible for commemorating the dead and for offering prayers and masses for the souls of the deceased. In this final chapter the impact that the dead had on the living community, the benefits, opportunities and threats that the dead afforded, will be addressed. The chapter addresses the function of funerals for the living community, the employment opportunities afforded by the funerary industry, the value of the remains of some prestigious individuals for the living, and the impact that periods of exceptionally high mortality, such as that following the outbreak of the Black Death, had on society.

Funerals

Although funerals were conducted for the express purpose of committing the remains of individuals to the ground and of setting their soul on the path to whatever awaited them in the afterlife, funerals were really primarily of value to the living. Ultimately funerals were a means by which the living community adjusted itself to the loss of one of its members. Medieval funerals have recently been described as involving a series of ritual processes (Dinn 1992). What has been dubbed the 'ritual of separation' involved the preparation of the dying person for death, the marking of the moment of death (with, for example, bell-ringing), the wrapping of the body in a shroud, and the saying of prayers. The next part of the funerary procedures has been described as a liminal phase, in which the body is taken in a coffin to church accompanied by the appropriate number and rank of people, and, after prayers have been offered in the church, the coffin is taken to the graveside. Finally the funeral may be said to enter a stage of 'ritual reintegration' as the body is buried, a requiem mass is celebrated and a funeral feast is held which was a step on the path towards the healing of the social wound caused by the death, and which helped to restore cohesion to the various groups and communities to which the dead person had belonged.

The death of those individuals who had led the most public lives created the greatest amount of disruption to the status quo. This commonly led to a great deal of time being taken and investment made in the funeral and in the funerary monuments dedicated to that person. The attention paid to such important individuals was not simply a reflection of their intrinsic importance within society, but a means by which the surviving community could both deal with their loss and also establish who was to replace them. We often see individuals in positions of authority in the Middle Ages establishing their authority by reference to the dead, through the bequests and prayers offered for the dead, through pilgrimages to pray and make offerings at their shrines and tombs and through the creation of monuments to them. The dead could give the living legitimacy, if the living made sufficient effort to highlight this (see below, pp.176-7).

In many ways death can be said to have involved two distinct processes — bodily death, which was immediate, and the more protracted process by which the deceased was separated from the living (which for some groups, such as monks and lepers, began even before bodily death had occurred). In fact, however, the on-going masses and prayers for the dead effectively meant that the dead were never completely separated from the living.

The appropriation of ecclesiastical space

The erection of monuments to the dead and the creation of chantry chapels and guilds impacted on the living in more than one way. In addition to providing commemoration and spiritual support for some, they also had an impact on those parishioners who did not have monuments or chantries and who were not members of guilds, since they took over so much space within parish churches. Some churches, as we have seen, became effectively the mausolea of particular families, and social groups. This encroachment on the space of parish churches was not insignificant. Not only did it impress the social importance of certain individuals and groups within local society, but it also affected the ways in which parishioners related to their parish church and to the religious services they attended. Ecclesiastical spaces were regularly transformed as new monuments were erected, and new building programmes started and completed. Throughout all of this, public worship normally continued.

The performance of the liturgy in medieval parish churches was a highly visual affair, which involved the priest processing around the church in a set order, sprinkling the various altars with holy water and eventually coming to the high altar where the Mass was celebrated. The visible routine of ecclesiastical services was extremely important to the meanings that they conveyed to the parishioners. Clearly, then, as new monuments and chantry chapels and guild chapels were built the processional would have been changed, and the experiences of the parishioners altered accordingly. Moreover, the visibility of the Host during the eucharist might also be affected by building programmes, and this not uncommonly led to disputes as parishioners complained that they could not see it. Although the basic layout of a church was determined by liturgical requirements, and involved a basic division between the areas for the parishioners (in the nave) and for the priest (in the chancel), ecclesiastical space was soon transformed under secular influence. The funerary and post-mortem requirements of the wealthy and influential were a major part of this transformation.

Churchyards

Churchyards were not simply places where the dead were buried; they were also where people gathered together for social activities. Churchyards were meeting places and sometimes played host to festivals, plays and markets. They were also places where people played games, such as football, wrestling, ninepins, marbles and quoits. Sometimes this revelry spilled over into violence. Fighting in churchyards would lead to cessation of burials if blood was shed, as happened at Beverley (Yorks) in 1306, and at Grantham (Lincs) in 1468. The churchyard would then have to be reconsecrated. At Grantham the person who had initiated the assault that caused blood to be shed was forced to walk barefoot carrying a wax taper during the reconsecration ceremony attended by the bishop, and he had to kneel down in the corners of the churchyard where he was flogged. This penance was to be repeated on the following Saturdays (at the time when the local market was full of people) and Sundays. For the next seven years on the eight annual vigils of the Virgin he was to have only bread and water. The ghost stories from Byland Abbey (Yorks) from *c.*1400 remind us that the inhabitants of churchyards were not always peacefully at rest, but often roamed the earth seeking assistance for their souls. As such, churchyards might be alarming places, particularly at night.

Buildings have been excavated in churchyards, and this shows that churchyards were often busy places in which a variety of activities took place, not simply the burial of the dead. Some of these buildings may have had religious functions, and may have housed clergy, chantry priests or other religious groups, such as beguines (informal communities of religious women), or have been hospitals or maisonsdieu (as in the churchyard at St Andrew's, York). Adjacent to the later Anglo-Saxon church of St Peter's, Barton-upon-Humber (Lincs) a structure has been excavated which had a flue and stokepit, and which has been interpreted — in the absence of any evidence of slag, waste or other residues — as an ecclesiastical bread oven.

Saints and cults

Saints were important for the living. They were focal points for local allegiances, and attracted much patronage to the churches where they were held. Saints' cults attracted pilgrims, who brought with them wealth, and who served to foster trade. Margery Kempe (*c.*1373-*c.*1440), the mystic from King's Lynn (Norfolk) travelled to York to visit the shrine of St William and to Bridlington to the shrine of St John of Bridlington. Pilgrimage was not, however, without its dangers. Margery was regarded with suspicion in York and there was an attempt to put her in prison because of the disquiet that her long stay caused. She was ordered to appear before the Archbishop of York, and although he found no fault with her she was later taken prisoner in Beverley.

Saints were believed to have miraculous powers. This is demonstrated by a window in York Minster, which shows a man holding up a wax effigy of a leg as a votive offering at the shrine of St William of York, probably in the hope of acquiring a miracle. Saints also offered intercession for the soul of the deceased, and they also had political value for the living. One of the most actively promoted cults in our region was that of St Cuthbert. The possession of his relics by a very wealthy religious community which had close links with successive kings, the periodic translations of his body, the subsequent enrichment of his tomb, the multiple miracles ascribed to him, and the commissioning of *Lives* of the saint, did much to enhance the fame of St Cuthbert, and to underpin the political role of the religious community associated with him. In the 880s, according to the anonymous *Historia de Sancto Cuthberto*, St Cuthbert is said to have appeared to the Abbot of Carlisle, who was told to cross the Tyne to the army of the Danes and to seek out Guthred, son of Harthacnut, and to have him elected as king. The abbot was to lead Guthred 'with the whole army to the hill which is called 'Oswiu's down, and there place on his right arm a gold armlet, and thus they all may acknowledge him as king'. In addition to drawing on the support of St Cuthbert, Guthred was also seen to have acquired the support of Oswiu, who was a famous and sainted seventh-century king of Northumbria. Guthred was later permitted burial in the 'high church at York' in 895 by the Archbishop of York.

The *Historia de Sancto Cuthberto* contains an account of the miracles that St Cuthbert allegedly performed for King Alfred of Wessex while he was in hiding from Scandinavian raiders in the Somerset marshlands in 878. It is unlikely that the house of Wessex and the community of St Cuthbert were seeking alliances in 878, but they certainly needed the support of each other 40 or 50 years later. The West Saxons needed to draw on the influence of important cults, and their associated religious communities, as they sought to take control of northern England in the early tenth century, and the community of St Cuthbert may have developed an interest in forging links with the West Saxons following their loss of land in the early tenth century to Scandinavian raiders. In 934 King Athelstan of Wessex made lavish gifts to the community, and although West Saxon authority in the North was lost after Athelstan's death, his successor, Edmund, granted privileges to the community in 944. This may have been the context for the addition to the *Historia* of the miraculous appearance to King Alfred in 878, when St Cuthbert assured Alfred of his, and his descendants', future rulership over all Britain. Saints could be very useful during times of political and military struggle.

Churchmen played an important role in publicising cults, and in particular the miracles that saints performed. Bede for example learned of the miracles of certain saints from fellow churchmen. In addition to the pious motifs for such interest, saints also provided useful protection for claims to land. In the *Life of St Wilfrid* the lands given by Northumbrian kings to Wilfrid were recorded, and this text was preserved by the religious community at Ripon, where it may have been read aloud at certain times, perhaps on the feast-day of the saint (which at Ripon was every Thursday). In effect, a saint's *Life* formed an everlasting record of the possessions of a church. When this record is combined with tales of the terrible fate that might befall someone who attacked the possessions of the church — in the case of St Wilfrid some of the men who burned the monastery where he died at Oundle were subsequently blinded — it can be seen that in the cases of saints, the dead continued to exert an important influence on society and politics for decades, if not centuries.

The translation of saints' relics from northern England to southern monasteries and cathedrals was a prominent feature of the tenth century, and must, in part, reflect the growing assertion of West Saxon domination of the North. While we should not overlook the pious motives of the house of Wessex, nor, perhaps, their desire both to protect relics from the Scandinavians and to benefit from their spiritual power, there was clearly also political capital to be gained from the acquisition of relics, as they were used to reward churches long-established with the West Saxon kings or churches in newly conquered territories within Mercia. The importance of saints' relics, and the implications of their loss, should not be underestimated. They were central to the lives of the religious communities who possessed them, and were also important to the local laity.

Not all saints and cults were officially sanctioned and the clergy often condemned them, particularly those that the peasantry promoted. For example, at Rippingale (Lincs) villagers set up a cross in the fields at which they prayed, held processions and made offerings, because they attributed miraculous happenings to it. The bishop of Lincoln, John Buckingham, ordered an enquiry in 1386 and condemned the practice, but ironically six years later the pope permitted a chapel of the Holy Cross to be set up at Rippingale. It may have seemed unreasonable to contemporaries that such practices were condemned when earlier bishops such as St Hugh had been avid collectors of relics. Indeed, the accounts of the ways in which St Hugh acquired relics reveal the almost depraved lengths that ecclesiastics would go to build their collections of relics. At the abbey of Fécamp he horrified the monks by using a knife to cut the cloth which was wrapped around the body of Mary Magdalen, and then by biting off two small bones from the arm. At Meulan, near Paris, St Hugh visited the shrine of the martyred Bishop Nicasius of Rheims, where he

> Put his fingers in the nostrils which had always breathed the good odour of Christ, and easily removed a delicate little bone which had separated the martyr's two eye-sockets.

This was after his attempts to extract one of the teeth of the saint had failed!

The funerary industry

Death and the rituals and paraphernalia surrounding it required a veritable industry of workers to support it. Although we know little about their production, coffins had to be made in both wood and stone right the way through our period. The study of excavated coffins reveals that different forms of coffin were used even in the same cemetery, as we have already seen at Swinegate in York, Barton-upon-Humber and York Minster. Coffin-makers were innovative and often fashioned wooden coffins out of other items, such as chests (as at York and Ripon) and pieces of domestic furniture (as at Barton-upon-Humber). Whether this is an indication of thrift, of the informal nature of coffin making (at least in the Anglo-Saxon period), or represents some 'symbolic' reuse of wooden items for coffins is unclear. Excavations at the Augustinian Priory in Hull have revealed a number of coffins made from Baltic oak (above, p.115) (see 37, 38), and such analyses enable us to see something of the economy of the coffin industry. Customs accounts from a number of ports in eastern England reveal that a great deal of Baltic timber was imported from the early fourteenth century, and that it typically arrived in plank form. Such timbers have been discovered used for boat planking, barrel staves, doors, cupboards, wall and ceiling panels, church altars and screens, and panel paintings. The Hull friary site provided the first example yet discovered in England of the use of Baltic oak for coffins. Dendrochronological dates reveal that most of the timbers were felled between 1327 and 1349, and the rest after 1362.

Stone coffins were also extremely varied in their form and decoration. During the Anglo-Saxon period stone coffins were sometimes highly decorated, and these were presumably made for holy or otherwise important individuals, and may have been intended to be on display rather than buried (*see* **3**). Stone coffins were also capable of reuse.

We know rather more about the production of funerary monuments. In the Anglo-Saxon period, the products of a small number of workshops have been identified by detailed study of the stone monuments of the region. Analysis of cutting techniques, styles and the layout of designs have permitted students of this art form to identify the products of workshops probably located in York, Bakewell (Derbs) and in the Ryedale district (Yorks), for example. It has also been demonstrated that workshops were innovative and able to produce a wide variety of types of monument. Recent detailed work on cutting techniques, the methods of laying out the decorative scheme and the dimensions of particular motifs has provided new insights into sculpture production. These elements of sculptural production are precise and idiosyncratic, and their study has permitted the recognition that the same workshop could produce monuments with radical differences in ornament and form. For example, it has been shown that a round cross-shaft at Masham was produced by the same hand as a squared cross-shaft from Cundall (Yorks), whereas previously these monuments had been ascribed very different chronologies because of the differences in design. This redefinition of typologies serves as a reminder that craftspeople may produce artefacts in response to demand, and not simply because of some inert following of fashion, or because they were only able or inclined to produce a single type of monument. Those who commissioned, bought and used stone funerary monuments during the Anglo-Saxon period were offered a choice. Thus, it may be that regional forms of monument may not have been simply the product of continually evolving styles of sculpture or because it was all that was available, but because lords wanted to express themselves and their allegiances through the commissioning of monuments with regionally-recognizable motifs.

In the later Middle Ages there was a wider diversity of funerary monuments than in the Anglo-Saxon centuries. We know comparatively quite a lot about the later medieval funerary industry, and it is apparent that there were important connections between the various craftworkers. Traditionally, comparison has been drawn between brasses and effigial sculpture, and while this is understandable given that the subject matter is commonly the same, there may be greater similarities, on a technical level, between brasses and other two-dimensional art forms, such as other forms of metal engraving, and painting on walls and glass and in manuscripts. There are, for example, striking similarities between the brass made for Archbishop Greenfield and the work of glaziers in the window glass of York Minster. Indeed, the brass may have been the work of a glazier given the contrast with brasses being produced in experienced workshops in London. Brass manufacture also required cooperation between metalworkers and marblers, although we do not know very much about how this relationship worked and who had the greater impact on the evolution of new styles. One useful insight, from outside our region, comes from the accounts of the executors of the will of Dean Kilkenny of Exeter Cathedral (d.1302) which show that the design was executed by John the Painter and then followed by masons and a metalworker. It may be, however, that the initial impetus for laying brass in stone or marble came from the masons or marblers, since the skills required to work with this material would have been the major determinant on how brass could be inset.

The brass industry is comparatively well known. While there is much that is common to brasses of various periods and workshops, there is also much that is peculiar to particular workshops or periods. There is, for example, a big difference between the rigid figures of many brasses and the swaying mobility of the figures of the so-called Hastings style (named after the finest example of this style made for Sir Hugh Hastings of Elsing (Norfolk) (d.1347)) manufactured in London. This style is similar to that of a brass from Linwood (Lincs) made for Sir Henry de Bayous (d.1328-32), an incised slab at Lincoln made in the 1340s and also on some of the figures in the clerestory windows in the Lady Chapel at York Minster. This style appears to have disappeared after the 1340s, and it may be that the workshop producing brasses in the Hastings style was wiped out by the Black Death in 1348-9. The relationship between the workshops in London and those in the provinces is unclear, and while there are many similarities of style it is also clear that there was a wide range of different designs emanating from the northern workshops. Indeed, there may have been more experimentation there than in London, where the workshops were designing and manufacturing for the market place items of distinctive and high quality, whereas some of the northern workshops seem to have been producing a wide range of monuments from the very elaborate to the very simple, low quality items. The northern workshops did not, as far as we know, begin to produce figure brasses much before 1300, and, as had happened earlier in London, inlayers of brass letters eventually moved on to producing grander creations in the fourteenth century. Even in the production of simple inlays of letters, however, there were to be distinctive northern forms as new types of lettering emerged, although letters for inlaying continued to be acquired from London throughout. The influence of the Flemish workshops is also noticeable on northern brasses, and was doubtless a product of the trading connections between English ports on the east coast and the continent. Clearly the brass industry was dynamic, and demand ebbed and flowed, meaning that brass workshops had to be prepared to respond to changing demand, in addition to leading that demand.

The alabaster industry in England was largely limited to the study area considered by this book. The alabaster used for effigies and slabs was largely quarried from a comparatively small area in the Trent Valley, with the main quarries apparently being located near to Tutbury (Staffs) and Chellaston (Notts). The earliest known use of alabaster in England comes from the later twelfth century when it was used in the west door of Tutbury Priory church, and the earliest surviving alabaster effigy dates to *c.*1300, at Hanbury (Staffs). By the eighteenth century alabaster was also being quarried from Red Hill (Notts) and the site may conceivably have been exploited in the Middle Ages. Alabaster workers are known to have been at work in York in the fifteenth century and they may have been acquiring their alabaster from a local source (possibly from the alabaster deposits at Ledsham or Buttercrambe). The main centre of carving of alabaster in the later Middle Ages appears from documentary evidence to have been Nottingham, although there were also concentrations of alabaster workers in York, Lincoln, Chellaston, Coventry (Warws) and Burton-on-Trent (Staffs). The Nottingham alabastermen seem to have specialised in producing panels, figures and altarpieces, while the alabaster workshops at Chellaston, for example, are a well-documented centre of the production of alabaster tombs. The alabaster workers of York made altarpieces (as can be seen from the discovery of several large panels from an altarpiece of the life of St William of York), and they may have made the alabaster tombs found nearby at Haworth, Methley and Sheriff Hutton (Yorks). In 1525-6 a guild of painters, gilders, stainers and alabastermen is recorded in Lincoln. Here the alabastermen were probably tomb carvers.

The names of the alabaster workers that are recorded in documentary sources from numerous places are all of English type and this suggests that this was an indigenous industry, rather than one involving foreign craft workers. That it was a family industry is suggested by references at Nottingham to the alabaster craftsmen Nicholas Hill and Thomas Hill in the 1490s and 1500s, and Walter Hilton and Edward Hilton in the 1480s, and at York a father and son, John and Thomas Roper, are recorded in the later fifteenth century. There is also slight evidence that women might be involved in the alabaster industry, such as Margery Walker of Burton-on-Trent and Emma Spenser of Nottingham.

The Black Death

The Black Death first arrived in England at the end of 1348 and successive outbreaks were to follow through the later fourteenth and fifteenth centuries. There has been much debate about the extent of its impact, and it has become common to set the impact of the Back Death in a broader context, and to draw attention to other factors affecting fourteenth-century society, such as war, the harvest failure, famines and cattle diseases of the early part of the century, ecclesiastical conflict, and so on. Yet while it is true that the Black Death was not the only factor that caused social and economic change in the fourteenth and fifteenth centuries, nonetheless the documentary evidence suggests that at least a third of the population died in the first outbreak of plague and that the plague was a powerful force for change. Some have argued that the fact that England was overpopulated in 1348 and that there was great demand for land meant that the first outbreak of plague was not catastrophic because there were so many people available to fill gaps in the ranks of tenants. Indeed, they have sometimes gone as far as to say that the plague was beneficial to the economy in the short term because it restored a balance between the demand and availability of land. However, Rosemary Horrox (1994, 236) has recently suggested that the notion that life continued pretty much as before in 1349 seems barely credible, and it would be better to describe the changes that the first outbreak of the plague caused as being 'contained', but that that the situation became 'unmanageable' following successive outbreaks in the 1360s.

Central government initially did little to respond to changing circumstances beyond trying to reinforce the status quo. For example, tax assessments remained fixed at the pre-plague levels (of 1334) for nearly half a century and the government attempted to collect taxation much as it had done previously. The Ordinance of Labourers was issued in June 1349 and it was an attempt to keep wage-rates at their pre-plague levels and to force the able-bodied to work. The subsequent Statute of Labourers (February 1351) indicates that there had been widespread evasion, and it sought to establish more precisely how these labour laws were to be put into effect. Clerical avarice was also a problem, or at least it was perceived to be, and various episcopal measures were taken to limit the wages of priests (see above, p.88). The problems of recruitment to the priestly lifestyle have already been mentioned (p.87). That priests were no longer prepared to accept the terms that they had been accustomed to is indicated by various cases in which incumbencies lay vacant, and recruitment was problematic, and by such measures as those taken in 1365 by Roger of Chesterfield, rector of the parish church of Wigginton (Lincoln), to revise the statutes of a chantry in Chesterfield (Derbs) to make it more attractive to future applicants to the job. As a priest himself, Roger presumably knew of the complaints and attitudes of his contemporaries, and the requirements of the job were scaled down and the chantry priest was even to be allowed occasional trips to the local taverns.

If the plague gave employees an opportunity to improve their lot, it also brought with it the danger of legal sanction and also moral outrage. It is clear that many contemporary observations about the behaviour of the laity had a strong moral component. By improving their circumstances and, for example, dressing above their natural station in life they were perceived by some commentators as threatening the divinely sanctioned natural order of the world. The Leicester chronicler Henry Knighton, writing in the 1390s, observed that

> The pride of the lower orders has so blossomed forth and grown these days in fine dress and splendid display . . . that one can hardly distinguish one person from another, because of their gorgeous clothes and accessories . . . each [strives] to excel his superior by wearing even grander clothes.

Moreover, by engaging in frivolity and by being lazy, workers were running the risk of seeing their soul damned. Contemporaries were of the opinion that the post-plague world was characterized by moral degeneracy: greedy and quarrelsome men, sexually active women, drunken and lecherous clergy, and a general threat to the social order. However, what contemporaries saw as moral degeneracy may be viewed very differently from our perspective. Whatever its psychological impact, which may have been terrible, the ramifications of the plague did provide new opportunities for workers, and an improved bargaining position with both employers and landlords.

Whether contemporaries were glad of these opportunities and how they felt about reaping the benefits of the deaths of so many of their friends, family and compatriots is difficult to judge. A certain level of vulnerability and guilt may have been experienced by the survivors, and although we have no real insight into medieval psychology the fact that the image of Fortune's Wheel became very common in the art and literature of the fifteenth century suggests a strong awareness of how fragile success might be.

The decline in population had a major impact on the landscape. Many settlements were eventually to be entirely deserted, and others shrank in size. There is little evidence that the population of any village was completely wiped out by a single visitation of plague. Most rural settlements appear to have been deserted gradually, or as a result of a combination of factors. Some of those that were eventually to be deserted showed signs of problems, such as an inability to pay taxes, even before the outbreak of plague. Some villages may have been deserted because the inhabitants chose to move elsewhere to take up more favourable tenancies and employment opportunities. This may help to explain why it was that many of the villages in the supposedly better and more fertile agricultural lands of the river valleys were deserted, and why settlements on the more marginal, less productive agricultural lands, which were also typically less burdened with rents and demands for labour services, were able to survive. Settlements in the more fertile agricultural lands where large open-field systems were prevalent often suffered because the community obligation and cooperation that was required to run these field systems was inflexible and prone to come under great stress when there was even a small decline in population. Settlements that operated a more mixed economy, and where fields were enclosed and run by individual families, were more flexible and better able to cope with the changed social and economic circumstances of the later fourteenth and fifteenth century.

The forcible eviction of peasants from land in order that lords could enclose the land and graze sheep on it is certainly known from the region, but it is something that often appears to have followed in the wake of a long period of decline. Villages such as Snarford, Kettleby Thorpe, Audleby, Wharton, Buslingthorpe and Wharton (Lincs) all appear to have disappeared during the course of the fifteenth century, and enclosure for pasture probably explains most of these desertions. Towns were also affected in different ways. Even within a single town some districts were badly hit, but others prospered. In the 1530s when John Leland passed through Boston he commented that 'fair dwellings' and 'sore decay' coexisted in the town. Thus, in both the countryside and the town, disaster for one man may have meant success for his neighbour.

The Black Death also had a major impact on artistic production. As we have seen (above p.90), there is little evidence that the artistic world was completely transformed, as most artistic styles common in the later fourteenth and fifteenth century can be found prior to 1348, but the Black Death certainly transformed the industry. For example, the brass manufacturer who was responsible for the so-called Hastings style of brass appears to have died in 1348-9 and his style with him. Building projects at some churches may have been interrupted following the death of craftsmen. For example, the master mason of York Minster, Thomas de Pacenham, appears to have died in 1349, the Beverley school of sculptures appears to have virtually disappeared after 1348, and the York school of glass painting and design also appears to have been severely disrupted at this time, and may still have been affected in 1405 when the east window of the choir was commissioned and the contract went outside York to John Thornton of Coventry (Warws). However, it was not simply the death of prominent craft workers that affected artistic production. The exorbitant wages charged by those who survived may also have had an impact. In 1349 the crown issued the Ordinance of Labourers, which sought to limit wages to their level in 1346, and in 1351 the Statute of Labourers sought to make the labour laws even more precise. One of the regulations of the Statute stated that 'carpenters, masons, tilers and other roofers of houses shall not take more for their day's work than the accustomed amount', which it then goes on to recount. The shortage of skilled workers meant that the crown sometimes had to resort to impressment to acquire them (although this was a practice that had occasionally occurred before 1348), particularly between 1350 and 1380, and one contemporary commentator observed that 'almost all the masons and carpenters throughout the whole of England were brought to [Windsor], so that hardly anyone could have any good mason or carpenter except in secret'. This often led to patrons competing with each other to offer better wages to acquire the services of master craftsmen.

Conclusions

As we have seen throughout this book, death was a complex, multi-faceted business, surrounded by a diverse range of rituals. It is clear that any study of death in the Middle Ages that wishes to understand the place of death in medieval life should not limit itself only to excavated cemeteries. Even a widening of focus to include funerary monuments will not really suffice, and we have to explore documentary sources and visual evidence. We also have to remember that official Church doctrine was not the only factor that determined the way in which the dead were treated, and popular customs and folkloric belief, and individual affection or repulsion for the dead, played their part in determining the fate of the dead.

There is certainly evidence to indicate a reciprocal relationship between the living and the dead throughout our period. However, we also have to remember that the dead often posed a threat to the living, in the form of their ghostly return, the repulsiveness of their state and the demands they made for prayer and commemoration. Moreover, the living were often ambivalent about the dead, as graves were disturbed, chantries left unfounded or allowed to fall into disuse, wills ignored and commemoration abandoned. While there was an obligation on medieval communities to remember the dead, there was also the impulse to forget. The relationship between the living and the dead was complex and ever changing.

At the end of our period the Reformation swept away many of the props and paraphernalia of the Church, and fundamentally affected the ways in which the dead were treated. Certainly there has been much debate about exactly how fundamental was the break in traditions brought about by the Reformation, and whatever the teachings of the Church the dead continued to be of importance and to be commemorated on a personal level, if no longer at the institutional level. Moreover, the dead were still commonly buried in the same places as the dead of previous generations. Northern and western England appear to have been slower to abandon Catholic traditions. On his translation from London to the see of York in 1570 Edmund Grindal commented:

> I am informed that the greatest part of our gentlemen are not well affected to godly religion, and that among the people there are many remnants of the old. They keep holy days and fasts abrogated, they offer money, eggs etc. at the burial of their dead: they pray on beads etc.: so this seemeth to be, as it were, another church, rather than a member of the rest.

Yet in spite of such remarks, things had changed. Gone were the monasteries and chantry chapels where the wealthier dead were laid to rest and provided with post-mortem prayers. Wall paintings were lime-washed over and replaced with texts of scripture. Monuments were destroyed or hidden away. The saints were swept away, and with this an important means by which even the humble dead were remembered.

Bibliography

1 General: death in the Middle Ages

S.R. Bassett (ed.), *Death in Towns. Urban responses to the Dying and the Dead, 400-1600* (Leicester, 1992)

N.L. Beaty, *The craft of dying: a study in the literary tradition of the Ars moriendi* (New Haven, 1970)

P. Binski, *Medieval Death. Ritual and Representation* (London, 1996)

D. Crouch, 'The culture of death in the Anglo-Norman world', in C.W. Hollister (ed.), *Anglo-Norman Political Culture and the Twelfth-Century Renaissance* (Woodbridge, 1997), 157-80

C. Daniell, *Death and Burial in Medieval England* (London, 1997)

C. Daniell and V. Thompson, 'Pagans and Christians, 400-1150', in P. Jupp and C. Gittings, *Death in England: an illustrated history* (Manchester, 1999), 65-89

R. Dinn, 'Death and rebirth in late medieval Bury St Edmunds', in S.R. Bassett (ed.), *Death in Towns. Urban responses to the Dying and the Dead, 400-1600* (Leicester, 1992), 152-69

B. Effros, '*De Partibus Saxoniae* and the regulation of mortuary custom: a Carolingian campaign of Christianization or the suppression of Saxon identity?', *Revue Belge de Philologie et d'Histoire* 75, fasc. 2 (1995), 267-86

R.C. Finucane, 'Sacred corpse, profane carrion: social ideals and death rituals in the later Middle Ages', in J. Whaley (ed.), *Mirrors of Mortality. Studies in the Social History of Death* (London, 1981), 40-60

R. Gilchrist, 'Christian bodies and souls: the archaeology of life and death in later medieval hospitals', in S. Bassett (ed.), *Death in Towns. Urban Responses to the Dying and the Dead, 400-1600* (Leicester, 1992), 101-18

A. Gill, 'Heart burials', *Proceedings of the Yorkshire Architectural and Archaeological Society*, 7 (4) (1936), 3-18

B. Golding, 'Anglo-Norman knightly burials', in C. Harper-Bill and R. Harvey (ed.), *The Ideals and Practice of Knighthood* (Woodbridge, 1986), 35-48

P. Heath, 'Urban piety in the later Middle Ages: the evidence of Hull wills', in D.B. Dobson (ed.), *The Church, Politics and Patronage in the Fifteenth Century* (Gloucester, 1984), 209-34

R. Horrox, 'Purgatory, prayer and plague, 1150-1380, in P. Jupp and C. Gittings, *Death in England: an illustrated history* (Manchester, 1999), 90-118

P. Jupp and C. Gittings (ed.), *Death in England: an illustrated history* (Manchester, 1999)

C. Karkov, 'Whitby, Jarrow and the commemoration of death in Northumbria', in J. Hawkes and S. Mills (ed.), *Northumbria's Golden Age* (Stroud, 1999), 126-35

P. Morgan, 'Of worms and war, 1380-1558', in P. Jupp and C. Gittings, *Death in England: an illustrated history* (Manchester, 1999), 119-46

R.K. Morris, *Churches in the Landscape* (London, 1989)

C. Platt, *King Death: The Black Death and its aftermath in Late Medieval England* (London, 1996)

R. Samson, 'The Church lends a hand', in J. Downes and T. Pollard (ed.), *The Loved Body's Corruption* (Glasgow, 1999), 120-44

2 General : the Church and religion in the Middle Ages

i) Early medieval

M. Biddle, 'Archaeology, architecture and the cult of saints', in L.A.S. Butler and R.K. Morris (ed.), *The Anglo-Saxon Church* (CBA Research Report, 60, 1986), 1-31

J. Blair (ed.), *Minsters and Parish Churches. The Local Church in Transition, 950-1200*, ed. J. Blair (Oxford, 1988)

J. Blair, 'Ecclesiastical organization and pastoral care in Anglo-Saxon England', *Early Medieval Europe*, 4 (2) (1996), 193-212

J. Blair and R. Sharpe, *Pastoral Care Before the Parish* (Leicester, 1992)

D. Bullough, 'Burial, community and belief in the early medieval West', in P. Wormald (ed.), *Ideal and Reality in Frankish and Anglo-Saxon Society* (Oxford, 1983), 77-201

L. Butler and R.K. Morris, *The Anglo-Saxon Church* (CBA Research Report, 60, 1986)

E. Cambridge and D.W. Rollason, 'The pastoral organization of the Anglo-Saxon church: review of the "minster hypothesis"', *Early Medieval Europe* 4 (1) (1995), 87-104

C. Karkov, 'Whitby, Jarrow and the commemoration of death in Northumbria', in J. Hawkes and S. Mills (ed.), *Northumbria's Golden Age* (Stroud, 1999), 126-35

R.K. Morris, *The Church in British Archaeology* (CBA Research Report, 47, 1983)

ii) Later medieval

P. Cullum and J. Goldberg, 'Charitable provision in late medieval York: "To the praise of God and the use of the poor"', *Northern History*, 29 (1993), 24-39

R. Gilchrist, *Gender and Material Culture. The Archaeology of Religious Women* (London, 1994)

R. Gilchrist, *Contemplation and Action. The Other Monasticism* (London, 1995)

R.K. Morris, *The Church in British Archaeology* (CBA Research Report, 47, 1983)

D. Owen, *Church and Society in Medieval Lincolnshire* (Lincoln, 1971)

C. Platt, *The Parish Churches of Medieval England* (London, 1981)

C. Platt, *The Abbeys and Priories of Medieval England* (London, 1984)

R.N. Swanson, *Church and society in late medieval England* (Oxford, 1989)

M. Vale, *Piety, Charity and Literacy among the Yorkshire Gentry, 1370-1480* (York, 1976)

3 Excavated cemeteries

This includes the cemeteries referred to in the book that have been published.

i) Early Anglo-Saxon cemeteries (fifth to seventh centuries)

A. Boddington, 'Modes of burial, settlement and worship: the final phase reviewed', in E. Southworth (ed.), *Anglo-Saxon Cemeteries: A Reappraisal* (Stroud, 1990), 177-99

H. Geake, *The Use of Grave-Goods in Conversion-Period England, c.600-c.850* (BAR British Series, 261, 1997)

S. Lucy, *The Early Anglo-Saxon Cemeteries of East Yorkshire. An Analysis and Reinterpretation* (BAR, British Series, 272, 1998)

S. Lucy, *The Anglo-Saxon Way of Death* (Stroud, 2000)

A.L. Meaney and S.C. Hawkes, *Two Anglo-Saxon Cemeteries at Winnall, Winchester, Hampshire*, Society for Medieval Archaeology Monograph, IV (1970)

J.R. Mortimer, *Forty Years Researches on British and Saxon Burial Mounds of East Yorkshire* (London, 1905)

R. van de Noort, 'The context of early medieval barrows in western Europe', *Antiquity*, 67 (1993), 66-73

ii) Mid- and later Anglo-Saxon cemeteries

K. Adams, 'Monastery and village at Crayke, North Yorkshire', *Yorkshire Archaeological Journal*, 62 (1990), 29-50

M. Adams, 'Excavation of a pre-Conquest cemetery at Addingham, West Yorkshire', *Medieval Archaeology*, 40 (1996), 151-91

J. Blair, *Anglo-Saxon Oxfordshire* (Stroud, 1994)

R. Cramp, 'A reconsideration of the monastic site of Whitby', in R.M. Spearman and J. Higgitt (ed.), *The Age of Migrating Ideas* (Stroud, 1993), 64-73

S. Crawford, 'The Anglo-Saxon cemetery at Chimney, Oxfordshire', *Oxoniensia*, 54 (1989), 45-56

R. Daniels, 'The Anglo-Saxon monastery at Church Close, Hartlepool, Cleveland', *Archaeological Journal*, 145 (1988), 158-210

N. Field, 'Fillingham', *Lincolnshire History and Archaeology*, 18 (1983), 96-7

N. Field, 'A possible Saxon cemetery at Swaby', *Lincolnshire History and Archaeology*, 28 (1993), 45-6

D.M. Hadley, 'Burial Practices in the Northern Danelaw, c.650-1100', *Northern History*, 36 (2) (2000), 199-216

D.M. Hadley, 'Equality, humility and non-materialism? Christianity and Anglo-Saxon burial practices', *Archaeological Review from Cambridge*, 17 (2) (2000), 149-78

R.A. Hall and M. Whyman, 'Settlement and monasticism at Ripon, North Yorkshire, from the seventh to eleventh centuries AD', *Medieval Archaeology*, 40 (1996), 62-150

D. Hinton, 'A smith's hoard from Tattershall Thorpe, Lincolnshire: a synopsis', *Anglo-Saxon England*, 22 (1994), 147-66

C. Loveluck, 'A high-status Anglo-Saxon settlement at Flixborough, Lincolnshire', *Antiquity*, 72 (1998), 146-61

A. Morton, 'Burial in middle Saxon Southampton', in S. Bassett (ed.), *Death in Towns. Urban responses to the Dying and the Dead 400-1600* (Leicester, 1992), 68-77

H. Mytum, 'Kellington church', *Current Archaeology*, 133 (1993), 15-17

M. Parker Pearson and N. Field, 'Fiskerton. An Iron Age timber causeway with Iron Age and Roman votive offerings' (2001, forthcoming)

D. Philips, *Excavations at York Minster, Volume I* (2 parts) (London, 1995)

J. Samuels, 'Newark Castle', *Current Archaeology*, 156 (1998), 458-61

J. Sills, 'St Peter's church, Holton-le-Clay, Lincolnshire', *Lincolnshire History and Archaeology*, 17 (1982), 29-42

P. Rahtz, 'Anglo-Saxon and later Whitby', in L. Hoey (ed.), *Yorkshire Monasticism. Archaeology, Art and Architecture from the seventh to sixteenth Centuries AD*, (London, 1995), 1-11

P. Rahtz, and L. Watts, 'Kirkdale Anglo-Saxon minster', *Current Archaeology*, 155 (1998), 419-22

W. Rodwell and K. Rodwell, 'St Peter's church, Barton-upon-Humber: excavation and structural study, 1978-81', *Antiquaries Journal*, 62 (1982), 283-315

T. Wilmott, 'Pontefract', *Current Archaeology*, 106 (1987), 340-4

iii) 'Viking' burials

M. Biddle, 'A parcel of pennies from a mass-burial associated with the Viking wintering at Repton in 873-4', *British Numismatic Journal*, 56 (1986), 25-30

M. Biddle and B. Kjølbye-Biddle, 'Repton and the Vikings', *Antiquity*, 250 (March, 1992), 36-51

J. Graham-Campbell, 'The Scandinavian Viking-Age burials of England — some problems of interpretation', in P. Rahtz, T. Dickinson and L. Watts (ed.), *Anglo-Saxon Cemeteries* (BAR British Series, 82, 1980), 379-82

J. Graham-Campbell, 'Pagans and Christians', *History Today*, 36 (October, 1986), 24-8

G. Halsall, 'The Viking presence in England? The

burial evidence reconsidered', in D.M. Hadley and J.D. Richards (ed.), *Cultures in Contact: Scandinavian Settlement in England in the ninth and tenth centuries* (Turnhout, 2000), 259-76

D. O'Sullivan, 'A group of pagan burials from Cumbria?', *Anglo-Saxon Studies in Archaeology and History*, 9 (1996), 15-23

M. Posnansky, 'The pagan-Danish barrow cemetery at Heath Wood, Ingleby: 1955 excavations', *Derbyshire Archaeological Journal*, 76 (1956), 40-51

J.D. Richards, *Viking Age England* (London, 1991; 2nd revised edition, Stroud, 2000)

J.D. Richards, M. Jecock, L. Richmond and C. Tuck, 'The Viking barrow cemetery at Heath Wood, Ingleby, Derbyshire', *Medieval Archaeology*, 39 (1995), 51-70

iv) Later medieval cemeteries

E. Baldi, 'Conservation of a pewter chalice from the priory of St Mary Magdalene of Monk Bretton, South Yorkshire', *Yorkshire Archaeological Journal*, 72 (2000), 59-65

J. Barrow, 'Urban cemetery location in the high Middle Ages', in S.R. Bassett (ed.), *Death in Towns. Urban responses to the Dying and the Dead, 400-1600* (Leicester, 1992), 78-100

M. Beresford and J. Hurst, *Wharram Percy Deserted Medieval Village* (London, 1990)

R. Bruce-Mitford, 'The Chapter House Vestibule graves at Lincoln and the body of St Hugh of Avalon', in F. Emmison and R. Stephens (ed.), *Tribute to an Antiquary* (London, 1976), 127-40

C. Coppack, 'Excavations at Chapel Garth, Bolton, Fangfoss, Yorks', *Yorkshire Archaeological Journal*, 50 (1978), 93-150

G. Coppack, 'St Lawrence church, Burnham, South Humberside. The excavation of a parochial chapel', *Lincolnshire History and Archaeology*, 21 (1986), 39-60

J. Dawes and J. Magilton, *The Cemetery of St Helen-on-the-Walls, Aldwark*, The Archaeology of York, 12 (1) (London, 1980)

R.B. Dobson and S. Donaghey, *The History of Clementhorpe Nunnery*, The Archaeology of York, 2 (1) (London, 1984)

V. Fiorato, A. Boylston and C. Knüsel (ed.), *Blood Red Roses. The Archaeology of a Mass Grave from the Battle of Towton AD 1461* (Oxford, 2000)

B. Gilmour and D. Stocker, *St Mark's Church and Cemetery*, The Archaeology of Lincoln, 13 (1) (London, 1986)

D. Hawkins, 'The Black Death and the new London cemeteries of 1348', *Antiquity*, 64 (1990), 637-42

R. Kemp and C.P. Graves, *The Church and Gilbertine Priory of St Andrew, Fishergate*, The Archaeology of York, 11 (2) (London, 1996)

P. Lilley, *The Jewish Burial Ground at Jewbury*, The Archaeology of York, 12 (3) (London, 1994)

J. Magilton, *The Church of St Helen-on-the-Walls, Aldwark*, The Archaeology of York, 10 (1) (London, 1980)

H. Mytum, 'Kellington church', *Current Archaeology*, 133 (1993), 15-17

H. Mytum, 'Parish and people: excavations at Kellington church', *Medieval Life*, I (1994), 19-22

H.G. Ramm, 'The tombs of Archbishops Walter de Gray (1216-55) and Godfrey de Ludham (1258-65) in York Minster and their contents', *Archaeologia*, 103 (1971), 101-48

W. Rodwell, *Church Archaeology* (London, 1984)

G. Stroud and R. Kemp, *Cemeteries of the Church and Priory of St Andrew, Fishergate*, The Archaeology of York, 12 (2) (London, 1993)

4 Anglo-Saxon Stone Sculpture

i) Guides to the location of sculpture in the region

W.G. Collingwood, 'Anglian and Anglo-Danish sculpture in the North Riding of Yorkshire', *Yorkshire Arcaeological Journal*, 19 (1907), 267-413

W.G. Collingwood, 'Anglian and Anglo-Danish sculpture in the West Riding of Yorkshire', *Yorkshire Archaeological Journal*, 23 (1915), 129-299

W.G. Collingwood, *Northumbrian Crosses of the Pre-Norman Age* (London, 1927)

D. Davies, 'Pre-Conquest carved stones in Lincolnshire', *Archaeological Journal*, 83 (1926), 1-20

P. Everson and D. Stocker, *Corpus of Anglo-Saxon Stone Sculpture, V. Lincolnshire* (London, 1999)

J. Lang, *Corpus of Anglo-Saxon Stone Sculpture, III. York and Eastern Yorkshire* (London, 1991)

T. Routh, 'A corpus of pre-Conquest carved stones of Derbyshire', *Derbyshire Archaeological Journal*, 71 (1937), 1-46

ii) Analyses of the significance of Anglo-Saxon stone sculpture

R. Bailey, *Viking Age Sculpture in Northern England* (London, 1980)

R. Bailey, *England's Earliest Sculptors* (Toronto, 1997)

M. Biddle and B. Kjølbye-Biddle, 'The Repton stone', *Anglo-Saxon England*, 14 (1985), 233-92

R. Cockerton, 'The Wirksworth slab', *Derbyshire Archaeological Journal*, 82 (1962), 1-20

J. Hawkes, 'Mary and the Cycle of Resurrection: the iconography of the Hovingham panel', in R.M. Spearman and J. Higgitt (ed.), *The Age of Migrating Ideas* (1993), 254-60

J. Lang, 'Sigurd and Welland in pre-Conquest carving from northern England', *Yorkshire Archaeological Journal*, 48 (1976), 83-94

J. Lang, 'Anglo-Scandinavian sculpture in Yorkshire', in R. Hall (ed.), *Viking Age York and the North* (CBA Research Report, 27, 1978), 11-20

J. Lang, 'Recent studies in the pre-Conquest sculpture of Northumbria', in F. Thompson (ed.), *Studies in Medieval Sculpture* (1983), 177-89

J. Lang (ed.) *Anglo-Saxon and Viking Age Sculpture and its*

Context (BAR British Series, 49, 1978)
P. Sidebottom, 'Viking Age stone monuments and social identity in Derbyshire', in D.M. Hadley and J.D. Richards (ed.), *Cultures in Contact: Scandinavian Settlement in England in the ninth and tenth centuries* (Turnhout, 2000), 213-35
D. Stocker, 'Monuments and merchants: irregularities in the distribution of stone sculpture in Lincolnshire and Yorkshire in the tenth century', in D.M. Hadley and J.D. Richards (ed.), *Cultures in Contact: Scandinavian Settlement in England in the ninth and tenth centuries* (Turnhout, 2000), 179-212
L. Watts and P. Rahtz, 'Kirkdale — the inscriptions', *Medieval Archaeology*, 41 (1997), 51-99
I. Wood, 'Anglo-Saxon Otley: an archiepiscopal estate and its crosses in a Northumbrian context', *Northern History*, 23 (1987), 20-38

5 Saints

M. Biddle, 'Archaeology, architecture and the cult of saints', in L.A.S. Butler and R.K. Morris (ed.), *The Anglo-Saxon Church* (CBA Research Report, 60, 1986), 1-31
D.W. Rollason, 'List of saint's resting-places in Anglo-Saxon England', *Anglo-Saxon England*, 7 (1978), 61-94
D.W. Rollason, 'The cults of murdered royal saints in Anglo-Saxon England', *Anglo-Saxon England*, 11 (1983), 1-22
D.W. Rollason, 'The shrines of saints in later Anglo-Saxon England: distribution and significance', in L. Butler and R. Morris (ed.), *The Anglo-Saxon Church* (CBA Research Report, 60, 1986), 32-43
D.W. Rollason, 'Relic-cults as an instrument of royal policy *c*.900-*c*.1050', *Anglo-Saxon England*, 15 (1987), 91-103
D.W. Rollason, *Saints and Relics in Anglo-Saxon England* (Cambridge, 1989)
L. Simpson, 'The King Alfred/St Cuthbert episode in the *Historia de Sancto Cuthberto*: its significance for mid-tenth-century English History', in G. Bonner, C. Stancliffe and D. Rollason (ed.) *St Cuthbert, His Cult and Community to AD 1200* (1989), 397-411

6 Documents
i) Anglo-Saxon
A. Campbell (ed.), *Æthelwulf de Abbatibus* (Oxford, 1967)
B. Colgrave (ed.), *The Life of Bishop Wilfrid by Eddius Stephanus* (Cambridge, 1927)
B. Colgrave (ed.), *Two Lives of Saint Cuthbert* (Cambridge, 1940)
B. Colgrave, *Felix's Life of St Guthlac* (Cambridge, 1956)
B. Colgrave and R.A.B. Mynors (ed.) *Bede's Ecclesiastical History of the English People* (Oxford, 1969)
C. Morris, *Marriage and Murder in eleventh-century Northumbria: a study of 'De Obsessione Dunelmi'*, (York, 1992)
D. Whitelock (ed.), *Anglo-Saxon Wills* (Cambridge, 1930)
D. Whitelock (ed.), *English Historical Documents I, c.500-1042*, (London, 1955; 2nd edn 1979)

ii) Later Medieval
A. Clark (ed.), *Lincoln Diocese Documents 1450-1544*, Early English Text Society (1914)
D. Douglas and W. Greenaway (ed.), *English Historical Documents II, 1042-1189* (London, 1981)
A. Grant, 'Twelve medieval ghost stories', *Yorkshire Archaeological Journal*, 27 (1924), 363-79
D. Edwards, *Derbyshire Wills proved in the Prerogative Court at Canterbury 1393-1574*, Derbyshire Record Society, 27 (1998)
C. Foster (ed.), *Lincoln Wills Registered in the District Probate Registry at Lincoln*, Lincoln Record Society 1 (1914)
R. Horrox (ed.), *The Black Death* (Manchester, 1994)
P. Matarasso, *The Cistercian World. Monastic Writings of the Twelfth Century* (London, 1993)
A.R. Myers (ed.), *English Historical Documents IV, 1327-1485* (London, 1969)
H. Rothwell (ed.), *English Historical Documents III, 1189-1327* (London, 1975)
B. Windeatt, *The Book of Margery Kempe* (London, 1985)

7 Guilds and Chantry Chapels

G.H. Cook, *Medieval Chantries and Chantry Chapels* (London, 1947)
R.B. Dobson, 'The foundation of perpetual chantries by the citizens of medieval York', *Studies in Church History*, 4 (1967), 22-38
R.B. Dobson, 'Citizens and chantries in late medieval York', in D. Abulafia, M. Franklin and M. Rubin (ed.), *Church and City, 1000-1500* (Cambridge, 1992), 311-32
J. Toulmin Smith *English Gilds*, Early English Text Society, 40 (1870)
E. Gee, 'The topography of altars, chantries and shrines in York Minster', *Antiquaries Journal*
B. Hanawalt, 'Keepers of the lights: late medieval English parish gilds', *Journal of Medieval and Renaissance Studies*, 14 (1984), 21-37
A. Saltman, *The Cartulary of the Wakebridge Chantries at Crich*, Derbyshire Record Series, 6 (1976)
H.F. Westlake, *The Parish Gilds of Medieval England* (London, 1919)

8 Later Medieval Funerary Monuments
i) Brasses
P. Binski, 'The stylistic sequence of London figure brasses', in J. Colaes (ed.), *The Earliest English Brasses: patronage, style and workshops, 1270-1350*

(London, 1987), 69-131
J. Coales (ed.), *The Earliest English Brasses: patronage, style and workshops, 1270-1350* (London, 1987)
M. Norris, 'Later medieval monumental brasses: an urban funerary industry and its representation of death', in S.R. Bassett (ed.), *Death in Towns. Urban responses to the Dying and the Dead, 400-1600* (Leicester, 1992), 184-209
M. Stephenson, 'Monumental brasses in the West Riding', *Yorkshire Archaeological Journal*, 15 (1898), 1-60

ii) Grave slabs
L.A.S. Butler, 'Some early northern grave covers — a reassessment', *Archaeologia Aeliana*, 4th series, 36 (1958), 207-20
L.A.S. Butler, 'Minor medieval monumental sculpture in the east Midlands', *Archaeological Journal*, 16 (1964), 111-53
P. Coss, *The Lady in Medieval England, 1000-1500* (Stroud, 1998)
P. Ryder, *Medieval Cross Slab Covers in West Yorkshire* (Wakefield, 1991)

iii) Tombs and effigies
F. Cheetham, *English Medieval Alabasters* (Oxford, 1984)
B. Gittos and M. Gittos, 'The fourteenth-century monuments in the Saltmarshe chapel at Howden, Yorkshire: their history and context', *Yorkshire Archaeological Journal*, 68 (1996), 113-55
A. Martindale, 'Patrons and minders: the intrusion of the secular into sacred spaces in the Late Middle Ages', in D. Wood (ed.), *The Church and the Arts* (Oxford, 1992), 143-78
S. Oosterwijk, 'Lost, found and lost again? The continuing enigma of the Gisborough Priory effigies', *Journal of the British Archaeological Association*, 151 (1998), 190-202
C. Ryde, 'Chellaston standing angels with shields at Aston on Trent: their wider distribution 1400-50', *Derbyshire Archaeological Journal*, 113 (1993), 69-90

9 Ecclesiastical Artß
i) Wall-paintings
R. Gem, 'Documentary references to Anglo-Saxon painted architecture', in S. Cather, D. Park and P. Williamson (ed.), *Early Medieval Wall Painting and Painted Sculpture* (BAR British Series, 216, 1990), 1-12
E. Rouse, *Medieval Wall Paintings* (Princes Risborough, 1991)
E.C. Williams, 'The Dance of Death in painting and sculpture in the Middle Ages', *Journal of the British Archaeological Association*, 1 (1937), 229-50
E.C. Williams, 'Mural paintings of the Three Living and the Three Dead in England', *Journal of the British Archaeological Association*, 7 (1942), 31-40

ii) Stained-Glass Windows
S. Crewe, *Stained Glass in England 1180-1540* (London, 1987)
P. Hebgin-Barnes, 'The medieval stained glass of Lincolnshire', *Lincolnshire Past and Present*, 22 (1995), 3-7
S. Pedersen, 'Piety and charity in the painted glass of late medieval York', *Northern History*, 36 (1) (2000), 33-42

iii) Sculpture
J. Bilson, 'On a sculptured representation of Hell cauldron recently found in York', *Yorkshire Archaeological Journal*, 19 (1907), 434-45

iv) Illuminated manuscripts
S.G. Bell, 'Medieval women book owners: arbiters of lay piety and ambassadors of culture', *Signs* 7 (4) (0000), 742-68
M. Camille, *Mirror in Parchment. The Luttrell Psalter and the Making of England* (London, 1998)
M.H. Caviness, 'Patron or matron? A Capetian Bride and a vade mecum for her marriage bed', *Speculum* 68 (1993), 333-62
J. Harthan, *Books of Hours* (London, 1977)

10 The Black Death and its impact
M. Beresford and J. Hurst, *Wharram Percy Deserted Medieval Village* (London, 1990)
C.C. Dyer, 'Deserted medieval villages in the West Midlands', *Economic History Review*, 35 (1982), 15-31
C. Harper-Bill, 'The English church and English religion after the Black Death', in W.M. Ormrod and P. Lindley (ed.), *The Black Death in England* (Stamford, 1996), 79-123
J. Hatcher, *Plague, population and the English economy, 1348-1530* (London, 1977)
R. Horrox (ed.), *The Black Death* (Manchester, 1994)
P. Lindley, 'The Black Death and English art: a debate and some assumptions', in W.M. Ormrod and P. Lindley (ed.), *The Black Death in England* (Stamford, 1996), 125-46
C. Platt, *King Death: The Black Death and its aftermath in Late Medieval England* (London, 1996)
B.H. Putnam, 'Maximum wage-laws for priests after the Black Death, 1348-81', *American Historical Review*, 21 (1915-16), 12-32

Index

Ælflaed, abbess 18, 127, 132
Ælfric, archbishop of York 169
Ælfric, monk 59, 61
Ælfwini, king of Deira 18
Æthelbald, king of Mercia 19, 62, 128-9
Æthelburh, St 32, 132
Æthelhun, child of King Edwin 18
Æthelred, king of Mercia 18, 32, 62
Æthelred, king of England 36
Æthelthryth, child of King Edwin 18
Ackworth (Yorks) 147
Adam 68-9,
Addingham (Yorks) 10, 26-7, 65-6, 103, 107-8
Aelred, abbot of Rievalux 72-5
Alkmund, St 20, 31-2, 104
Ars moriendi 71
Ashbourne (Derbs) 164
Aston-on-Trent (Derbs) 160
Augustine, St 16
Aunsby (Lincs) 143
Badsworth (Yorks) 80
Bakewell (Derbs) 42-3, 81, 83, 127, 145-7, 161, 179
Bampton (Oxon) 38,
Bardney (Lincs) 18, 32-3, 62,
barrow burials 29-31, 34, 36, 63, 93-5, 130
Barrow-upon-Humber (Lincs) 30-1, 108
Barton (Yorks) 49
Barton, John 159-60, 164-5
Barton-upon-Humber (Lincs) 10, 30, 100, 103-5, 108, 163, 176, 178
Baslow (Yorks) 146-8
Baston (Lincs) 83, 85
Beckingham (Lincs) 167
Bedale (Yorks) 109
Bede, monk and scholar 11, 18-19, 31-2, 41, 58-61, 102-3, 131-2
Bedlington (Yorks) 109
Belton (Lincs) 37
Benty Grange (Derbs) 29, 93-4
Bertun, St 32
Beverley (Yorks) 18, 32, 48, 61, 67, 83, 85, 113, 169, 176, 183
Bicker (Lincs) 138
Black Death 12, 49, 87-90, 164-5,
181-4
Blyth (Notts) 48, 68
Bolsover (Derbs) 42, 48
Bolton (Yorks) 44
Boston (Lincs) 83, 86, 150, 168, 183
Bradbourne (Derbs) 129, 148
Brailsford (Derbs) 139
Brandesburton (Yorks) 152-3
brasses 10-11, 14, 147-53, 179-80
Bridlington (Yorks) 53, 143
Brinton, Thomas, bishop of Rochester 70
Bromyard, John, preacher 70
Brotton (Yorks) 49
Brough Bridge (Yorks) hospital 50
Burgh (Lincs) 83
burials
  cremation 11, 17, 34, 110, 140
  early Anglo-Saxon 11, 13, 17, 95
  mid- to late Anglo-Saxon 64-6, 92-112
  later medieval 112-24
Burnham (Lincs) 44
Burnsall (Yorks) 136
Burton Agnes (Yorks) 170
Byland Abbey (Yorks) 122, 166-7, 176
Caenby (Lincs) 29, 94
Calver Low (Debrs) 30
Cambois (Yorks) 109
Carlton (Yorks) 42
Castle Bytham (Lincs) 143
castles 28, 40-1, 143
Catton (Yorks) 147
Chad, St 31
Cedd, bishop 18
chantry chapels 45, 47, 80-1, 165-9, 175, 182
charcoal, in burials 99
Chellaston (Derbs) 11, 180
Chesterfield (Derbs) 10, 82-4, 182
  hospital 10, 50, 113-15, 118
Cleasby (Yorks) 49
coffins 25, 64-5, 93, 97-101, 103-6, 115-18, 122-3, 127, 178-9
Conisborough (Yorks) 143
Corby Glen (Lincs) 69-70, 170
Cottam (Yorks) 30
Cow Low (Derbs) 29, 93-4
Cowthorpe (Yorks) 151-2
Crayke (Yorks) 25-6, 33, 65, 103

cremation (see burials)
Crich (Derbs) 81
Crowland (Lincs) 31, 40, 62, 84, 142
Cumberworth, Sir Thomas 71, 78, 162-3
Cundall (Yorks) 179
Cuthbert, St 19, 25, 33, 60, 93, 127, 129, 131-2, 176-7
Dalderby, John, bishop of Lincoln 53,
Daniel, Walter, biographer 72-3, 75,
Darrington (Yorks) 147-8
Day of Judgement 67, 90
De Abbatibus, poem 58, 129
de Ghant, Gilbert 143
de Grey, Walter, archbishop of York 113-15
de Lacy, Robert 41, 142
de Ludham, Godfrey, archbishop of York 74, 114,
Derby 20-21, 31-2, 45, 104, 130
Dewsbury (Yorks) 70, 141, 143
Digby (Lincs) 143
Doncaster (Yorks) 43-4, 47, 86-7
Dronfield (Derbs) 83-4
Dryhthelm, vision of 58-60
Eadberht, king of Northumbria 18
Eadburh, St 31
Eadred, king of Wessex 28, 33
Ealdred, archbishop of York 40, 61, 63
Eanbald, archbishop of York 18,
Eanflaed, queen of Bernicia 18, 132
Easby (Yorks) 49
East Kirkby (Lincs) 167
Edgar, king of England 36
Edmund, king of Wessex 33, 36
Edwin, king of Deira 18, 59, 132
effigies, later medieval 14, 115, 149, 153-61, 180-1
Egbert, archbishop of York 18-19
Egbert, St 18, 31, 99
Egton (Yorks) 49
Eleanor, queen of England 74, 80, 145, 169
embalming 74, 114
Etritha, St 32
excommunicates 50-1
Eve 68-9

Index

Felix, biographer 58, 131
Fenny Bentley (Derbs) 159-60
Fillingham (Lincs) 10, 13, 37, 39, 97, 100, 106
Fimber (Yorks) 30
Fitz Payn, Joan 79, 173
Fitzherbert, Anthony 149
Fitzherbert, Elizabeth 147-8, 154
Fitzherbert, Henry 154-5
Fitzherbert, Nicholas 149, 159
Fitzherbert, Ralph 147, 154, 157
Fitzherbert, William, archbishop of York 53, 176, 181
Flawford (Notts) 113
Flixborough (Lincs) 10, 13, 23-4, 65, 103, 130
Fulford (Yorks) 49,
funerals 75, 77, 82, 86-7, 90-1, 174-5
Fursa, monk 58
Gainthorpe (Lincs) 84
Garton Slack (Yorks) 30, 94-5
Gedney (Lincs) 84
ghosts 166-7, 176
Gilling (Yorks) 49
Gisborough Priory (Yorks) 153
Glentworth (Lincs) 144
Gosburton (Lincs) 168
Grantham (Lincs) 10, 32, 84-6, 145, 176
   hospital 10, 50, 52-3
grave goods 11-13, 17, 30, 34, 37, 63, 92-7, 100-1, 110-1, 113-14
grave slabs
   Anglo-Saxon 18, 27, 31, 143
   later medieval 14, 41, 118, 145-8, 180
Great Hale (Lincs) 37, 144
Greenfield, William, archbishop of York 150-1, 179
Grimsby (Lincs) 86
Grosseteste, bishop of Lincoln 150
guilds 45, 81-5, 165-9
Gunby (Lincs) 157
Guthlac, St 31, 40, 57-8, 62, 131-2
Hackness (Yorks) 32, 57, 126, 128, 132
Haddon (Derbs) 90
Hagworthingham (Lincs) 168
Hampole (Yorks) 53, 162
Hampsthwaite Yorks) 149-50
Harby (Notts) 74, 80, 145
Harewood (Yorks) 67, 154, 158-60
Harrington (Lincs) 167
Hartlepool (Cleveland) 111, 127
Healaugh Priory (Yorks) 87, 91
Heaven 15, 66-7, 76, 90
Hell 15, 66-9, 71, 90

Hemswell (Lincs) 44, 46
Hesket-in-the-Forest (Cumbria) 34
Heynings (Lincs) 48
Hibaldstow (Lincs) 31
Hild, abbess 32-3, 57, 132
hoards 109
Hogsthorpe (Lincs) 168
Holbeach (Lincs) 84
Holme (Notts) 159-60, 164-5
Holton-le-Clay (Lincs) 31
Hornsea (Yorks) 86
hospitals 50, 52-3, 82, 113-15, 118
Hougham (Lincs) 144
Hovingham (Yorks) 21, 33, 105, 130
Hugh Candidus 32
Hugh, St, bishop of Lincoln 50, 54, 75-6, 80, 91, 169, 178
Hull (Yorks) 10, 44, 78, 82, 171
   Augustinian friary 10, 48, 76-7, 113, 115-17, 178
Hurdlow (Derbs) 30
Hygbald, St 31
Indulgences 83, 85-6
Ingleby (Derbs)
   Heath Wood cemetery 10, 34, 109-110, 140-1
Jews 10, 51, 122-4
John, bishop of York 18, 31, 40
John, St of Bridlington 53, 176
Keddington (Lincs) 143
Kellington (Yorks) 10, 31, 42-3, 48, 97, 99-100, 108
Kempe, Margery 176
Kildale (Yorks) 110
Kilham (Yorks) 37
Kirkby cum Osgodby (Lincs) 168
Kirkdale (Yorks) 18, 21, 27-8, 105-6, 130, 144
Kirkham Priory (Yorks) 153, 161
Kirklevington (Yorks) 137-9
Kirton Lindsey (Lincs) 168
Langland, William 88, 144
Langtoft (Lincs) 86,
Lastingham (Yorks) 18
law-codes 34, 36, 43, 51, 181-2
Lazarus 71, 74
Leatham (Yorks) 49,
Leeds (Yorks) 137, 153
lepers, leprosy 50, 52-3, 72
Levisham (Yorks) 139
Lincoln 10, 45, 51, 54, 68, 74, 80, 82-4, 123, 145, 150, 162, 170-1, 180-1
   Cathedral 68, 113-14, 143, 149-50, 169, 180
   St Botolph's 143

St Mark's 10, 14, 42, 99, 103, 106, 108, 113, 119-21, 133, 138, 143
St Mary-le-Wigford 138, 144
River Witham at 109, 122
Londonthorpe (Lincs) 143
Long Sutton (Lincs) 120
Ludham, Godfrey, archbishop of York 74,
Luttrell, Sir Geoffrey 78, 162-3, 171-3
Lythe (Yorks) 49, 139
Malmesbury, William 32-3
Mannyng, Robert 144, 166
manuscript illuminations 11, 15, 79, 171-3
Masham (Yorks) 137, 179
Meaux Abbey (Yoks) 88
Melbourne (Derbs) 69
Merewalh, king of Magonsætan 18
Methley (Yorks) 147, 157, 181
Methley, Richard 53
Michael, St 68
Middle Rasen (Lincs) 44, 46
Middleton (Yorks) 136, 139-40
Minting (Lincs) 143
Mirk, John 96
Monk Bretton Priory (Yorks) 113, 146
monks
   death of 47, 72, 88
Morley (Derbs) 152
mortuaries 86-7, 122
Moulton (Lincs) 86
Mount Grace Priory (Yorks) 53, 76
Nettleham (Lincs) 89
Newark-on-Trent (Notts) 40-1, 49, 81, 90, 100, 106, 108, 168
Norbury (Derbs) 112, 139, 147-9, 153-5, 157, 160
Norman Conquest 11, 39-42, 142-3
Normanby le Wold (Lincs) 86
Nottingham 11, 45, 180-1
Nunburnhome (Yorks) 136
Osbald, king of Northumbria 18
Osthryth, queen of Mercia 18, 32, 62
Oswald, king of Northumbria 32, 61-2, 127
Oswy, king of Bernicia 18, 177
Otley (Yorks) 136
Owersby (Lincs) 168
Owston (Lincs) 168
Painsthorpe Wold (Yorks) 29-30, 94,
Patrington (Yorks) 164
penance 60, 76, 79, 131

191

Index

Pickering (Yorks) 68, 170-1
Pickworth (Lincs) 90
pilgrims, pilgrimage 77, 83, 85, 176
Pontefract (Yorks) 13, 28-9, 41, 66, 96, 103, 107, 142
Purgatory 15, 43, 50, 56, 66-7, 69, 72, 85
radiocarbon dating (see skeletal analysis)
Raunds (Northants) 47, 108, 112
reliquaries 24, 130-1
Repton (Derbs) 10, 13, 18-19, 21, 23-4, 29, 31, 34, 42, 62, 65, 96, 99-103, 107-8, 110-11, 128-9, 144
Riplingham (Yorks) 51
Ripon (Yorks) 10, 13, 21-3, 29, 33-4, 57, 65, 96, 99-100, 106, 108, 112, 177-8
Rippingale (Yorks) 89, 178
Rolle, Richard 53, 73
Rudby (Yorks) 49
saints' cults 21, 31-3, 53-4, 57-8, 62, 162-3, 169, 176-8
saints' *Lives* 15, 19, 31-3, 40, 57-60, 131-2, 176-8
Scarborough (Yorks) 86, 96
Scredington (Lincs) 165
Scrope, Richard, archbishop of York 53,
Seaham (Co. Durham) 37
Seamer (Yorks) 49
shrouds 64-5, 74, 103
Sigewine, abbot 129
Sigglesthorpe (Yorks) 153
Skeletal analysis
  age 14
  disease 50, 53, 100
  DNA 14
  radiocarbon dating 13-14, 22-3, 25-6, 28, 30, 37, 95-6, 99-100, 102, 106, 114
  sex 14, 47
Skelton (Yorks) 49
Skerne (Lincs) 109
Skipwith (yorks) 139
Sleaford (Lincs) 69
Snaith (Yorks) 42
South Kelsey (Lincs) 44, 46
South Kyme (Lincs) 21, 33, 105, 130
Southampton 112
Southwell (Notts) 31
Spalding (Lincs) 83-4, 86
Sprotborough (Yorks) 147, 150, 154, 157
Stamford (Lincs) 82-3, 85, 145, 150

Stanwick (Yorks) 49,
Stokesley (Yorks) 49
stone-lined graves 30, 37, 39-40, 100, 106, 116, 119
  'ear-muffs', pillow stones 98-100, 106
stone sculpture 10, 14,
  Anglo-Saxon 10, 19-22, 25, 61, 63-5, 126-9, 132, 144, 165
  Anglo-Scandinavian 10, 31, 39, 111-12, 133-42,
Stow (Lincs) 29, 118, 150
Swaby (Lincs) 37, 96
Swinhope (Lincs) 30
Symphorianus, St 32
Tattershall (Lincs) 167-8
Tattershall Thorpe (Lincs) 94
Theodore, archbishop of Canterbury 60, 131
Thirsk (Yorks) 164-5
Thoresby, John, archbishop of York 49, 89
Thornhill (Yorks) 64-5, 126, 153, 156
Thornton-le-Moor (Lincs) 150
Three Living and Three Dead, medieval legend 9, 90
Thwing (Yorks) 10, 30, 64, 95, 103, 110, 128
Tickhill (Yorks) 87
Tideswell (Derbs) 151, 154, 156, 164
tombs, later medieval 14, 43-4, 153-61
Topcliffe (Yorks) 149
Towton (Yorks) 47, 49, 168
Tydd (Lincs) 83
Uncleby (Yorks) 30
'Viking' burials 23, 33-5, 100-2, 109-11, 140-2
Waddingham (Lincs) 44
Wakebridge, William 81
Walkington Wold (Yorks) 36, 106
wall paintings 11, 15, 61, 67-9, 90, 170-1
Waltheof, earl 40, 142
Wensley (Yorks) 90, 110
Werburgh, St 33
West Tanfield (Yorks) 168
Weston (Yorks) 139
Whaplode (Lincs) 83
Wharram Percy (Yorks) 10, 113, 164
Whitby (Yorks) 10, 18-19, 23-4, 32, 41, 57, 65, 97, 103, 106, 110, 127, 131-2
Whitton (Lincs) 37-8
Wigber Low (Derbs) 10, 94

Wiglaf, king of Mercia 19
Wigtoft (Lincs) 84
Wihtberht, St 18, 31, 99
Wilfrid, St 18, 22, 31, 33, 57, 60, 99, 131, 177
William I, king of England 40-1, 142
wills 15, 43-5, 48, 57, 62-3, 74, 76-9, 81, 90, 108, 117-18, 147, 153, 162-4, 166, 170-1
Wilton (Yorks) 49
window glass 11, 15, 68-70, 73, 78, 117, 156, 161-5, 170-1, 179, 183
Winster Moor (Derbs) 94
Wirksworth (Derbs) 20-1, 33, 105
Worsborough (Yorks) 160
Wulfrannus, St 32
Wulfric Spott 63, 108
Wystan, St 19, 31
Yarm (Yorks) 139
York 10, 80-1, 142, 150, 168-70, 176
  All Saints, North Street 73, 78, 161-2, 166, 170
  All Saints, Peasholme Green 113
  Clementhorpe nunnery 116
  Corpus Christi guild 84-5
  Jewbury 10, 51, 122-4,
  Minster 14, 18-19, 21, 69, 96-100, 106, 108, 113, 127, 133-6, 139, 176, 178-80, 183
  St Andrew's, Fishergate 96, 100, 102, 104, 106-7,
  St Andrew's, Gilbertine priory 10, 42-3, 47-8, 115-23, 176
  St Benet's, Swinegate 12, 104, 108, 122, 178
  St Denys 163
  St Helen-on-the-Walls 10, 42, 96, 99, 113, 118-19, 121,
  St Leonard's 50
  St Martin, Coney Street 170
  St Mary Bishophill Junior 96
  St Mary Bishophill Senior 96, 138
  St Mary, Castlegate 136
  St Michael, Spurriergate 69
  St Olaf's 43, 49
Zouche, William, archbishop of York 49, 87, 89